THE CHRISTIAN REFORMED CHURCH

The Christian Reformed Church

IN NORTH AMERICA

ITS HISTORY, SCHOOLS, MISSIONS, CREED AND
LITURGY, DISTINCTIVE PRINCIPLES AND
PRACTICES AND ITS CHURCH GOVERNMENT

BY

DR. HENRY BEETS 1869—

EASTERN AVENUE BOOK STORE
GRAND RAPIDS, MICH.

1923

Presented to..

On the occasion of..

By...

Place..

Date..

6882

Foreword

"THE CHRISTIAN REFORMED CHURCH, its History, Schools, Missions, Creed and Liturgy, distinctive Principles and Practices, and its Church Government", was written with the distinct purpose of enabling our people, particularly our young people, to know and to appreciate their denomination, and willingly to devote their prayers, their means, and their services to the promotion of its highest and best interests and the carrying out of its mission, to the coming of God's Kingdom, to the praise of God and the salvation of men.

Just like the true religion involves knowing, loving, and serving the true God, so we believe that the proper kind of church membership requires that we know the Church we belong to, its right to exist, its principles, and its activities, that we love it properly and consecrate to it and to its work, its preservation and extension, such contributions as grace enables us to make.

If, in order to prove our right to exist, parts of Chapter II are somewhat polemical and apologetical in character, such was demanded by the nature of the case, and is in nowise meant as speaking disparagingly of a respected sister denomination. We particularly disclaim responsibility for the harsh statements and sweeping indictments of the Reformed Church occasionally made by overly-zealous champions, and also found in the LETTER which we give as Appendix I, as a long lost historical document which we, during the summer of 1923, discovered in the

Netherlands. ("De Wachter", October 24, 1923.) The Letter seems to reveal the authorship of the "Andrew Jackson" of our early history—Chapter III, §4.

This volume will, we trust, be useful as a textbook for study in Societies of various kinds, (for that purpose we gave review questions and references), as well as for reading purposes and for reference, as a "Manual" or "Handbook" of our Church. With a view to that last-named aim we furnish a full Index of names, and we believe that the maps will also prove useful. We are indebted to Dr. L. S. Huizenga for the map of the Chinese Mission and the article on the China work; to the well known historian Rev. J. C. Rullmann of Utrecht, for valuable ideas as to the services of Drs. Kuyper and Bavinck, to Prof. Dr. H. Bouwman of Kampen, for matters pertaining to Church Polity, and to Dr. S. Volbeda for carefully going over the first two chapters and making various suggestions improving their contents.

Mr. D. Lam of the Independent Art Studio, Grand Rapids, helped us greatly in perfecting the China map, and the Rev. L. P. Brink in bringing the Indian map up to date.

In the paragraphs devoted to the Christian School, friends of the cause whose writings on the subject helped us, are mentioned by name.

Finally we thank all brethren who encouraged us with advance orders, and above all do we ascribe praise to our gracious Lord who gave sufficient time and strength to finish this work—a labor of love—to which we gladly devoted the spare time of many years.

HENRY BEETS.

Grand Rapids, Mich., Thanksgiving, 1923.

The CHRISTIAN REFORMED CHURCH

CHAPTER I

THE PEOPLE AND THE CHURCH OF OUR FATHERS
ACROSS THE SEA

Introductory: Why the Study of Denominational History. §1. Our Pagan Ancestors and their Condition. §2. Missionaries Among Them. §3. Impurity of the Church they Planted. §4. The Reformation: Its Forerunners, Leaders, Principles, and Grounds. §5. The Reformation in the Netherlands. §6. The Reformed Church of Holland: Its Construction, Systematization and Corruption. §7. The Secession Movement: Its Grounds and its Adherents. §8. Emigration to the United States: Objections to it; Settlements, Spirit, and Objectives of our Pioneers.

INTRODUCTORY: WHY THE STUDY OF DENOMINATIONAL HISTORY

HISTORY is a systematic record of past events. Church history describes the events intimately connected with the visible Church of Christ as an historical phenomenon, an organization with its office-bearers, services, activities, and ideals. The visible Church may be defined as a formal organization consisting of all those throughout the world who profess their faith in the Lord Jesus Christ and obedience to His Word, together with their children. A denomination indicates a particular group of christians, with a distinct history, creed, form of worship, government, etc.

Why the *study* of denominational history? First, to help the people belonging to a distinct denomination to know and evaluate the religious heritage conferred upon them by their ancestors, the principles they stood for, clung to, and bequeathed.

Second: such a study tends to weld together in one brotherhood the various congregations of such a denomination, scattered far and wide, so that a distance-overcoming spirit of oneness may be created or strengthened, and efficient co-operation is possible, to reach goals set before the group.

Third: such a study assists to avoid pitfalls in which these ancestors may have fallen, to the loss of precious principles, or at least to the obscuring of the vision of the God-assigned task.

Fourth: denominational history properly studied, brings out that a denomination is only a part of the one Catholic Church of God, and cannot and should not lead a life of harmful isolation. As Dr. H. Bavinck put it: "Every sect which considers its own group the *only* Church of Christ, in exclusive possession of the truth, dries up and dies as a branch torn from its trunk."

Finally: such a study is instrumental in showing that no Church has yet reached its goal and realized its ideals. The Church on earth, during this dispensation, is and should be a "militant" or fighting Church, never resting on the laurels of past victories. It should be an Army, ever on the move, till Christ be "Lord of all." (Compare Chapter V, § 9.)

§1.   OUR PAGAN ANCESTORS AND THEIR CONDITIONS

The ancestral home of our people is the Netherlands and adjacent regions, East Friesland and Bentheim, in northwestern Europe. Our forebears were pagans long after Christianity had been planted in southern Europe by the Apostle Paul and others. In common with all their Teutonic kindred peoples, our ancestors were polytheists, worshiping many gods. Wodan or Odin, was their chief divinity after whom Wednesday is still named. They also paid divine honor to Wodan's son Thor, the god of thunder, of war, and of agriculture, after whom Thursday was called, while our Friday reminds of Frigga, Wodan's wife, the goddess of marriage. Two other days of the week, Sunday and Monday, show that the sun and moon, after which they were named, also received homage. Our forefathers worshiped their gods in the depths of their great forests, under large trees, considered sacred, and at times human sacrifices were slain on huge stone altars. While the ancient Germanic peoples possessed several virtues, such as love of liberty, bravery, chastity, and hospitality, their lives were defiled by such vices as drunkenness, gambling, and cruelty towards prisoners of war. They believed strongly in sorcery and witchcraft, in omens, in spooks, and werwolves.

§2. MISSIONARIES AMONG THEM

Up to about the year 600 after Christ, our forefathers remained pagans. Then the set time of God's favor arrived. From France and Great Britain missionaries of the Christian religion, such as they knew it, arrived to acquaint our ancestors with Christianity. From France came Amand, whose king, Dagobert I, in the year 630 or 632, erected a Christian chapel on the place now occupied by the famous cathedral of the city of Utrecht, in the heart of the Netherlands. Later on Eloi of Eligius, at one time bishop of Noyon, in France, brought the gospel to the people of Zeeland and Friesland. At times he suffered severely for his witnessing for Christ. From Great Britain came Wilfred, a monk and a bishop, in 677 cast by a storm upon the Friesian coast. He labored with success, baptizing the ruler of the country, Adgild, and thousands of his people. But he remained only one year in Friesland. The real apostle of the Friesians was Wilfred's disciple Willibrord, who, with twelve fellow-missionaries from Great Britain, began work in Frankish Frisia in 690. Six years later he became archbishop of the Friesians, with his residence in Utrecht. Boniface, the apostle of central Germany, likewise a British monk, also labored diligently to bring about the conversion of our ancestors, not alone during the early part of his life, 716, but also at its close, sealing his ministry among our people with his death as a martyr, June 5, 755, near the Friesian town of Dokkum.

Many others of less renown devoted years of labor toward the christianizing of the Netherlands and adjacent territory, among them Ludger, a native Friesian, who preached the gospel to many people in Friesland, Groningen, and Westphalia.

§3. IMPURITY OF THE EARLY CHURCH

But the Christianity these men brought was not that of the New Testament in its simplicity and purity. It was the Roman type of church life and that meant three kinds of serious departure from Bible precept and example. In the first place unscriptural *doctrines* were taught. They were the placing of tradition (overlevering) on equal footing with the written Word of God, justification, in part at least, by works, and transubstantiation, i.e., the doctrine that the bread of Communion changes into the body of our Lord, and its wine into His blood. The claim that besides a heaven and a hell there is a purgatory beyond the grave, and the demand of submission to the pope and his hierarchy (priest-rule), also involved false doctrines.

In the second place, the Christianity brought to our fathers involved unscriptural *practices,* such as the withholding of the communion cup from the ordinary church-members, the laity, (so-called in distinction from the clergy or priests); the invocation of the Virgin Mary and of the saints, the use of images as books for the laity, and severe restrictions as to the reading of the Bible in the vernacular. In the third place there were serious *abuses* which had crept into the Church, such as the sale of offices and indulgences, immorality of the priesthood, and the instituting of the Inquisition to compel the people by cruel tortures to submit to the popes and their creed.

§4. THE REFORMATION: ITS FORERUNNERS, LEADERS, PRINCIPLES AND GROUNDS

In the early part of the sixteenth century opposition to these things, considerably aided by social conditions, and influenced by a Revival of Learning, led to the *Reformation,* a great religious movement, which purified the Church.

Forerunners of the *Reformation* were such men as the German Tauler, the Englishman Wycliff, the Bohemian Hus, the Italian Savonarola, and, particularly, in the Netherlands, an organization called "the Brethren of the Common Life", which included the eloquent John Brugman, the learned Wessel Gansfort, called "Lux Mundi" (Light of the World), and Thomas à Kempis, famous as the author of the *Imitation of Christ.* Later on three men became known as the great *Reformers:* Luther, Zwingli, and Calvin.

Martin Luther was a German, born in 1483. After many soul struggles he found peace for his troubled conscience in the great doctrine of the justification of a sinner before God in the way of faith alone. He boldly proclaimed this, rallying many of the German princes as well as hosts of the common people around him. He died in 1546.

Ulrich Zwingli (1484—1531), was a Swiss priest, who through study of the Bible was led step by step, to break away from Rome's errors in doctrine and practice and who obtained a considerable following in Zurich and other cantons of his native land.   (Cf. Chapter VIII, §4.)

John Calvin (1509—1564), was a Frenchman, born in Noyon.   He studied law and theology and was preparing for the priesthood when converted to Protestantism.   Most of his life as a Reformer was spent in the Swiss city of Geneva.   His chief work, *The Institutes of the Christian Religion,* is the great literary monument of the Reformation.

In the great struggle to purify or "reform" the Church, three great *principles* were enunciated.   They have become the fundamentals of Protestantism, the *grounds* of the Reformation.

The first, or *objective* principle, affirms that the Bible is the supreme and infallible rule of our faith and practice.   The second, or *subjective* principle of Protestantism, is that we are justified before God by a true and living faith, without any merits of ours, merely of grace.   The third Reformation principle is called the *social* one. Christ is the King of the Church, and, subject to Him, all believers are of equal spiritual rank.   This involves the general priesthood of believers, the right to interpret the Bible, and to share in the government of the Church. (Cf. Chapter X, §2.)

It will be seen at once that in these principles are involved a *protest* against what we named in §3, speaking of the impurity of the Church of the Middle Ages as to doctrine and practice.   The Roman Church was manifesting in these matters, defended and maintained with might and main, even with recourse to the cruelest measures, its serious departure from the original purity of the early Church as founded by our Lord and His Apostles.   To put it in other words, the papal organization no longer revealed what our fathers later on described as "the *marks* by which the true Church is known: if the true doctrine of the Gospel is preached therein; if she maintains the pure administration of the Sacraments as instituted by Christ; if Church discipline is exercised in the punishing of sin; in short, if all things are managed according to the pure Word of God, and all things contrary thereto rejected and Jesus Christ acknowledged as the only Head of the Church." (Confession, Article 29.) We shall see that these marks as grounds for reformatory action figure later on in the history we are giving.

§5. THE REFORMATION IN THE NETHERLANDS

While all the Reformers were a unit on the principles we named above, there soon appeared considerable difference mong them regarding minor points, particularly concerning the Lord's Supper, and to some extent also with reference to church government. Those who followed Martin Luther in his conception of the matters at issue, became known as Lutherans. Their churches are found in Germany, Scandinavia, and throughout the world. The followers of Calvin and Zwingli formed the Reformed churches of Christendom. The Church of our fathers across the sea belongs to the last-named family of denominations.

Not all of the Dutch people, however, became Reformed or Calvinistic. Many remained Roman Catholics. Quite a number of Netherlanders became Lutherans, especilly during the earlier years of the Reformation period, but Lutheranism never was strong in Holland. At one time, 1531—1560, there were many *Anabaptists* in the Netherlands. Anabaptism has been called the "radical Reformation". It rejected infant baptism along with the abuses of Rome which all the Reformers condemned and discarded. At one time some of the Anabaptists tried to establish a visible Kingdom of God in the city of Munster.

Bitterly persecuted at times, the scattered Anabaptists were reorganized later on by the Friesian ex-priest Menno Simons, after whom the Mennonites in the Old as well as in the New World call themselves. At about 1560 the Calvinists became predominant in the Netherlands, although during the first decade or two of the Eighty Years' War between Holland and Spain (1568—1648), they formed only one-tenth part of the entire population of the Netherlands. Calvinism obtained a foothold in Holland not alone because the Dutch as well as the Scotch are adapted temperamentally for the stern type of religion Calvin stood for, but also because fiery preachers of Calvinism went up and down the Low Countries to proclaim the Reformed religion. Some of these heralds of Calvinism were native Netherlanders, others came from what is now called Belgium, among them Petrus Dathenus, born 1531, formerly a monk. He versified the Psalms and translated the Heidelberg Catechism, which had been prepared by the German scholars Ursinus and Olevianus, at that time living in Heidelberg in the Palatinate, southern Germany, and which had appeared in 1563 (Chapter VIII, §1). Another preacher of Belgian birth, Guy de Bray, exerted a strong influence on the Reformation in the Netherlands through the "Belgian Confession", of which he was the author. (Chapter VIII, §2.)

§6. THE REFORMED CHURCH OF HOLLAND

Out of the stress and struggle of an Eighty Years' War with all its horrors, there arose in the Netherlands the Reformed Church, the old Church of our Fathers, of the *Calvinistic* faith (see Chapter IX, §1), and of the Presbyterian order of church government. The Synods which prepared or perfected the organization of this Church and developed a Church Order, were held at Wesel, 1568; Emden, 1571; Dordrecht, 1574 and 1578; Middelburg, 1581, and The Hague, 1586. At the great National Synod of Dordrecht, held in 1618–'19, the Church Order received its final form, the Heidelberg Catechism and the Belgian Confession were revised, and the Canons of Dordrecht were promulgated to be a part of the standards of the Reformed Church, or the Formulas of Unity (see Chapter VIII). For Church Government and Church Order, see Chapter X.

But the Reformed Church of the Netherlands did not long maintain the high standard of doctrinal purity expressed in its creed, nor did its membership perpetuate the heroic "Golden Age" of wonderful enterprise and achievement politically, and of noble zeal for religion, not alone for the Church at home, but also for heathen peoples far away, as shown in attempts to evangelize the natives of the Dutch East Indies.

The history of the Church usually goes through a cycle of four distinct periods. First there is construction, then systematization, then corruption, and finally in the good providence of God, restoration. Such marked the life of the Christian Church before the Reformation, and this cycle also appears in the history of the Reformed Church of our Fathers.

The *construction* period, from the beginning of the Eighty Years' War till the great Synod of Dordrecht, 1618–1619, was followed by that of *systematization,* when learned theologians worked out the great principles of Calvinism as a religious system. We name as the most important of them Gysbert Voet or Voetius (1588—1676), famous as a theologian and as an authority on church government; Petrus van Mastricht, (1630—1706); W. à Brakel, (1635—1711); Johannes à Marck, (1655—1731); A. Hellenbroek, (1658—1731); and A. Francken, (1676—1743). These men belonged to what was called the Voetian school of theologians, as opposed to the Cocceian school, composed of followers of John Cocceius, (1603 —

1669), who emphasized the Covenant idea in theology, but whose views of Bible interpretation and Sabbath-keeping were considered departures from Reformed truth. F. A. Lampe, (1683—1729), was a gifted theologian who laid stress on experimental religion, and so did writers like the Teelincks and P. Immens and others.

But even while this constructive and systematizing work was going on, alarming signs of *corruption* were seen. James Arminius and his followers tried to eviscerate the Calvinistic creed by erroneous views about predestination, atonement, conversion, and other doctrines. Their errors were condemned and erring ministers who were unwilling to recant or remain silent, were exiled as a result of the decisions of the Synod of Dordrecht, 1618–'19, (Chapter VIII, §3). But the spirit of liberalism was not killed. About the year 1648 the corruption period of the Dutch Church opened. Rationalism started to poison the minds of many, worldliness conquered still more of the Reformed people of Holland, while some of its truly pious people were falling into the extreme of Labadism—a very subjective type of religion fathered by a certain John de la Badie, formerly a French priest, later a clergyman in the Reformed Church, (1674). Practically in vain did the godly J. Van Lodenstein, (1620—1677), and J. Koelman, (1632—1695), and others, plead with the nation to return to God and godliness of life, while men like A. Comrie, (1708—1774), tried to revive the orthodoxy of the days of Dordt. The process of decay could not be arrested. When the French Revolution swept over Europe, it led to the disestablishment of the Reformed Church of Holland, i.e., it ceased to be the official national or privileged Church, such as it had been from 1651. King William I of the new Kingdom of the Netherlands in 1816, in an autocratic fashion, forced a new organization upon the old Church, placing it more or less in bondage to the State, and to that of oligarchies or administrative bodies (Besturen), contrary to the *Presbyterian order*. (Chapter X.) Doctrinally there was very flagrant departure from the official standards of the Church of the Fathers, and the ordination vows were changed in such a way that ministers could preach practically what they liked (Leervrijheid). Only here and there were men who still proclaimed the old-time religion of free grace. Corruption in life as well as in doctrine wrought fearful havoc during this third period of the cycle of Church history, particularly during the first decades of the nineteenth century.

§7. THE SECESSION, ITS GROUNDS AND ITS ADHERENTS

In the year 1834 the period of *restoration* opened. In the village of Ulrum, in the province of Groningen, the Rev. Hendrik De Cock was graciously led to see the unsatisfactory nature of the popular religious views of his days. In the theology as set forth by the *Institutes* of Calvin, already named, he found peace of mind and joy of heart. When with whole-hearted devotion he began to proclaim the truth as he saw and felt it, hundreds if not thousands from near and far flocked to hear him. Some persisted to have him baptize their children, although living in different congregations. De Cock's activity, in defiance of existing regulations, his witnessing against "wolves" in the sheepfold, and his seconding of a very severe condemning of the hymns of his Church, led to his suspension and finally to what has been called the SECESSION, which is usually dated from 1834, when, October 14th, De Cock and his followers at Ulrum signed an Act of Separation. In accordance with the office of believers (Article 28 of the Confession), they announced to the world their separation "from those who were not of the Church", refusing to fellowship any longer with the Established Church "until it return to the true service of God", and inviting fellowshipping with all Reformed church members and assemblies united on the basis of the Word of God. That Word was accepted as rule of faith and life, and, as based thereon, the old Standards of the Reformed Church. Its ancient Liturgy (Chapter VIII), was adopted, as well as the Church Order of Dordrecht (see Chapter X).

The Revs. H. P. Scholte, S. Van Velzen, A. Brummelkamp, and G. F. G. Meerburg, who had come under the influence of a Revival which had originated in Switzerland, with their congregations, soon after followed the example of Ulrum's pastor and people. March 2 to 12, 1836, the churches of the Secession held their first Synod, in Amsterdam, at which meeting the Candidate A. C. Van Raalte was examined and ordained. The meeting called itself the "General Synod of the Christian Reformed Church in the Netherlands". And it had grounds for styling itself General Synod because when it met there were "provincial assemblies" already in nine of the eleven Dutch provinces. Most of the Seceders lived in the northern provinces of the Netherlands: Groningen, Friesland, Drenthe, and Overijsel. A large proportion was found in South Holland, but many less in North Holland, although in populous Amsterdam a congregation had been organized in 1835. We have no statistics covering these early years, but by 1857 the membership of the Christian Seceder Church amounted to about 50,000—the approximate number of the Jews who returned from the Babylonian captivity.

The Secession movement spread even beyond the boundaries of the Netherlands to Eastfriesland, under leadership at first of the Rev. R. W. Duin, and to Bentheim (also in Germany), where the "exhorters" J. B. Sundag and H. H. Schoemaker were instrumental in arousing a number of the "Graafschappers" (as the Bentheimers were usually called), to return to the old-time religion. Being close to the Dutch boundaries, and still using the

Holland tongue, the people of the two districts just named were soon and strongly influenced by the Secession in the Netherlands. The Old Reformed Church, as their denomination was called, kept up close contact with the Reformed Churches of the Low Countries, and in 1923 united formally with them as a Particular Synod, at least for the time being.

The *grounds* for the Secession movement as given by De Cock and his followers are chiefly these five:

1) A falling away from the pure doctrine of the Reformed Church, as expressed in its standards.

2) A hierarchial form of church government and arbitrary regulations.

3) The introduction of unsound hymns.

4) A new and dubious-sounding formula of subscription. Reformed doctrine was to be taught not because (*quia*) but in so far (*quatenus*) as it was contained in the Word of God.

5) Unfaithfulness of preachers regarding their ordination vows.

It will be seen at a glance that in this case, as in that of the Reformation, §4 above, it was the departure of the dominant church from what were considered the marks of the true church, that furnished the reasons for separation. (Cf. Chapter II, §8.)

THE ADHERENTS OF THE SECESSION

Who were the men and women who separated themselves from what they considered a spurious Reformed Church, in so far at least as its ruling bodies were concerned? The reply of some has been far from favorable. The leader of the Secession, De Cock, has been called a fanatic, a sectarian, and a separatist. An American writer, as late as 1922, spoke of the seceders of 1834 as people "who vociferated their appeals to the fathers of Dordt, but in their ignorance and anger tore the doctrines and practices of these fathers to shreds". (W. O. Van Eyck's *Landmarks of the Reformed Fathers*, p. 86.) No doubt they were far from perfect. Being as the christians of Paul's days: "Not many wise men after the flesh, not many mighty, not many noble", their cultural horizon was very limited. Some were not free from narrow-mindedness and held labadistic views as to christian experience. Others laid undue emphasis on the doctrine of predestination and failed to appreciate the covenant relationship of the seed of the Church. Uncharitable condemnation of those who lived outside of their circles was at times in evidence. There were some who stressed justification far more than sanctification, no doubt brought to this through reaction from the prevailing Christianity of that day which consisted largely of attempts at self-improvement, (werkheiligheid). There were testy sermons-testers among them, soulless weighers of souls, merciless critics, people who themselves had not entered the Kingdom and were hindering anxious inquirers. Antinomians and Pharisees, they also were not lacking here and there, and now and then.

The Seceders bitterly quarreled among themselves as to the real nature of the Church, and the privileges of its baptized membership. There was acrimonious controversy about the garb of the clergy and prohibiting degrees of blood-relationship in marriage. Particularly about the binding power of the old Church Order and Scholte's petition for liberty of worship, from the side of the government, involving a surrender of the name and claim of being a continuation of the old Reformed Church, great internal dissension arose. The discontented churches in 1840 united as "the Reformed Congregations under the

Cross"—and continued separate existence till 1869, when reunion took place.

But we should not wonder unduly at these imperfections and controversies. They have appeared in the history of the Church whenever new reforms had to right ancient wrongs. Such things as we named are also found in the history of the Pilgrims and Puritans. Indeed, there is much similarity between both the rise and the ideals of the founders of New England and those of the founders of the Secession Church. Both were essentially *reform* parties. The Puritan movement arose as protest against the formalism of the Church of England and the worldliness of its people. The roots of the Dutch Secession lie in the movement started by Voetius, and fostered by Lodenstein and Brakel—that of the Dutch Pietists or perhaps more correctly, the Dutch Puritans, a people protesting against the departures of the Church of their days from the standards they heartily believed in.

The Pilgrims and Puritan pioneers of New England, notwithstanding all their faults, tried to stand bravely for the great fundamentals of the Calvinistic view of God and the world. And so did those Dutch forebears of ours, thank God! Notwithstanding their faults and limitations—and exceptions,—the rank and file of the Dutch Secession people bowed humbly before God as their Sovereign, and sought Him as their Father, through Christ. They unhesitatingly accepted the Bible as the inspired Word. They believed in salvation by free grace, beginning, middle, and end. They aimed at the glorification of God, at the mortification of the old man. They endeavored to do justly, to love kindness, and to walk humbly with their God.

The history of the Secession Church of the Netherlands has shown that after its "crisis of youth", the expulsive power of new affections and convictions threw off many of the dead old leaves, while faithful preaching and disci-

plining removed many of the excrescences of the early
growth.

No, we do not join those who may condemn the fathers
of 1834, as those "who tore to shreds the doctrines and
practices of Dordt". While not blind to their limitations
and faults, we honor them as those who stood for the
"faith of our Fathers", the doctrine of free grace. We
also praise them for their insistence on catechism preaching and teaching, their maintaining of the Psalter as the
chief manual of praise, and their stress on the necessity
of leading the separated life, be it that anabaptistic extremes at times revealed themselves in this respect. We
also revere them for what they practised about the christian school, and, soon after their early years of internal
struggle were over, proclaimed and planned about throwing out the life-line in missionary endeavor.

Finally we mention to their honor their demonstration
of the possibility of a free church, maintained by the offerings of a willing people, entirely without state support.

§8. EMIGRATION TO THE UNITED STATES: OBJECTIONS
TO IT; SETTLEMENTS; SPIRIT AND OBJECTIVES
OF OUR PIONEERS

It was largely from among the people who sided with
De Cock and his associates that the great movement of
migration to the United States originated. There were
two great causes for this. The first in historical order was
the bitter persecution which some of the followers of De
Cock and his fellow-reformers endured. Well might the
seceders speak of their "Church Under the Cross". The
Government at times cruelly persecuted God-fearing men
and women whose chief desire was to worship God according to the dictates of their conscience and according
to the creed which had made old Holland great. Cruel
dragonading, heavy fining, and needless imprisonment,

ineffaceably blotted the fair pages of the history of the Netherlands as a country of religious liberty. Bitterly some of our forebears suffered at times. They were ejected from their rented farms, boycotted in their business and ostracized socially. Even their little children were pelted with stones going to and from church or school. It was this persecution which led some of them to look for a land somewhere in which religious liberty could be enjoyed.

But a second cause leading to emigration became even more prominent and dominant. To the burden of the petty but painful persecutions which we enumerated, were added those of unusually hard times. These were the aftermath of the wars of Napoleon and others, and caused particularly at that time by the temporary upsetting of the labor market, owing to the introduction of machinery. Taxes were tremendously high, while wages were so low during the closing years of the first half of the nineteenth century, that in the Betuwe, one of the best parts of Gelderland, the poor had to content themselves with eating at each meal nothing but cabbage and turnips, without any bread. And no wonder,since some heads of families earned only 16 cents (about 6c American) per day. And they were glad to have work at all. Those out of work, and others who were indigent, were helped only very niggardly by the authorities. In Herwijnen, e.g., the poor received no better support than a quart of horse-beans and two stivers (4 cents American) per week, per person. (De Liefde-Lens, *Vaderlandsche Geschiedenis,* p. 652.)

Russian wheat and other grains also began to flood the Dutch markets, forcing prices down and throwing farmhands out of employment.

When, owing to disease, the potato crop, the poor man's staple food, failed in these years, and the winter of 1844-'45 was unusually severe, philanthropists like Rev. O. G. Heldring and some of the leaders of the Secession, thought of plans of migration to relieve the desperate situation. But as soon as they were broached, many objections were made to these projects. Especially when the name "America" was mentioned, many of the people spoke warningly of the "Indian raids" which rendered life insecure in the United States. Our climate was said to be unbearable, medical help was lacking, mail connections with the Netherlands were impossible, etc.

But besides these objections of a material sort, which Scholte was fully able to prove unfounded or exaggerated, some advanced arguments against migration which were of a *religious* character, and no doubt these at first weighed heavily on the minds of some of our forebears. Many quoted the case of Naomi as a deterring example in leaving the native land, and particularly Romans 13: 1-7, about subjection to the higher powers, was quoted, as if the Dutch themselves in the long ago had not "migrated" to the Low Lands and had not changed masters during the Eighty Years' War! And as to "Amerika"—when that was mentioned more and more as the "land of hope"—many took pains to picture it as dominated by the spirit of the French Revolution—as if Holland itself had escaped that. Moreover, some pleaded that, if the old home land were really as wicked as claimed, the pious people had the more reason to remain, in order to ward off or mitigate its merited doom. Particularly the motive to improve economic conditions was condemned, though without good grounds, as we shall see presently.

But while numbers were no doubt deterred by these objections, there were a few hundreds of people, mainly followers of Brummelkamp, Van Raalte and Scholte, who were not convinced. They quoted the Bible command to replenish the earth (Genesis 9: 1), as sufficient to offset all arguments advanced.

In order to act in unison, *Emigration Societies* were formed, and many joined them, although, in true Dutch fashion, several independent parties followed their own initiative, leading to unprofitable scattering of our people.

SETTLEMENTS IN AMERICA. SPIRIT OF THE PIONEERS

Favorable reports from a few Dutch people already settled in the United States, led to the decision to go thither instead of to the Dutch East Indies or South Africa as mentioned at times. On November 17, 1846, in the bark *Southerner,* the Rev. A. C. Van Raalte and his family arrived in New York, accompanied by some fifty Hollanders and Bentheimers. Soon they were on their way westward, wintering in and near Detroit, Mich. While there it was decided to settle in the Black River district in western Michigan.

Two days after Van Raalte had arrived at New York, the "voortrekkers" of Scholte's party of immigrants, led by Hendrik Barendregt, landed at New Orleans, Nov. 19, 1846. The next spring Scholte himself, in the *Sarah Sand,* came to America by way of Boston.

In a letter dated January 30, 1847, written in Detroit, Van Raalte expressed the hope that Scholte also would settle in Michigan, if not in the Black River district, then at least in the Grand River or Kalamazoo River valley, or in a more northerly part of Michigan. But, contrary to the advice of the Dutch motto: "Eendracht maakt macht", which Van Raalte quoted, Scholte, who was strongly individualistic, chose and followed his own way, thus leading to a division of forces, which, at first at least, sadly crippled the strength of the migration movement. He settled with some 800 followers in the heart of Iowa, founding the Pella Colony, later the mother of the Sioux County, Iowa, settlements of our people.

But these well known pioneer parties were not the only ones to arrive on our shores during the days of the "Great Trek", as we may call the period from 1845 to 1850, when our people founded colonies in Michigan and Iowa under the leadership of Van Raalte and Scholte. Various bands of Dutch people came hither and many displayed the same spirit.

If the hand of God is seen in American history at the time of bringing hither the best blood of the nations of western Europe, in the period of the colonizing of the Atlantic colonies, this same hand can be observed directing the footsteps of some of the most God-fearing men and women of Holland and adjoining regions to the United States during the middle of the nineteenth century.

The Wisconsin settlements, founded by the Revs. P. Zonne and G. Baay in 1847 and 1848, consisted of people who reckoned with God and His Word as much as their kinsmen across Lake Michigan, even though they did not influence the life of the Holland-Americans as much as those who lived in larger colonies.

Take also the Dutch settlements in what was formerly called Low and High Prairies, south of Chicago, Illinois. Low Prairie, since 1869, called South Holland, was founded by deeply religious people, such as the Killewinger, the De Jong, the Gouwens, the Van Vuuren, and the Benschop families. John Killewinger and Hendrik De Jong came there as the pioneers, in 1847, arriving direct from the province of South Holland, hence the name of their settlements.

From the province of North Holland came their neighbors to the north, living at what formerly was called High Prairie, now Roseland, a part of Chicago, Ill. The leader of the Roseland pioneers, who arrived in the spring of 1849, was Peter De Jong, a godly man, one of the small but faithful band of Seceders then living some miles north of Alkmaar. While he was a teacher at Kerkebuurt, celebrating a feast or "gastdag", so popular in that part of the Netherlands, some of De Jong's relatives mentioned their plan of going to America. He made it a subject of earnest prayer. When he had reached the conclusion that his Lord and Master wanted him to go, and he discovered that his relatives had changed their mind, De Jong insisted on going, and persuaded the others to follow. (Cf. Chapter VI, §6.)

Men of such positive convictions, men who reckoned with God in their planning, have started practically every Dutch settlement in the United States. Such was the case also with the colony at Fulton, Ill., whose founders, led by Vander Meulen, all came from Warffum, Groningen, members of the little Seceder church there which dates from 1835. At Fowler and Lafayette, Ind., and elsewhere, there were men of such type from the beginning, people of positive religious convictions.

That also applies to later settlements such as Holland, Neb., where in 1874, three "Seceder" families from the heart of "modern" North Holland settled, those of Klerk, Slot, and Smit.

The Roman Catholic Hollanders also, who founded the colonies of their people at Green Bay and near the Fox River, in Wisconsin, were led thither by a man whose name deserves to be remembered—the Rev. T. J. Vanden Broek, who spent many years of service in that region among the Indians.

Indeed, we know of no Holland settlement of any significance which did not have a strong religious element among it at the start. Surely, the hand of God was in this.

What the spirit of these pioneers was, has not been shown, however, by their later history alone, but was proclaimed from the very genesis of the movement, during the middle of the nineteenth century. The statutes of the Emigration Societies, above alluded to, breathe a positively christian spirit. The Utrecht organization, of which Scholte was the soul, had embodied in its articles of incorporation that only men of christian principles could join it, men who without subterfuge or evasion accepted the Word of God as authoritative. The Society formed under the auspices of Brummelkamp and Van Raalte expressed in Article 7 of its Rules: "The first duty is to make the colony christian, therefore it is recommended to the care of the committees which are to be concerned with accepting, aiding, and sending emigrants, to seek such a salting element for the colony as shall be necessary to give it a christian majority. For that reason they shall not accept any other persons for colonization than those from whom it may be expected that they will subject themselves to the Word of God, so that in that way there may be established not only a christian church government, but also a christian civil government for the maintaining of God's command which is the strength ("vastigheid") of every state." (*Leven van Prof. A. Brummelkamp,* p. 206. Cf. H. S. Lucas, *Michigan History Magazine,* Vol. VI, p. 670.)

The same spirit of the famous *Mayflower* compact breathing in these articles is also evident in a LETTER written by Brummelkamp and Van Raalte, dated May 25, 1846, addressed "to the Believers in North America", and given along with some parties who constituted the vanguard of the movement furthered by the men just named. It stated that the Dutch immigrants, soon due on our shores, maligned as they were in their old home, and considered the offscouring of the nation, came here with *objectives* that could bear investigation.

OBJECTIVES

Three purposes were announced. The first was to improve the social condition of the immigrants. Many of them, it was stated, were bowed down under the heavy burdens of the times in the Old World.

The second aim was: the desire to enjoy the great privilege of having their children taught in christian schools, "a privilege that we lack here, since in the public schools a general moral instruction is given which may offend neither Jew nor Romanist, while free schools are barred".

The third reason for coming to the United States was, they stated, "the sincere desire to have an active part in the propagation of God's truth among the heathen, something for which many of us have a desire, but power to do it begins to fail". To do this, they aimed at a fourth objective, viz., to live in groups, "dorpsgewijze", as they called it, to prevent scattering and all its dangers, and to insure the interests or worship and education. "Eendracht maakt macht" was quoted here also.

Would these pioneers and their posterity reach these objectives? And would they remain loyal to the principles of the Secession people to which we alluded in the preceding paragraph? The prosperity of the Holland-American people almost everywhere evident in their many settlements from coast to coast, shows that the first objective has been reached. Incidentally this is manifest in the many activities carried on and institutions maintained by our churches. In how far the other matters we named were kept in mind, this volume aims to show.

TEST QUESTIONS

1. Why should we make a study of denominational history?

2. What were the social and religious conditions of our ancestors?

3. When did the first missionaries reach them? Who were they?

4. Mention some of the unscriptural doctrines and practices of the Roman Church.

5. Name some of the forerunners of the Reformation; its leaders and grounds.

6. What can you relate about the Reformed Church of Holland, its Synod of Dordt, and its theologians during the seventeenth century?

7. Name the cause of the Secession, its leaders and grounds, and characterize its people, and the things they stood for.

8. Which two great causes led to Emigration to the United States?

9. Name the chief settlements of our people, and describe the spirit of our pioneers.

10. What can you say about the objectives of the immigrants?

WORKS OF REFERENCE

"The Reformed Reformation", J. I. Good.

"The Reformed Church in the Netherlands, 1340—1840", M. G. Hansen.

"The Dutch Reformation in the 16th Century", W. C. Martyn.

"A Church and Her Martyrs", D. Van Pelt.

"A. C. Van Raalte" (Dutch), H. E. Dosker.

Same, by J. A. Wormser.

"Hendrik Peter Scholte", J. A. Wormser.

"The Hollanders in Iowa", J. Vander Zee.

"A Dutch Settlement in Michigan", A. J. Pieters.

"Religious Thought in Holland During the 19th Century", J. H. Mackay.

"De Chr. Geref. Kerk, Zestig Jaren van Strijd en Zegen", Henry Beets, Chapters I and II.

Cf. works on the Dutch Secession by J. C. Rullmann, J. A. Wormser, H. Bouwman, J. H. Landwehr, and others.

CHAPTER II

THE CHURCH OF OUR PIONEERS, ORGANIZED, UNITED AND DISUNITED

§1. The Struggles of our Pioneers. §2. The Reformed Church in America in Its History. §3. First Contact with the R. C. A. §4. Dr. Wyckoff's Visit and Report. §5. The Union with its Ommitted Reservation. §6. Dissatisfaction in Michigan and the Grounds for it. §7. The Parting of the Ways, April 8, 1857. §8. The Right to a Place in the Sun. §9. The Pluriformity of the Church. Our Mission.

§1. THE STRUGGLES OF OUR PIONEERS

THE FOUNDATIONS of the early settlements of our people in America have been laid not alone at the expense of brain, brawn, and sweat, like all such new beginnings in the untrodden wildernesses of our land, but of many tears and prayers as well. Yea, at the expense of many lives. "Settlements are built on the bones of the settlers"—something like that has become a proverb, based on reality.

The colonies of our people in Wisconsin, in Illinois, and in Indiana all went through trying privations, untold hardships, and various afflictions. In 1848 the *Mayflower,* with several Dutch immigrants aboard, caught fire when near Sheboygan, Wis., on Lake Michigan—a panic ensued and several Hollanders perished miserably. Even the Iowa settlement has known years of stress and struggle, although Scholte is said to have led "the flower of the Dutch emigration of that day"—many men with means being among them. In the central portion of Iowa, in Marion County, title had been secured to 18,000 acres of excellent land. The eight hundred people who belonged to Scholte's first party immediately provided shelter in the shape of sheds made of lumber they had found on hand. Soon after they built dug-outs, sod-houses, partly above and partly below the ground. Pella, laid out in the fall of 1847, became known as the "Straw Town" (Strooien Stad), from the appearance of the straw roofs of these huts. But the spring of 1848 brought a terrible windstorm which razed many buildings under construction and wrecked some already occupied. The winter of 1848–'49 was unusually severe. Snow covered the ground from November, 1848, to May, 1849, at an average depth of three feet, and for weeks the temperature was twenty degrees below zero. Much live stock perished and many people suffered severely from lack of fuel. In the spring of 1849 came disastrous floods which killed still more cattle, unable to extricate themselves from the miry bottom lands in which they grazed. During 1849 many of the Iowa colonists had exhausted their supply of money. Truly, it was a testing-time they passed through in Pella.

But God provided relief in the way of His Providence. Gold had been discovered in California. One of the main trails thither led through Pella, and the colonists were able to dispose of their produce for ready money. During 1849, two hundred and fifty more Hollanders came to the Pella colony. When the government census was taken in 1850, there lived in Iowa 1,108 Hollanders of foreign birth, by 1856 increased to 2,077.

Many more of our people, however, had during that period gone to Van Raalte's colony in western Michigan. Most of them were of the poorer class, compared to Scholte's followers. They had but little money, not enough to buy prairie land, like Scholte's followers were able to purchase. That fact evidently was the chief reason for Van Raalte selecting Michigan. It was not alone closer to Detroit, where his party had wintered from 1846–'47, as we already recorded, thus saving traveling expense, but also cheaper. We find him writing to Brummelkamp that he would not dare to plant a colony on the prairies, since it demanded too much money. A well-wooded section would also mean the building of houses at small cost. But, oh what a price, in other respects than money, our pioneers paid at first to carve their homes and fortunes out of the forest primeval of Michigan!

Van Raalte's vanguard arrived on the evening of February 9, 1847, at what now is the site of Holland, Mich. Soon others came to join the little band. The Rev. M. A. Ypma reached Holland during June, 1847, with 49 Friesians, to found the Vriesland colony nearby. Closely in their wake came a company of people from Bentheim, to found Graafschap. The Rev. H. G. Klyn became their pastor the next year. Next came a strong party of immigrants hailing from the province of Zeeland, led by such strong men as the Rev. C. Vander Meulen, and J. Vande Luyster and J. Steketee. They settled between Holland and Vriesland. "Brothertown", thus Vander Meulen had intended to call the centre of the settlement, but "Zeeland" was chosen. Near Zeeland was Groningen, whose founder was the enterprising John Rabbers. Drenthe, settled in 1847, shows the provincial origin of its pioneers sufficiently, and so does Overisel, whose first settlers came there in 1848. Noordeloos was started during the year last named by a few people from the province of Groningen. North Holland, settled in 1849, was doubtless named thus after its location, five or six miles northeast of the chief place of the Dutch colony, usually called "de Stad", Holland. By October, 1847, there were already some two thousand in the various places we enumerated.

But, as in Iowa, the colony was soon to be tried, and even a great deal worse. The work of clearing the ground was very arduous. Food was in many cases insufficient. The homes of our Michigan pioneers were of a very primitive kind: huts covered with bark, or cloth, and but poor shelter for men and women accustomed to good houses. The furniture was a kind of makeshift. Clothes were not what our people were used to wearing. The little money they had was soon spent or tied up in land and tools. The exposure and poverty involved in the above, as well as the dampness of swamp lands and clearings, brought all kinds of sickness, such as malarial fever, dissentery, bilious fever, scarlet fever, and smallpox. Before long the Colony looked like a large hospital. Many families died out completely, and practically all suffered grievous bereavements. Of a company of Friesians, twenty-two in number, which had arrived in 1847, only eleven survived by April, 1848. The population of Groningen was diminished by one-half. In Graafschap the living scarcely had strength enough to dig a grave for their dead. During the late summer of 1847, when Van Raalte preached to a small band of colonists, he broke out in a weeping ejaculation while at prayer: "O Lord, must we all die?" Quite a number left the Colony in disgust, to settle elsewhere. A few, we are told, had lost their faith as well as their possessions.

But not so, thank God, the great mass of our people. Those driven through force of economic circumstances to neighboring towns like Grand Haven, Kalamazoo, and particularly Grand Rapids, started religious services from the very beginning. In the Colony itself, notwithstanding all trials and tribulations, regular Sunday services were held in all the congregations, catechetical classes were taught, the sick visited, discipline exercised, in short, all the religious interests were attended to, although services were held at first amidst primitive conditions. In the beginning open-air services were held, the preacher standing on a rude platform, his audience seated around him on logs, and stumps, and other things which could serve the purpose. But before long log churches were built and the Colonial Church at Holland, erected in 1856, shows laudable sacrifice of labor and money, as well as an eye for architectural design. Schools were opened in various

places, as related in Chapter VI, §6. During the summer
of 1849 the church at Holland was reported to number
225 families; Zeeland, 175; Vriesland, 69; and Overisel
135, while Graafschap's congregation numbered 50 families, Drenthe 45, and Groningen 30. Altogether there were
in 1849—928 communicant members, and a total of some
3,000 souls.

Some of these immigrant congregations were not organized in a formal way, notably thet First Church of Holland, Mich., shepherded by Rev. Van Raalte, the acknowledged leader of the Colony, and its pastor till 1867. Consistory-members who had served in the churches of our
Fathers across the sea re-assumed their functions here without a formal vote. So it came to pass that, for instance, in
the Zeeland church at first 16 elders were functioning, and
14 deacons. The Secession of 1834 for that matter, while
strong as to dogmatic principles, did not excel in clear in-
sight into Reformed Church polity. That was to be a root
of trouble later on. But our pioneers felt enough for Presbyterian principles of church government to realize the
need of some judicatory of broader scope and jurisdiction
than a local consistory, and so as early as April 23, 1848,
consistory-members and their pastors organized what they
called a classical meeting, later known as the Classis of
Holland. At first, however, they did not strictly follow
historical precedent. All consistory-members were seated
as members of Classis, and not alone ecclesiastical subjects were discussed in those early days, but also matters
pertaining to education and such common interests as the
making of roads, the building of bridges, etc.

As things were brightening up by the spring of 1849,
economically speaking, and under the shepherding care
of faithful pastors and capable elders, it seemed that the
future held the promise of a vigorous church life, according to the principles of the Church of the fathers across the
sea and in close connection with that body. But, strange

to say, no arrangements had been made with the denomination in the Netherlands as to ecclesiastical *relationship*. And instead of developing a church life of their own, as the Pilgrims of New England had done, our Michigan pioneers were led to connect themselves with another denomination whose history we must trace first to fully understand the situation.

§2.   THE   REFORMED   CHURCH   IN   AMERICA—ITS   HISTORY

When the "Pilgrims of the West" arrived in the United States they were welcomed by a few leaders of a denomination which, within a decade of the meeting of the great Synod of Dordrecht, had been planted in the New World as an offshoot of the old Church of the fathers. It was the Reformed Church in America, at the time officially known as the Reformed Protestant Dutch Church. During Holland's Golden Age, while the Eighty Years' War was still raging, the enterprising Netherlanders had wrested much territory from the hands of their foes. Not alone the East Indian Islands, already named in Chapter I, became Dutch possessions, but, after Henry Hudson, in 1609, had sailed up the river to be named after him, the country along the Atlantic sea coast, between Virginia and what was then known as New France, between the fortieth and forty-ninth degree of latitude, was also claimed by the Hollanders as theirs, by right of discovery, and in 1614 named New Netherland. On Manhattan Island, bought from the Indians for "the value of sixty guilders", or about $24, divine services were begun at least as early as the spring of 1624. In the course of time, as other Dutch settlers came to the New Netherlands, joined by religious refugees from Belgium, France, and the Palatinate, congregations of the Reformed faith and order were established in different places along the Hudson, Mohawk, and Raritan rivers, and in adjacent territory. In 1846, when our pioneers arrived in the United States, there were 271 Reformed Churches, served by 280 ministers. The denomination numbered 23,301 families, embracing 32,209 communicant members and totaling 104,098 souls. While the name "Dutch" was still a part of the official denominational title, the language of Holland had ceased to be that of public worship, although quite a number of the older people were able to converse in what was called "Jersey Dutch", and among prominent families in New York and New Jersey, some were considerably interested in Old Holland.

§3. FIRST CONTACT WITH THE REFORMED CHURCH

When tidings of the persecution entailed by the Secession reached America, they provoked sympathy, already as early as 1838, when the Classis of Poughkeepsie called the attention of General Synod to it, but found this body unable to express its judgment because of lack of information. In 1846 the Rev. Th. De Witt signified to the General Synod that he intended to visit Holland that summer. Synod *resolved* to recommend him "to the entire confidence and affection of the brethren and judicatories of the General Synod [of the Netherland Reformed Church] from which the Dutch Reformed Church in the United States had sprung and toward which it continues to cherish the most affectionate regards". Evidently, it was not realized at the time how some of these very "brethren" had considerable to do with the persecutions of the Seceders. But the Lord overruled it for good, for Dr. De Witt reported to the General Synod of 1847 that: "When in Holland I received information of a rising spirit of emigration to America and especially among the (afgescheiden) seceders from the Established Church, and had a short interview with the Rev. Mr. Scholte of Utrecht, recently arrived in this country". (*Minutes General Synod,* p. 135.)

The "Letter" of the Revs. Brummelkamp and Van Raalte to the American believers, (Chapter I, §7), was handed to the Rev. I. N. Wyckoff, who translated it and had it published, October 15, 1846, in the columns of *The Christian Intelligencer,* the organ of the Reformed Church. In Albany, where he was pastor at the time, (from 1836— 1866), Dr. Wyckoff organized a "Holland Emigration Society" to aid "the new body of Pilgrims who reached our shores from Holland, the land of our fathers and the shelter, in ages gone by, to outcasts by persecution". The General Synod of 1848 *resolved,* in view of the great number of Hollanders coming to this country, that the students at New Brunswick Seminary should learn Dutch, to be able to preach to the newcomers in their own language. The Board of Domestic Missions was charged "to give special attention to the wants of the Protestant Hollanders, with a view to bring them into connection with our Church". The Reformed congregation at Grand Rapids, dating from 1840, frequently opened its pulpit to "the Holland ministers in that vicinity who dispensed the Word and ordinances to the people who recently settled there from the land of our forefathers". (*Minutes* 1849, p. 503.)

§4.   DR. WYCKOFF'S VISIT AND REPORT

Finally, on the last day of May, 1849, Dr. Wyckoff himself appeared upon the scene at Holland, Mich., as "special agent" sent by the Board of Domestic Missions of the Reformed Church to inquire "into the religious and ecclesiastical relations of this people, to express to them the sympathy of our Church, to make overtures for church relation, and to offer such aid in their straitness as might be necessary and desirable".

Dr. Wyckoff found our pioneers indeed in "straitness", outwardly. Their funds were exhausted in the purchase of land and in making improvements. "The pastors have but little support, some of them literally none, from their churches". But they were reported to live in faith and hope of better times, rejoicing that the Lord had kept them alive during their first and bitter struggle with the forest, with disease and disappointment in "the dark and untrodden wilderness". There was much joy in the Colony when Dr. Wyckoff showed the interest of the Church of the East in the Hollanders of the West, "who had mourned that the Dutch Church (had) counted them strangers, and had no word of encouragement, no hand of help for them", as he expressed it later in his report to his Board. Rev. Van Raalte "dispatched letters and messengers to the several ministers and consistories, inviting them to a conference with me on Monday, June 4th. Quite a large company attended......At the Classical meeting it was soon made known that the brethren were a little afraid of entering into ecclesiastical connection with us, although they believe in the union of brethren and sigh for christian sympathy and association. They have so felt to the quick the galling chain of ecclesiastical domination, and have seen with sorrow how exact organization, according to human rules, leads to formality on the one hand, and to oppression of tender consciences on the other, that they hardly knew what to say. I protested, of course, that it was the farthest from our thoughts to bring them in bondage to men, or to exercise ecclesiastical tyranny over them. And I stated that they would be most perfectly free, at any time they found an ecclesiastical connection opposed to their religious prosperity or enjoyment, to bid us a fraternal adieu, and be by themselves again". "On comparison of doctrine, a perfect agreement with our standards was found. In the Order of their churches, they believe each church and consistory should direct and manage its own concerns, and incline to the idea that an appellate jurisdiction of superior judicatories is not so scriptural as a kind and fraternal conference and advice. Each of their churches appoints as many elders as seems desirable, and they are always in office until they are dismissed as guilty and unworthy, or removed by death. As the result, they agreed, with those explanations, to join our Synod".

§5. THE UNION AND ITS OMMITTED RESERVATION

"They agreed to join our Synod". So Dr. Wyckoff stated in the Report of the June, 1849, meeting from which we quoted. Evidently on the basis of this agreement the Rev. A. C. Van Raalte attended the meeting of the Particular Synod of Albany. "We authorize him in our name to give and ask all necessary information which can facilitate the desired union", so it was stated in his credentials, signed by the president of Classis, the Rev. S. Bolks. The Albany Synod agreed to this union, and at the General Synod, held at Pougkeepsie, N. Y., a little later, the Classis of Holland was received under its care.

It seems incredible that our Holland pioneers rushed this union matter through the way they did. There had been no newspaper discussion about it to explain the pros and cons of such an important matter as a union with a body whose very name was not correctly known among them, even by the ministers, as the records show. No congregational meeting had been held to weigh the matter. There is no record of any consistorial discussion on the subject or any instruction given to delegates at Classis. Fact is, there is not even a record of any *motion* of Classis passed as the basis of the letter of President Bolks, although this is considered the "formal application" of the Classis of Holland to be received into the Reformed Church. But it only mentions authorization to "give and ask all such information as may be necessary to pro-

mote the desired union". Moreover, there had been absolutely no investigation made by a committee of Classis to
find out all it could about the body they had been asked
to join. Indeed, of such a loose mode of procedure, and such
a haste in forming an ecclesiastical union we have not
found a parallel anywhere in Church History. In our days
people would speak of "railroading it through". We repeat: it seems incredible the way our sensible pioneers
rushed the matter. Did they not know: haste makes
waste? And a second thing looks incredible: the way the
reservation of Dr. Wyckoff was omitted from all official
documents. But others had not forgotten that stipulation
about freedom to be by themselves in case they found the
connection opposed to their religious prosperity or enjoyment. It was too vital a matter to them. Our pioneers
were Calvinists. A Calvinist ever is, as Bancroft stated,
a fanatic for liberty. Could they sign away their ecclesiastical freedom without the calm investigation the
Dutchman usually institutes before he acts? Indeed, it
has occurred to the writer that it was this very reservation
which made our pioneers go as unexpectedly swift as they
did. The "union" was, at best, only conditional and tenta-
tive, so, it appears to us, was the popular impression.

It seems to us that the responsibility for this rests particularly on the shoulders of Dr. Wyckoff. We fail to see
that he was at liberty to make such a reservation as he did.
The formation of a church union is more than merely an
ecclesiastical business transaction. It involves spiritual
and moral interests as well. Had he foreseen the use to
be made of it later, he no doubt would have refrained
from offering it.

And the men of the convention of 1849 should have
realized also that such a stipulation was not proper. They
should have investigated thoroughly what kind of a
church they were about to join. What a large amount of
misery they might have prevented. Had they forgotten

the question of the prophet of old: "Shall two walk together, except they have agreed?" (Amos 3: 3.)

In our work *De Christelijke Gereformeerde Kerk*, p. 72, we made the statement that in so far as the union with the R. C. A. took place in the West it was contrary to Reformed Church polity, because the men who attended the meeting with Dr. Wyckoff were not properly delegated to transact the business of the day—not having been authorized by their consistories in so far as the records show. In fact, the meeting was not a classical one at all, but simply a convention, a meeting of ministers and consistory members hastily called together. The later action of the Classis, too, was not strictly formal; the action, we mean, was not based on a properly passed motion. In so far as the union took place in the East, we asserted it was illegal because no mention was made at all of the reservation.

We have not seen any reason as yet to alter the statements involved in the above. And we are glad that no less an authority on Church Polity than Prof. Dr. H. Bouwman of the Kampen Theological School wrote in his *Amerika*, p. 136: "No doubt in regard to the manner in which union was decided from the side of the Classis of Holland it was not according to Church polity as to its form", (niet kerkrechtelijk juist in den vorm), while on p. 137 the admission is made: "the legality of this union consequently is subject to just objection" (de wettigheid van deze vereeniging is dus aan rechtmatige bedenking onderhevig.)

How Dr. Bouwman expresses agreement with our assertion, p. 38 of the *Gedenkboek* as to the separation being a matter of duty (plichtmatig), we shall see later on.

§6.   DISSATISFACTION

In the Church of our pioneers there was not a perfect oneness of opinion on all matters ecclesiastical. For one thing: it certainly was not the common view that, as Dr.

Wyckoff stated: each church and consistory should direct and manage its own affairs, and the inclination to the idea that the jurisdiction of superior judicatories is not so scriptural as a kind and fraternal conference and advice could not have been that of all. Such would be in perfect harmony with the independent theory of church government (see Chapter X, §1), but it certainly is not the Reformed or Presbyterian conception. There was difference of opinion also about the Church Order. The Holland Classis had adopted the entire *Handbook* ("Kerkelijk Handboekje") containing the regulations of all the Synods of the Dutch Churches held prior to 1618–'19, and not simply the Rules of the Synod of Dordt of the last named years—something which was bound to cause confusion.

Again, there were differences among our people about the length of the term of service of elders and deacons— the meeting of 1849 seemingly favored life-tenure—whereas the Church Order of Dordt spoke of two years' terms. Some of our pioneers believed that all children of the Church should be baptized, others only those whose parents, one or both, had made confession of faith. Some favored celebrating the great feasts of the Church with a two days' celebration, others considered one day quite enough. In Holland, Mich., the hierarchial bearing of Rev. Van Raalte and his consistory, by one, (Krabshuis?) dubbed the Pope and his cardinals", led to friction as well as other matters, inevitable since in those days consistories busied themselves with material as well as with spiritual things. In other places, too, there were disputes which originated in or were increased by strife about land contracts and other material things.

But the ever-recurring and constantly increasing source of unrest and dissatisfaction centered in and was fed by the hasty "union" of 1849–'50. It was an ever-growing conviction: we joined a Church we should not have united with.

What a committee should have detected was discovered by men who, during a shorter or longer period, sojourned in the East, notably Gysbert Haan, formerly from Hilversum, friend of the Rev. S. Van Velzen, the sternest Calvinist among the men who led the Secession movement. These men saw and heard different things about the doctrines and practices of the Reformed Church which filled them with amazement and alarm. They also learned various things from men who belonged to the True Reformed Dutch Church, in New Jersey and New York, which already in 1822 had found grounds for a secession from the judicatories of the Reformed Church. These grounds, they claimed, were the toleration of Hopkinsian errors, Arminian teachings on the atonement and election, abuse of sealing ordinances, and fraternization with Arminians.

When these things became known to the people in the Colony—voices of protest were soon raised. The first ominous sign of the approaching storm was seen at the consistory meeting of Rev. Van Raalte's church, held August 22, 1853.

Article 4: "Deacon (T.) Keppel had learned from Plaggermars, that the church-member Hoffman, farmer, already during more than a year spreads slander about our minister, viz., that his reverence for the sake of money, has brought our congregation into an impure church". Of course, our soul revolts at this mention of mercenary motives. Van Raalte stood far too high for this. But that the Church which had been joined in such unexplainable or at least unjustifiable haste, was *impure,* became the conviction of an ever-increasing number of people in the Colony. The following is a resumé of what was usually objected to:

(1) Departure from the Calvinism of the standards— particularly as to the two points just mentioned, atonement and election.

(2) Neglect of Catechism-preaching and teaching.

(3) The use of 800 hymns, contrary to the Church Order of Dordrecht—a matter, by the way, which had been discussed vehemently in Holland, early in the nineteenth century in what was called "Gezangenstrijd" or controversy about the hymns which had been forced upon the Church.

(4) The toleration of Free Masons as members in good standing.

(5) Private baptisms taking the place of public administration of the sacrament in connection with preaching, according to Reformed principle.

(6) Admission of non-reformed people to the Communion table: open communion.

(7) Neglect of family-visiting as required by the Church Order.

Additional grievances were found with the opening of pulpits to preachers of various denominations, while several expressed disapproval of the way wherein the right of the Dutch Secession was denied. The fact that some of the pastors recommended Baxter's *Call,* condemned as Arminian by such men as Erskine, Marshall and Comrie, was also considered a severe grievance. (Compare *Acht Nacht-teekenen,* Appendix II. of this work.)

There was much debating of the matter among our people in those days in private conversation and at consistorial meetings. A "rain of protests" at Classis followed. There was evidently a pleading that *all* of the brethren might return to the "standpoint of 1849", as their former condition and position was called. But most of the clerical leaders defended the "East" as much and as long as they could. A breach appeared more and more unavoidable. It occurred less than a decade after our people settled in Michigan. The church of our pioneers, organized, united with the R. C. A., was soon to be disunited.

§7. THE PARTING OF THE WAYS, APRIL 8, 1857

As the Secession of 1834 had forerunners, so did the Movement of 1857. As early as 1853 the Rev. R. H. Smit and the greater part of his Drenthe church had severed connections with the Holland Classis and joined the Associate Reformed Church, usually called the "Scottish Church", a body which in 1858 was one of the two groups which combined to form the United Presbyterian Church.

During the spring of 1856, J. Gelock and G. Haan and others in Grand Rapids, sent their resignations to their consistory and began to hold separate divine services. A. Krabshuis had left the Holland congregation already during January of 1856, and H. W. Dam was dismissed from the Vriesland church, March, 1856. January 25, 1857, the Rev. H. G. Klyn, joined the brethren Gelock and Haan and their following. At the meeting of the Holland Classis on the 8th of April, 1857, formal *notices of withdrawal,* to return to the standpoint of 1849, were on the table from the congregations of Graafschap and Polkton, from the Rev. K. Vanden Bosch and his Noordeloos church, and from the Rev. H. G. Klyn. Rev. Vanden Bosch's letter was harsh, in keeping with his character, as we shall see later. Rev. Klyn's letter contained a pathetic plea for his brethren of the Classis to unite with him on the same platform. The missive of the Graafschap consistory—which reminded of Dr. Wyckoff's reservation—pleaded in the same way as Rev. Klyn's epistle. "Brethren, we rejoice that nearly the entire congregation....again occupies the platform (standpunt) on which our fathers enjoyed so much happiness (zaligheid), and O, we should rejoice still more if the King of the Church would persuade you that it is the duty of us all. The God of love may be your Counsellor and Leader to walk in the path of truth". The letter of Polkton's consistory also spoke of walking on the way of the fathers as its cordial wish and prayer.

But all this pleading was in vain. The Classis of Holland, in its majority, received and filed the communications alluded to, without further action. The Church of our pioneers was disunited. Its small minority effected a classical organization April, 1857, at Holland, Mich., the Rev. Klyn acting as president and the Rev. Vanden Bosch as clerk. The old standards were displayed and acknowledged—the Forms of Unity of the fathers, and their liturgy and Church Order—and it was resolved to notify the Seceder Church in the Old Home of what had transpired in the New World. In a *Letter,* sent to the Dutch Synod, and dated Grand Rapids, April 24, 1857, the Revs. Klyn and Vanden Bosch asserted that fundamental errors existed in the Reformed Church, especially as to general atonement, and the desire was expressed to be acknowledged as a part of the seceded Reformed Church in the Netherlands, that it might assist with counsel and help. (See Appendix I.) How Synod acted on this we shall see in Chapter III, §5.

§8. THE RIGHT TO A PLACE IN THE SUN

It was to be expected that the movement of 1857 was to be condemned by those who preferred to remain in the Reformed Church. History is full of parallel facts. The Roman Catholic Church anathematized the Reformers and to this day calls the Reformation a revolt. The Secession of 1834 has been branded by some champions of the Established Church as a denial of the work of God who made the "Hervormde" Church a mother of the nation, whereas the Secession was not the Lord's work but that of men. (De Stigter, *Vaderlandsche Kerk,* p. 90.) The second reformatory movement in the Netherlands which in 1886 led to the Doleantie under Dr. A. Kuyper, has been described as having started under the curse of God (*Banner,* January 4, 1923).

In Chapter I, §7 we already related that an author in America as late as 1922, characterized the Seceders of 1834 as men who vociferated their appeals to the Fathers of Dordt, but in their ignorance and anger tore the doctrines and practices of these fathers to shreds. When one so far removed from the time and scene as Mr. Van Eyck, feels thus about the men of 1834, there is but little room for wonder that he also was stirred up to write 300 pages, "to show that the Reformed Church of 1850 was the historical continuation of the real Reformed Church of the era of Dordt, comparatively unsullied by the waves of European or New England rationalism......*and of the unbalanced doctrines and extravagances of the Dutch Secession of eighty years ago*—a Church from which the Secession of the Western Hollanders in 1857 proved to be an illegal, unscriptural and unreformed schism, based not indeed entirely on wrong intentions, but on ignorance of the distinctive features of Reformed Churches", (p. 319). Over against these sweeping and harsh contentions, we claim that the movement of 1857 was *legal, scriptural,* and *Reformed,* and giving the Christian Reformed Church "a right to a place in the sun"—to borrow a well-known phrase.

(1)   The movement of 1857 was *legal* because it was in harmony with the reservation recorded in §4 above, giving our forebears liberty "at any time they found an ecclesiastical connection opposed to their religious prosperity or enjoyment to bid us [the Reformed Church] a fraternal adieu and be by themselves". This reservation was of much wider scope than some have been willing to admit. It referred not simply to "bondage" and "tyranny", named in the preceding sentence, but to prosperity and enjoyment—far broader conceptions. And about this prosperity and enjoyment "they", and not others, were to judge. As a lawyer who had carefully gone over the evidence submitted in the *Landmarks,* put it: "An impartial critic

cannot fail to read in these words so often quoted the possibility and opportunity for a separation. The question then presents itself as to how such desired separation was to be brought about. Was it to be through resolutions and acts of individuals of local congregations, or only through the actions of an organized body of superior jurisdiction? Where a formal union existed, the door was closed for the last named course. Only the other two avenues remained open and were followed when that step was taken. The brethren who left the Dutch Reformed Church, either individually or collectively, felt that by so doing they could preserve longer their individual characteristic and have greater opportunity for self-expression. Time and history have proven that to be a fact. The Christian Reformed Church fills its own place in the religious world of today, and does it well." (*The Banner,* February 15, 1923, p. 107.)

That this reservation was not mentioned later on, when the union was consummated, of course, does not alter the situation. It had been named at the June meeting (1849), which formed the basis for the later transactions. Its specific mention by Dr. Wyckoff explains what otherwise might be considered very unseemly haste and procedure, contrary to Reformed Church polity and Dutch character. Withdrawal on the basis of such a plain and broad stipulation was entirely *legal.*

(2) But, was it *scriptural?* People who place the Word of God above any human word, its holy Law above any other law, are mainly concerned with that question. And here, too, we do not hesitate to say: the movement of 1857 was not unscriptural, as charged, but in harmony with Holy Writ. In our *Christelijke Gereformeerde Kerk* we have devoted an entire chapter to prove the Return of 1857 legal, a matter of duty, and justified by history (Chapter V). Let us here name but one thing: Free Masonry. We have the assertions made at various times by leaders and classical meetings of the Reformed Church

that Free Masonry is "anti-republican, anti-christian, and anti-Reformed". These assertions were based on careful investigation of official Masonic literature and substantiated by the testimony of converted Masons. The Deism underlying Free Masonry, its exclusion of the Christ as the only Savior, in order to avoid giving offense to Jews and liberals, who belong to the Order, its fearful oaths, its bombastic nomenclature, its sinister influence on the Commonwealth, its honey-combing of the churches,—all these and more things prove Free Masonry to be contrary to the precepts of our Lord. Even the General Synod of the R. C. A. in 1870 declared officially, "the path of prudence and safety lies outside of all oath-bound secret societies". But a number of Reformed church-members, ministers as well as laymen, belonged to this Secret Order during the period of agitation which led to the movement of 1857. Neither at that time, nor before it, nor afterwards did the Reformed Church ever take a decided stand against it. Instead, the evil has been allowed to grow unhindered. We have the testimony of a man like Dr. H. Bavinck: "More than half of the preachers of the Reformed Church belong to the lodge". (*Dr. Herman Bavinck,* by V. Hepp, p. 308.)

Now what does the Bible say about such fellowshiping of the people of God with the children of the world? Paul tells us, 2 Cor. 6: 14-19: "Be not unequally yoked with unbelievers: for what fellowship have righteousness and iniquity? or what communion hath light with darkness? And what concord hath Christ with Belial? or what portion hath a believer with an unbeliever?......wherefore come out from among them and be ye separate saith the Lord, and touch no unclean thing; and I will receive you, and will be to you a Father, And ye shall be my sons and daughters, saith the Lord Almighty." In view of such apostolic injunction, and on the basis of what Reformed authorities have said about Free Masonry, we aver that the movement of 1857 was *scriptural*. The brethren of

Graafschap and others who discussed the subject as one of their grievances against the Reformed Church, were keen enough to see this, even in their day, when there was not as much light on it as we have at present.

(3) Was the movement of 1857 an *un-Reformed schism,* as claimed, or in line with Reformed precedent? And we assert that it was in harmony with what Protestants throughout the ages and in different countries have practised. The Reformation, as we saw in Chapter I, §4, was a *protest* against departures from the marks of the true Church and an endeavor to have the original purity of the body of Christ restored. The Secession of 1834, as related in §7 above, was, in its essence, a movement of the same character. So were the great Free Church movements in their days, the middle of the preceding century, in Scotland, Switzerland, and elsewhere, and long before them those of the Waldenses of Italy and the Hussites of Bohemia. Now, we claim that the withdrawal from the communion of the Reformed Church in America, in 1857, was a justifiable following of the precedents set by others. It, too, as related in §7 above, was a *protest* against departures from the marks of the true Church and an attempt to bring about the restoration of the purity of the Church which our forebears had come to understand and love in the Church across the Atlantic. They had serious scruples of conscience about a number of things they had discovered in the communion they had joined post haste. Lording it over their conscience—that would have been un-Reformed. To follow its dictates—has ever been considered a duty before God as well as men. And the more so, since their act of separation included what was quoted above: the preservation of their individual characteristics and greater opportunity for self-expression. Theirs were different ideals about the future as well as different conceptions of the past.

That leads us to one more observation confirming the right to separate denominational existence.

§9. THE PLURIFORMITY OF THE CHURCH. OUR MISSION

In the fact of the *pluriformity* of the Church of God we find our fourth ground for claiming a place in the sun. The acknowledgement of this pluriformity is of comparatively recent date. Augustine in his days sketched the ideal of one Church, embracing all mankind, a world-church, the City of God on earth. Something of that ideal led the popes to push their claims for supremacy among the rulers of the world. They found serious opposition in the appearing of new national ideals. Calvin in his days and in line with these new aspirations, spoke of national churches. The nation was to be the body, of which the Church was to be the soul. There was room in such a state for only one Church, the established one. What was outside of that was "false", spurious. It was something of that idea that caused Brakel to write as he did about those who "seceded"—sentiments which often have been quoted in condemnation of secession movements on both sides of the Atlantic.

But facts are stubborn things. As the Word of God was studied, as new church organizations appeared, manifesting the spirit of Christ, and doing His Kingdom work, people began to revise their opinion. It was assented to, in course of time, that during this dispensation, until Antichrist appears, the terms "false" and "true" are relative ideas and not absolute ones. (Cf. Kuyper, *Reformatie*, p. 114.) The one invisible Church of God reveals itself not exclusively in one manifestation, but in various groups of believers or denominations. Especially Dr. A. Kuyper brought out the idea of the pluriformity of the Church which expresses the above. It was God's design, that at Babel the one humanity should separate in order to develop human life in *national* manifestations. Each of the peoples was to carry out its own mission and to contribute what it, and only it, could contribute to the world's development. And so the one invisible Church evidently was designed to manifest itself in different forms, each to carry out its own particular mission and to furnish its own contribution to the Kingdom of God. As it requires all the saints to comprehend what is the breadth and length and height and depth and to know the love of Christ which passes knowledge (Eph. 3: 18, 19), so it takes more than one group of believers to manifest the riches of the counsel of our God in planning the one great body of Christ, to the praise of His glory, world without end. As Judge Brewer of the United States Supreme Court expressed it: "denominations exist, will exist and ought to exist. Their existence is in no manner inconsistent with the spirit of unity which should animate all. They only illustrate the great principle of the universe: unity in variety". Or, as Prof. Honig of Kampen stated it: "This pluriformity is in part the work of Him who loves variety". God's Old Testament people during their wilderness journey marched as tribes and pitched their tents as such, each tribe in its place. But the ark of the covenant was the common center. And so during the journey of the New Testament Church, God's Pilgrim Army marches and encamps as denominational regiments and national brigades. If only the One Covenant God be ever kept in the center and holy jealousy reign, instead of Ephraim envying Judah, and Judah vexing Ephraim, (Isaiah 11: 13).

As to the *mission* of the denomination here described, see Chapter V, §8. To once more quote Dr. H. Bouwman, "We agree, therefore, with what Dr. Beets writes on page 38 of the *Gedenkboek*: 'It was a matter of duty before God and men to be by themselves as they had begun to do, in the fear of the Lord. As an independent group leaning on God's might, standing at the side of other calvinistic manifestations of the body of Christ, they were to coöperate in the great work of the coming of God's Kingdom and the 'development of a typical American-Reformed Church as the final result'." (*Amerika,* p. 154.) We trust that on the grounds given no true lover of the Kingdom will deny the little Christian Reformed regiment its claim to separate existence, its right to "a place in the sun".

TEST QUESTIONS

1. What can you say about the church life of our pioneers?
2. What do you know of the history of the Reformed Church in America?
3. Tell of Dr. Wyckoff's visit and his report.
4. What was the reservation which he offered to the Michigan Dutch?
5. On what grounds were people in Michigan dissatisfied with the union?
6. What do you know about the men and the churches of the movement of 1857?
7. What was done at the first meeting of the separated churches, April, 1857?
8. What can you say about the movement of 1857 being legal, scriptural and Reformed?
9. What is meant by the pluriformity of the Church?
10. What should we consider our mission and contribution as a Church?

WORKS OF REFERENCE

Chapters II—V of "De Christelijke Gereformeerde Kerk".
"Het Rechtsbestaan der Hollandsche Christelijke Gereformeerde Kerk", G. K. Hemkes.
"Outline History of the Christian Reformed Church", H. Vander Werp.
"Amerika", Dr. H. Bouwman.
See also Dr. Bouwman's brochure on the Church Polity Grounds of the Secession. Published 1923.
Very valuable for the earliest history of the Reformed Church in America is Dr. A. Eekhof's "De Hervormde Kerk in Noord Amerika", 1624—1664.
Full of information: Dr. E. T. Corwin, "Manual of the Reformed Church", and his "Digest of Synodical Legislation".
Cf. the titles at the end of Chapter I.

CHAPTER III

THE CHRISTIAN REFORMED CHURCH DURING ITS PERIOD
OF STRUGGLING EARLY LIFE, 1857—1880

§1. The Name of the Church. §2. Periods of its History. §3. The
Struggle to Obtain a Foothold as an Organization. §4. The
Struggle as to Ministerial Forces. §5. Recognition Abroad.
§6. Struggles about Denominational Undertakings. §7. Petty
Points of Dispute, and Big Things Championed.

§1. THE NAME OF THE CHURCH

THE NAME of our denomination, Christian Reformed,
is a good name, because it stands for the essentials of
our religion. Presbyterian, Congregational, Episcopal,
these words simply indicate the system of church government accepted, i.e., rule respectively by elders, congregations or bishops. The name Baptist, singles out one sacrament as if preëminent. Methodist, that only stands for
certain "methods" in religious work. Lutheran, seems to
give undue honor to a man. But in our name, the adjective Christian, stands for the great truth that we are part
of Christianity, while Reformed, denotes that we belong
to the Re-formed or purified church, which went through
the Reformation struggle (Chapter I, §4). Essentials are
involved in this title, and rightly so. Moreover, it is of re-
spectable antecedents and age. When in 1609 it was necessary for John Robinson and his fellow-pilgrims in Leyden, to defend themselves as to their faith, they stated in
a petition to the magistracy that they were "of the Church
of the Christian Reformed religion".

And in 1637, during the heyday of Dutch Calvinism,
the name was used in the preface of the famous Dutch
Bible version issued by the authority of the States General of the United Netherlands, hence the name "States-
Bible" (Staten-Bijbel). Moreover, the first Synod of the

Dutch Seceders, held in 1836, repeatedly speaks in its Minutes of the body it represented as "Christelijke Gereformeerde Kerk".

But our Church has not always borne this title. It was a struggle to obtain it. Our denomination was officially nameless till 1859, when the title "Holland Reformed" was adopted, to be succeeded in 1861 by the name, "True Dutch Reformed", in order, as a resolution stated, to distinguish us from the Reformed Church and to retain our "Dutch character". This title remained in use, although not without protest, until 1880, when the name, "Holland Christian Reformed" was adopted. Ten years later it was agreed to drop the word "Holland" because American- and German-speaking churches had meanwhile become part of our organization. This title, "Christian Reformed" without any addition to it, is the official name of our denomination. That our title-page adds "in North America" is simply to differentiate it from a like named body in the Netherlands.

§2.   PERIODS OF ITS HISTORY

The history of a denomination may, to some extent, be compared to that of an individual human being. First is the period of struggling early life. A struggle it is indeed in many a case, physically frail as young life often is, entailing a battling with disease. There is a mental struggle as new sensations and experiences are met with day after day. Instinct impels to action rather than clear-cut ideas. Life is self-centered. Quarrels with comrades are not infrequent. Then comes the period of adolescence. It is marked by very rapid growth—physically, especially at first. Mentally it is a time of expansion; life is constantly widening its horizon. A spirit of teamwork shows itself. There is idealism, noble purposing—ambitious program. But also, at times, turmoil and confusion, with extremes

and contradictions, a period of "storm and stress". Finally
comes early manhood's day. Vigor marks manhood, and
active accomplishment rather than idealistic planning.
Contact with others is established for definite purposes,
there is fixing of principles, definition of a life-task; practical interests are advanced, and if need be, there is a reso-
lute facing and, if possible, settling of issues which seem
to conflict with the mapped-out program of life or the
adopted principle.

Somewhat following this analogy, we may distinguish
three periods in the history of the Christian Reformed
Church:

    I. *The Period of Struggling Early Life,* 1857—1880.
   II. *The Period of Adolescent Growth,* 1880—1900.
 III. *The Period of Early Manhood, Vigor and Strife,*
      1900—1920.

I.
THE PERIOD OF STRUGGLING EARLY LIFE,
1857—1880

§3. STRUGGLE TO OBTAIN A FOOTHOLD AS AN ORGANIZATION

Struggle may indeed be the guiding idea as we survey
the history of the denomination in its earliest period—like
childhood life in many ways is marked by it. There were
various *causes* for this. In the first place—there was the
smallness and *feebleness* of the movement of 1857.

At the classical meeting held October, 1857, the first one
whose Minutes are extant, only five congregations were
represented: Grand Rapids, Vriesland, Noordeloos, Graafschap, and Grand Haven. Polkton, which in April, 1857,
had notified the Classis of Holland of its withdrawal, had
by this time returned to the Reformed Church. At the
February, 1858, Classis, Grand Haven was not represented,
and both Polkton and Grand Haven are absent from the

roll of Classis for years. Up to 1864 we find only four congregations named in the Minutes: Grand Rapids, Vriesland, Graafschap, and Noordeloos. At times the name
Zeeland is joined to that of Noordeloos, and sometimes
substituted for it. How many communicant members had
withdrawn in 1857? Comparison of statistics shows the
following: Grand Rapids, 94 members; Graafschap, 113;
Vriesland, about 20; Noordeloos, 19; a total of about 250
communicants. The number of families probably was not
above 150; and the total number of souls, figured at an
average of five per family, must have been about 750 at
the highest. It was a slow, almost imperceptible growth at
first. We find no new churches organized until 1864, when
Zeeland's name is recorded separately. Attempts to establish congregations in some other places like Milwaukee,
brought no permanent results.

But a year before the close of the first decade a change
began to set in. Up to 1866 the True Dutch Reformed
Church was found only in the State of Michigan, in the
territory of the Grand and Black Rivers. But in the year
just named, a congregation was organized in Paterson,
N. J., in the East, and where from 1850 to 1855 a considerable number of Dutch people had settled, coming from
Goeree, Texel, and Gelderland. At Pella, Iowa, in the
West, as well as at Ridott, in Illinois, churches were established during that same year, 1866. In 1867 still other
churches were enrolled west of Lake Michigan, and at Cincinnati, in Ohio, so that it was resolved the next year to
constitute a second Classis, that of Illinois, consisting of
the congregations of Chicago, Low Prairie (South Holland) and Ridott, in the State of Illinois; Gibbsville (Oost-
burg), in Wisconsin; Cincinnati, in Ohio, and Steamboat
Rock (Wellsburg) and Pella, in Iowa. And so rapidly did
the new Classis grow, that by 1877 it was resolved to organize as its offshoot a new Classis, named after the State
of Iowa, and consisting of the congregations of Orange

City, Steamboat Rock, Hastings, Pella, Ackley, and Ridott. When the decision was made to constitute the Illinois Classis (1868), it was resolved that the Michigan churches should call their classical organization after their State. To this body the Paterson congregation belonged until 1878 when the Classis of Hudson could be organized, consisting of the churches of Paterson, Passaic, Hohokus, Sayville, and Rochester. These classical bodies met, as a rule, twice a year, composed of two delegates from each consistory. Since 1865 a joint meeting was held annually at which each congregation was represented, at first by four and later by two consistory members, either the pastor and an elder, or in the case of vacant charges, two elders. But even though the denominational machinery had thus been set up duly and was functioning regularly—what a small and feeble organization the denomination was up to 1880! After twenty-three years of existence there were only 39 widely scattered congregations! And most of them were so small that the entire Hudson Classis reported only 271 families; Illinois, still smaller, but 175. And the Iowa Classis totaled, in its seven churches, only 140 families! The entire denomination numbered no more than 3,566 confessing members. It had been indeed a day of continuous struggle to obtain "a place in the sun".

§4. STRUGGLE AS TO MINISTERIAL FORCES

There was a second cause for this struggling character of the first period. It was the smallness of its ministerial force. As related in Chapter II, §6, only two pastors served notices of withdrawal on the Classis of Holland on the notable day of April 8, 1857. There are evidences of attempts some years before '57 to have the Classis as a whole return to the standpoint of 1849. But, owing largely to the attitude of their leaders, the great majority of our pioneers was unwilling to sever relationship with the Reformed Church, and of the ministers, as already stated, but two cast in their lot with those who preferred independent denominational existence, namely, the Revs. H. G. Klyn and K. Vanden Bosch. At the first meeting of the delegates of the churches which had withdrawn, the former acted as president and the latter as secretary. But already at the very next meeting of the Classis it was reported that Rev. Klyn had returned to the Reformed Church. It seems that fears about his future motivated him in his action, and perhaps, trained as he was by the brilliant but erratic Scholte, he was not wholly at one with the leaders of the Michigan movement, who as a rule were followers of the more conservative wing of the Dutch Secession,· represented by De Cock and Van Velzen, over against the Rev. Brummelkamp and Van Raalte and particularly Scholte.

Moreover, a few other ministers who later on came from abroad to join the True Dutch Reformed Church, remained in the ranks but a brief season and their withdrawal caused confusion of mind in all cases, and defection in some. Even some of the most active leaders of 1857 among the laymen disappointed their followers at times, a few of them never re-joining the old colors, which at one time, they loudly shouted for.

These disheartening experiences impeded the growth of the organization perceptibly, especially because through them the number of ministers remained so small. Up to 1863 the Rev. K. Vanden Bosch was the only pastor to shepherd the flock of 1857. Born in 1818 with a limited education, he came as minister from Noordeloos in South Holland, to Noordeloos in Michigan, in 1856. He sided heartily with De Cock and Van Velzen in Holland. Vanden Bosch was a man of strong convictions and frequently revealed a violent temper. More than once strained relationship existed between him and his people, and at one time, in hot anger, because he felt unjustly treated, he temporarily withdrew from his brethren. He traveled much to reach the scattered churches, with a yoke of oxen going through the Michigan forests. He was a man of the Jacksonian type with its good and its bad.

Quite different from the Rev. Vanden Bosch was the REV. H. W. VAN LEEUWEN, born in 1807. He became Vanden Bosch's colleague in 1863, as pastor of the Grand Rapids church. Schoolmaster in the Netherlands at first, his pen was that of a ready writer, as his publications show, although he was at times at odds with his brethren about their contents. He evidently had progressive ideas, and as the better educated of the two pastors, he at the time was the first one to whom the training of young men for the ministry was entrusted as early as 1863, see Chapter VI, §1.

The third pastor of the True Dutch Reformed Church was the REV. D. J. VAN DER WERP, born in 1811, a man who, more than the two just named, labored with pen and tongue to promote the interests of the young denomination. Like the Rev. Van Leeuwen, he had been a school teacher in Holland. Persecuted for the sake of his expressed sympathy for De Cock and his doctrines, he had been led into the ministry. Arriving here in 1864, called by the Graafschap church, he at once gave himself with heart and soul to the cause for which the movement of 1857 stood. He traveled far and near to organize or strengthen churches. He trained quite a number of men for the ministry, while holding busy pastorates. He was the first Stated Clerk of the denomination (General Correspondent), 1868—1875, and editor of the denominational organ, *De Wachter*. If the Rev. Van den Bosch was of the Jacksonian type, his colleague may be compared to Alexander Hamilton in his wonderful leadership and great variety of patriotic activity when America was still young. The Church owes a great deal indeed to Rev. Van der Werp, as a gifted and consecrated man of God, a steady worker, a wise leader, and loyal to the core to the cause and creed of the True Dutch Reformed denomination.

Another valuable addition to the ministerial ranks was the fourth Netherland-ordained man who remained faithful to the end, the Rev. W. H. Frieling, who arrived in 1866, called by the Vriesland congregation. He was well-versed in church government and served acceptably for many years, much longer than the Rev. F. Hulst, who came in 1868, and who amply proved both his zeal and his loyalty to his denomination, but who died early. The Rev. S. Baron, arriving in 1869, as Niekerk's pastor, never took a prominent part in denominational affairs, much less than the Rev. W. Coelingh. Of the Rev. G. E. Boer, who came here in 1873, and the Rev. G. K. Hemkes, arriving in 1877, we shall hear more in Chapter VI.

The accession of these last named men was greatly instrumental toward the upbuilding of the church at home and the obtaining of a better standing abroad. We owe a heavy debt of gratitude to them for casting in their lot with our people, then still living amid pioneer conditions, with privations of all sorts, while the congregations as well as the denomination still were in their formative period with all the unpleasant features of such a critical time of youth.

But whatever meed of praise is due the pastors who came from abroad during the period of struggle, we should not fail to be appreciative also of the yeoman's services rendered by pioneer ministers who were more or less American-trained. As such we name the Rev. E. L. Meinders, graduate of the Dubuque Presbyterian School, and during January, 1869, ordained as minister of the Steamboat Rock, Iowa, church. Another worker, who, with his congregation, joined during the years of struggle, was the Rev. J. R. Schepers, of Lafayette, Ind., of the Associate Reformed Church mentioned in Chapter II, §6. He proved to be a worthy addition to the pioneer ministry, and so did his cousin, the Rev. J. Schepers, who had the distinction of being the first graduate trained in our circles and ordained as early as 1868. Closely rivaling him as to the honors of priority of education and ordination in America, is the REV. J. NOORDEWIER, who graduated February, 1869, together with Revs. W. Greve and J. Stadt, and who outlived all the ministers of the pioneer period as well as many of later decades. He excelled dozens in activities for Zion's welfare. Rev. Noordewier was Vice-President of several Synods, Treasurer of many funds, writer of numerous articles and several books, and Treasurer of Synod from 1883 onward, enjoying a green old age. Another man of importance in the period of struggle was the REV. L. RIETDYK who graduated in the fall of 1869. His election to the presidency of the major church judicatories three times shows that he was considered a strong man.

While mentioning the names of these preachers, we should not fail to note the service rendered by some *elders* of the period. Church history is more than a record of the doings of ministers, like the story of a war includes more than the activity of generals. Notable is the record of many a quiet worker of the period, especially among the eldership. When "Seceder" was still a name of scorn, when strength was feeble, and numbers small, when ministers quarrelled and some fled, many an elder stood loyally, bearing without complaint the heat of the day and the cold of the night for the sake of the Zion they had learned to love. The Christian Reformed Church should ever hold in grateful memory the names of men like J. Gelock, J. Gezon, G. Haan and others in Grand Rapids; J. F. Van Anrooy and H. Strabbing and others at Graafschap; A. Krabshuis and C. Vorst in Holland, and H. W. Dam and J. Groen at Vriesland. Even though some faltered at times, on the whole there must have been a faithful eldership in those days, men who were well grounded in the truth of the Reformed Standards, and thoroughly at home in the works of the writers we named in Chapter I, §6, especial Brakel's *Reasonable Religion*.

§5. STRUGGLE TO OBTAIN RECOGNITION ABROAD

A third cause of the struggle involved in the period here discussed was that to obtain recognition from the side of the Netherland Church. During early life we do not possess the independent spirit of later years. There is a leaning on the parents, a desire, in undertakings of any worth-whileness, of paternal approval. But in the case here described, many disappointments were experienced; hope deferred made the heart sick at times, and the work hard and heavy. Most of the pastors and professors of the Secession Church of Holland at first felt very unsympathetic toward the separation movement in America. This was quite generally the case with only a few notable exceptions, particularly that of Prof. Van Velzen, whose sympathies were from the start with men like G. Haan— one of his fellow-workers in early days. As already related, Chapter II, §7, at the Synod of 1857 a letter was read, signed by Rev. Klyn as president, and Rev. Vanden Bosch as secretary, "seeking union with the Christian Seceder Reformed Church of Holland". These men evidently desired thus to strengthen their own position, as well as to show that they had indeed returned to the standpoint of 1849. But they were disappointed. Synod stated that in view of contradictory reports from America, it was unable either to approve or to disapprove of the Secession here, and advised them to act carefully and according to God's Word. The Synod of 1860 read a letter from Rev. Vanden Bosch, complaining about the "stepsisterly" attitude of the Holland Church, and asked recognition of the American churches, but again in vain. Synod replied that it recognized all Churches of the Reformed faith and order, but refused to say anything beyond this. At the Synod of 1866, however, Dr. A. C. Van Raalte was warmly welcomed and in the name of the Netherland Church he received the right hand of fellowship for the denomination he represented. The separation here, he had declared to Synod, was not due to unorthodoxy, but the result of the presence in America of "different elements" and special causes. When in 1872 our first delegation appeared at Synod, J. Gelock, J. De Jonge, and B. De Graaf, they were seated only after considerable debate and with the expressed declaration of Synod that it refused to judge the case. This aloofness continued to the next period. Some of the first pastors even had difficulty in obtaining papers of dismissal to the American denomination. It was not till 1880, and consequently at the opening of the next period, that we read of the Christian Reformed Church of Holland extending an invitation to the American Church to be represented at its General Synod of 1882. (*Acta,* 1880, Article 17.)

§6. STRUGGLES ABOUT DENOMINATIONAL UNDERTAKINGS

Due largely to this attitude of the Netherland churches it was with difficulty that pastors from abroad could be obtained. This led to another struggle period, namely, the one to obtain a *Theological School* for the training of the ministry—a subject which for various reasons is discussed separately in Chapter VI. The struggle to obtain a foothold led to *home missionary* activity (see Chapter VII), while the endeavor to defend the position assumed led to the publication of a denominational *organ.* This was called *De Wachter,* whose first issue is dated February 14, 1868. Its first editor was the Rev. D. J. Vander Werp, while Mr. C. Vorst of Holland, Michigan, was the publisher and owner. But it was only with considerable difficulty that this small semi-monthly could be maintained, and decades passed by before it became a paying venture, although all these years it rendered valuable service, not alone in defending the movement of 1857 and the truth it stood for, but also in creating unity and coöperation among the constituency of the struggling infant Church. A *Yearbook for* 1875 proved to be an utter failure financially. Attempts to publish series of sermons also were far from successful. Fortunately for the cause, however, regardless of whether it "paid" or not, in 1869 there was published a booklet called *Brochure,* addressed to the Synod of the Netherland Church. Its title stated, that it was "An exposition based on official sources of the actual conditions of the Reformed Protestant (Dutch) Church in America and a defence of the basis of the return of the True Dutch Reformed Church in America to the old standpoint forsaken in 1849". Likewise in defence of the movement of 1857 was a *Zamenspraak* (dialogue), published in 1874 by the Rev. F. Hulst. Mr. G. Haan's booklet, *Stem Eens Belasterden* (Voice of a Slandered One), 1871, while more of a personal nature, served to throw valuable light on conditions prior to the withdrawal of 1857.

§7.   PETTY POINTS OF DISPUTE AND BIG THINGS CHAMPIONED

As we expressed it in our simile about Periods of History, there is a battling in life's early days against all kinds of infantile diseases as well as frequent quarreling with comrades. This also applies in a measure to the Church we are writing about. As to disease we shall say something in the next Chapter. As to quarreling—how frequently the pages of the Minutes of early meetings of consistories, Classes and General Meetings are disgraced with matters which mark unbrotherly strife! Petty things, most of them. For instance, in those days there was considerable diversity of opinion about the celebration of the day respectively following Christmas, Easter, and Pentecost. Some insisted on holding church services on these "second holidays" because prescribed by the Church Order, while others refused to observe them, claiming the practice smacked of Romanism. The question of the right of individuals to carry fire insurance disturbed many churches during a long period, and so did the discussion about the rights of baptized members to present their children at baptism. There was narrowness displayed at times in petty quarrels about non-essentials, such as some, for instance, objecting to have elders read sermons from the pulpit platform instead of from the reader's desk. Many saw great sin in having corpses in the church-buildings during funeral services. The vestibule had to suffice for showing the remains to the friends present. Flowers on the coffin were considered worldly, and the covering up of the excavated sand near the grave, was wicked hiding of death's horror. Some looked with disfavor upon the making of photographs as contrary to the Second Commandment. A few considered beards, and especially mustaches, taboo, while whistling was supposed to be "calling the devil". Ideas about personal adornment, somewhat reminding of those of Quakers and Mennonites, were entertained by a number. What might be called "tradition of the elders" was adhered to at times, as when the Rev. Van Leeuwen was compelled to retract that the Pope was not the Antichrist. That ever new light breaks forth from the Word, as John Robinson told the Pilgrim Fathers on their way to New England in 1621, and that there is and should be logical and biblical growth and development, also of the Calvinistic system of truth was, we presume, not grasped by many, if any, of our Pilgrim Fathers of Michigan. Repeated resolutions about the retention of the Dutch tongue "in generations" testified more of love for the old than of a sense of obligation to the new Fatherland, although it bore good fruit, at least in one respect: in fathering and fostering the *Christian School movement* (see Chapter VI, §6).

But at the same time, many big and noble things were championed also in those days, as even in childhood's

years there may be surprising idealism at times. Possibly,
as in a person's formative period of life, instinct impels to
action rather than clear-cut ideas and fixed principles, so
our fathers, we presume, were not always conscious of it
that this or that action was deduced from Reformed principle. But they somehow felt as a rule, intuitively, whether
or not it was in harmony with it. For instance, from the
very beginning, the Movement of 1857 stood foursquare
for the old unadulterated Calvinism of the Creed (Chapter IX, §1). Not alone were the Forms of Unity and Liturgy (Chapter VIII), and the Church Order of Dordrecht
(Chapter X), accepted as the fundamentals at the first
classical meeting, as we have already seen, but at the April
Classis of 1861 it was reiterated and affirmed unanimously
that ministers, elders, deacons, and school teachers should
subscribe to the standards of the Church unconditionally.
The preaching and teaching of Reformed truth was carried on regularly. That head knowledge was not considered sufficient to assume vows of church-membership is
plain from the decision of the time that the *Compendium*
should be the guiding line if people made confession of
faith, and that not alone as to doctrine but also as to life.
The Psalter in its new (Dutch) version was maintained,
and as to the separated life we find not alone the adherents of Free Masonry excluded, but all who joined secret
societies. There was testimony against the saloon as early
as 1861, and in the dark days of our Civil War, when dis-
loyalty reared its head here and there, a resolution was
adopted to censure the "copperhead".

No, indeed, they were far from perfect these pioneers
of our bands in America. They emphasized the "pilgrim"
part of the chrsitian life far more than the "soldier" side
of it—whereas christianity should include both. What is
worse—the pilgrims indulged far too much in fighting
among themselves instead of opposing the common foe
and forging ahead that God's Kingdom might come in

them, around them and through them. But while all this is true, there is also another statement due these fathers and founders of our Church.

A study of years, of documents and printed matter, has shown us to our own satisfaction, that the men of 1857 on the whole were men who, as true Calvinists, reckoned with God, who felt for the Reformed principle, and who revered the Old Bible, as God's inspired revelation of sovereign love. Indeed, it was early life's struggle, with childhood's limitations. But just like some children whose early years are filled with all kinds of privations, seem able to weather all storms and come out more vigorous than others, so it was also in the case of the Church whose history we sketch. Its early life might be full of struggle; its adolescence would reveal remarkable vitality.

TEST QUESTIONS

1. What can you say in defense of the name of our Church?
2. Describe the three Periods of its Church History.
3. Which are the four oldest churches of our denomination in Michigan?
4. Mention the first four Holland-trained ministers.
5. Mention the leading America-trained men among our pastors.
6. What was the attitude of the Church of the Fathers in the Netherlands?
7. What do you know about the earliest training of our ministers? Why was it undertaken, and when?
8. What can you say about missionary activities of the Period?
9. Mention the earliest Church publications.
10. Which were the nobler things advocated during the early Period?

WORKS OF REFERENCE

"De Christelijke Gereformeerde Kerk", Henry Beets, (Chap. VI).
"Het Rechtsbestaan der Hollandsche Christelijke Gereformeerde Kerk", G K. Hemkes.
"An Outline of the History of the Christian Reformed Church", Henry Vander Werp.

CHAPTER IV

THE CHRISTIAN REFORMED CHURCH DURING ITS ADOLESCENT PERIOD OF GROWTH, 1880—1900

§1. Growth in Numbers. §2. The Ministry as Factor in the Growth. §3. The Anti-Masonic Movement as Explaining the Increase. §4. The Growing German Element. §5. Growth Through Union with the Classis of Hackensack. §6. The Americanization Movement. §7. Growth in the Activities for the Kingdom of God—The Press and Society-life. §8. Adolescence's "Storm and Stress". Doctrinal Controversies. §9. The Broadening Horizon of Youth.

§1. GROWTH IN NUMBERS

IN HUMAN BEINGS the period of adolescence which follows early youth is marked, as we stated in the preceding chapter, by rapid physical growth, by a spirit of teamwork and idealism, noble purposing, ambitious program—but also at times by turmoil, storm and stress, while, as a rule, the mental horizon is broadened more or less. Much of this applies to the history of the Christian Reformed Church during its second period, from 1880 to the end of the nineteenth century.

To begin with growth—*the numerical increase* certainly was remarkable.

The following table shows this plainly at a glance:

	Classes	Churches	Ministers	Families	Communicants	Souls
1857	1	4	1	150	250	750
1880	4	39	19	2,014	3,566	12,001
1900	9	144	98	10,614	17,584	53,794

That shows, that during the twenty years covered by this second period, the classical organizations more than doubled, the churches trebled, the ministerial force was increased five-fold, the same as in the case of the families and communicants, while the number of souls in 1900 was considerably more than four times what it was in 1880. The five Classes added to the roll were those of Holland, dating from 1882; Muskegon, organized in 1888; and East Friesland, which in 1896 was formed as an offshoot of the Iowa Classis. The old Michigan Classis had changed its name in 1882, when Holland was formed, to Classis Grand Rapids, which latter body, in 1898, was split into two bodies, Grand Rapids East and Grand Rapids West. The fifth classical organization, added in 1890, was really the oldest one of them all—the Hackensack Classis, dating from 1822. (See §5 below.)

That this remarkable numerical increase can be recorded is due to various *factors*. One of them, and to some extent the most obvious, is the heavy *immigration* which marked particularly the first decade of the two covered by this Chapter. From 1841 to 1850 only 8,251 Netherlanders reached our shores. From 1870 to 1880 their number was doubled, totaling 16,541. But from 1880 to 1890, due largely to unfavorable industrial and social conditions in Holland, as many as 53,701 people arrived from the Low Countries, or more than three times the number of immigrants of the preceding decade. True, from 1891 to 1900 only 31,816 Netherlanders came to the United States, but even that was about twice as many as arrived from 1870 to 1880.

But the strong immigration from Holland was not the only thing explaining the rapid growth. Much of the increase could not have been recorded if it had not been for something else. It was:

§2. THE MINISTRY AS A FACTOR EXPLAINING THE GROWTH

In 1880 there were, as we stated, only 19 pastors. That meant that less than one-half of the congregations enjoyed regular ministerial labors. The entire Iowa Classis possessed only four preachers, the Revs. J. Schepers, S. Baron, W. Coelingh and J. Stadt. The Hudson Classis reported but two ministers in all, the Revs. L. Rietdyk and W. Greve. While the Illinois Classis was better supplied, having but two vacancies in 1880, in the Michigan Classis as many as twelve congregations were vacant—among them the two Grand Rapids congregations of the time (Spring Street and East Street).

But by 1900 what a difference—the ministry was numbering ninety-eight. That meant that instead of one pastor for every two churches, there was one for every one and one-half. That meant much more service, even in vacant charges, of the regular ministry. Moreover, these men were, as a rule, far better equipped for the work, due largely to better training in the Theological School (Chapter VI). Moreover, most of them having been reared in the same atmosphere, understanding one another better, these preachers were able to do team work much more effectively, while change of denominational affiliations was a rare thing, instead of being a frequent occurrence as formerly.

Besides this, some of those who had come from abroad to heed the Macedonian call from America were strong men, whose standing in the Old World meant a great deal for the Church in the New, as we shall see presently. They also proved to be good leaders at home. As such we may well single out the Rev. R. T. Kuiper, who presided at the Synod of 1880. Born in 1826, he had held two pastorates in Holland before coming here in 1879 to become Graafschap's minister. While in the Netherlands he published a book on the Levitical Marriage Laws. Soon after his arrival here his *Tijdwoord,* and *Stem* (1882), showed him to be a keen observer, while various articles in *De Wachter* revealed him as a man of vision and progress. The president of the 1883 Synod was another leading figure of the period here described, the Rev. J. H. Vos. He was a native of the Bentheim district of Germany. Born in 1826, a Kampen graduate in 1858, he had served important parishes in Holland before coming here in 1881 to take charge of the Spring Street church (First) of Grand Rapids, then the strongest of the denomination. Soon he became prominent in the affairs of the Theological School, in the mission cause, and as secretary of the Synodical Committee, and occupied a place of importance during many years. The REV. L. J. HULST, president of the 1884 and 1890 Synods, although a year older than the Revs. Vos and Kuiper, surpassed them and all the ministers of the denomination as to length of life (from 1825—1922), and years of service in the active ministry—from 1849 to 1910. He edited *De Wachter* from 1884 to 1888, wrote numberless articles in it since then, published catechism books, and *Supra en Infra, Oud en Nieuw Calvinisme,* and other pamphlets. He was the leader of the Anti-Masonic Movement (§3). The REV. E. Bos, who presided at the synodical meeting of 1888, was another forceful and influential personality during part of the period covered in this Chapter, though alas, only for a brief season.

Less in the eyes of the public, but equally devoted to the work and loyal to the core, were two of Rev. Vos' fellow-Bentheimers, the REVS. G. and E. BROENE, brothers, who both lived to a ripe old age. As to two other brothers, the REVS. C. and H. BODE, of East Friesian stock, while none of them ever presided at Synods, their influence in the West was strong and their work for church extension across the Mississippi very valuable.

Among those trained abroad, who, like the four just named, also missed presidential honors, was one whose services amply entitle him to reference in these pages, the REV. HENRY VANDER WERP, who arrived here in 1882. He was one of the best-educated, and what is more, one of the most gifted men our denomination ever had. He would have graced a chair in our Theological School and would have been able to preside at any Synod.   Yet these honors were withheld from him.   His remarkable versatility is shown by numberless articles in Christian Reformed church papers and in several booklets, both in poetry and in prose, in Dutch and in English.   He was a musician of ability as shown in his publication of a Psalter Version (compare Chapter IX, §3), in English.   To mention no more, the Rev. Vander Werp was the first one to give the English reading world an idea of our Church, its descent and history, in *An Outline of the History of the Christian Reformed Church of America,* pp. 49; (published in 1898).

Among the strong men of the period we should also name the REV. H. VAN HOOGEN, who, like the Revs. Boer and Hemkes (Chapter VI), belonged to the second generation of the Christian Reformed Church of Holland.   Graduating from the Kampen Theological School in 1865, he ministered to five churches in the Netherlands before coming here in 1894 to serve three congregations in three different States: Second Roseland, (Illinois) ; Central Avenue, in Holland, Mich.; and Prospect Park, Paterson, New Jersey, where he died in the harness, 1906.   He had the pen of a ready writer as well as the tongue of a gifted speaker and the intelligence of a wise counsellor.

Of longer sojourn in his adopted land, and of wider and more enduring influence speaks the record of the REV. K. KUIPER, who succeeded the Rev. Van Hoogen as pastor of Second Roseland.   His first American pastorate had been First Grand Haven, his last was Niekerk. Almost from the first year of his coming to America (1891), the Rev. Kuiper raised his voice in behalf of Christian Primary as well as of Higher education, and the entire movement owes a great debt to his wise, persistent and successful pleading for the cause he loved.   He served many years as writer of the Sunday School lessons in *De Wachter* and *Sabbatschool Bode,* and wrote a *Catechism.*

Speaking of gifted men of the period we should also name three who finished their ministry in the East—the REV. P. VAN VLAANDEREN, earnest champion of the Christian School Movement in his region; the REV. K. VAN GOOR, talented pulpit orator, and the REV. J. M. REMEIN, a quiet man with a good pen.

Moreover, mentioning valued forces, we should not fail to name the REV. E. R. HAAN, from 1873—1883 missionary-pastor on the island of Java, who in 1892, with his congregation of Midland Park, N. J., joined our denomination, like Second Paterson, with the REV. H. H. D. LANGEREIS, had done in 1888. Both of these last named men held pastorates in the West as well as in the East, as had been the case, for that matter, with the Revs. K. Van Goor, and W. Greve and others, whose memory ought to be kept green among us. Other men of note will be named in other connections.

What we gave suffices to show that the ministry of the period naturally was quite a factor in explaining the great accessions of membership and churches from 1880 to 1890, seconded as these ministerial leaders were by such strong men as the elders T. Keppel, H. Bosch, W. Brink, J. De Boer, E. Hekman, S. S. Postma, N. Silvius, A. Van Bree, F. Kniphuizen, J. W. Garvelink, G. W. Mokma, J. J. Heeringa, and others.

§3. THE ANTI-MASONIC MOVEMENT EXPLAINING THE INCREASE

Of considerable significance during the period was something which occurred during its early part, namely, the accession of a number of congregations which had withdrawn from the Reformed denomination as the result of what we already named, Masonic, or rather, Anti-Masonic agitation. That some of the men of the Reformed Church were Free Masons was already evident to our pioneers of 1857. In 1868 the Reformed Classes of Holland

and Wisconsin presented extended testimony against Free Masonry, and asked their General Synod to disapprove of it. But it refused to express an opinion. Two years later, however, General Synod issued the significant statement: "the path of prudence and safety lies outside of all oath-bound secret societies wherewith obligations may be exacted in conflict with the liberty of the individual conscience; the Christian religion furnishes all needful moral culture, and its pledges of mutual love represent a higher capacity for practical benevolence than the moral lessons of any mere human organization". But these declarations were prefaced by the words: "Synod cannot interfere with consistorial prerogatives of discipline". That meant practically the independent idea of absolute congregational autonomy, incompatible with the Presbyterian system of Church Government (Chapter X, §2). This standpoint was maintained, although Western Classes contended that Free Masonry was anti-republican, anti-christian and anti-Reformed.

It was felt that the attitude of the General Synod practically opened the door to Free Masons and led to the strange and unreformed practice that in one church some members could be in good standing who were rejected by sister congregations, leading to very awkward situations, subversive of church discipline.

The outcome of much agitation among the Western Hollanders was that during the years 1881 and 1882 eight Reformed congregations, under the leadership of the Rev. L. J. Hulst and others, severed their relationship with their denomination. They were the First Church of Holland (Van Raalte's Colonial Church), Coldbrook (Grand Rapids), East Saugatuck, Second Grand Haven, Graafschap, North Street (Zeeland), Montague, and Drenthe. Soon after they joined the Christian Reformed Church, with the exception of Graafschap which, with its pastor, the Rev. A. Zwemer, returned to the Reformed fold.

This accession not alone swelled the number of congregations and ministers, but in various localities individual members left the Reformed Church to join the churches of 1857. In a few places this led to the organization of new congregations: Zutphen, Beaverdam, Fremont, Spring Lake, Harderwijk, and Overisel (all in Michigan), and Alto, in Wisconsin.

However, the growth of the denomination was materially increased during this period not alone through the accessions just named, but also, as already alluded to, through a more favorable attitude toward the Christian Reformed Church assumed by the Church in the Netherlands. When the Rev. P. D. Van Cleef, a Reformed pastor, in 1882 stated in a letter to the Synod of Zwolle: "Many of our best and most orthodox ministers and church-members are Free Masons", and "Our Synod could not take action which would virtually excommunicate these brethren....what God hath cleansed that call thou not common or unclean"—the delegates shuddered. The result was the advice to the Netherland churches no longer to address membership papers to Reformed congregations until "turned from the abomination of Free Masonry". Consequently, the great stream of the immigration of Reformed Hollanders was turned into Christian Reformed channels, something which continued to be the case for decades.

§4. THE GROWING GERMAN ELEMENT

Among the classical organizations formed during this period we mentioned in §1 the Classis of *East Friesland*. This body embraced and was designed to embrace all of the German-speaking congregations. Their increase also explains the growth here discussed.

As stated in Chapter I, the Secession movement of Holland had spread to the adjacent districts of Germany:

Bentheim and East Friesland. Van Raalte, who had organized one or two "Seceder" churches in Bentheim, was on his trip to America, accompanied by some Bentheimers, who settled at Graafschap, Mich. Others came over in the course of succeeding years, and many joined the Christian Reformed denomination. The Fremont, Mich. church had from the start many members of Bentheim origin, and so did Overisel and East Saugatuck (formerly known as Collendoorn), in Michigan. East Friesland "Seceders" settled at first in Illinois and many joined the Presbyterian and Reformed denominations. But the Ammermann family in Stephenson County, Illinois, the East Friesian "Mother Colony", hearing of the existence of a Seceder (Afgescheiden) Church in Michigan, sought and found a church home in the denomination here described, by effecting, in 1866, the organization of a congregation at Ridott (German Valley), Illinois. The Rev. E. L. Meinders' accession brought Iowa East Friesians to the fold, and, especially due to the labors of the Rev. H. and C. Bode, and later by the sons of the latter, the Revs. H. C. and W. Bode, as well as by the Revs. J. Gulker, J. Plesscher, J. H. Schultz and others, the German element increased considerably, the East Friesland Classis in 1900 numbering as many as seventeen churches. Not all of them, however, used the German tongue in their divine services. In fact none of the older congregations did so exclusively because their founders were fully as well conversant with the Holland language as with High German, owing to close connections between the Netherlands and their old Home, in former centuries. But particularly during the last decade of the nineteenth century German was demanded increasingly, in part due to the fact that the later immigration had been taught the German tongue in the schools of their native places. That this transition of language entailed demands for training of future ministers in the language of the Fatherland and led to education effort, we shall see in Chapter VI, §5.

To serve as a means for the unification and propagation of this German element, a periodical called *Reformierte Monatschrift* began its career in 1891, to be succeeded after an interval by the *Reformierte Bote* (Reformed Messenger), a monthly dating from 1899, edited by the Rev. G. L. Hoefker, at first assisted by the Revs. J. Timmermann and J. H. Schultz.

§5. GROWTH THROUGH UNION WITH THE CLASSIS OF HACKENSACK

In Chapter II, §6, we mentioned the True Reformed Dutch Church. This body dated from 1822, when a group of churches in New Jersey and New York, led by the Rev. Dr. Solomon Froeligh, seceded from the parent body. With people of the Classis of Hackensack, at the time the remnant of the "True" Church, some of our pioneers came into contact before 1857. That they became a source of information on actual conditions in the East we have already related. In 1859 the Rev. J. Berdan of Passaic, who several times preached for some of our people in the East, proposed to the authorities of his denomination to seek closer contact with the Western churches, and ten years later we find the Rev. J. Y. De Baun and an elder heartily welcomed at a meeting of the Michigan Classis. In 1877, a federal union was formed, involving exchange of membership certificates, communion privileges, and voting at the meetings of major church courts. Closer contact in the East showed that the two federated bodies were so similar in belief and practice that the question arose involuntarily: why not unite fully? The Americanization movement in Michigan, sketched in the next section of this Chapter, was materially helped by the Hackensack brethren, and when the Rev. J. Y. De Baun, in 1887, took charge

of the LaGrave Avenue church, he made a most favorable
impression as to orthodoxy and earnestness.   No doubt
this paved the way for a still closer union consummated
at the Synod of 1890.

Serious objection was made to the fact that the Hackensack churches used fifty-two Hymns, appropriate to the
fifty-two Lord's Days of the Heidelberg Catechism, as appendix of their Psalter.   But when the stipulation was
made that Holland- and German-speaking churches were
prohibited from using hymns, the obstacle was overcome,
though not without protest from the side of the Rev. J. H.
Vos and his consistory, who spoke of the inconsistency of
having some of the churches use hymns while others were
forbidden to do so.   The Hackensack Classis, from its
side, had made certain reservations when by a majority
vote it decided to seek a closer union, and in them were
involved   causes   of   discontent   and   alienation   which
showed themselves already during the period here discussed, but which came to a head during the next.   (Chapter V, §7.)

Numerically the Classis of Hackensack was weak, only
numbering 507 families in the thirteen congregations on
its roll in 1890.   Still, its accession involved denominational growth, not simply because of the 2,000 souls added,
and some of the ministers proving to be valuable assets,
but particularly because in Passaic and Paterson they
served to "stop the leaks" that had been going on for years
on account of the language question.   A number of our
people, anxious to exchange the Dutch for the English as
their language of devotion, found church homes in the
congregations named, and thus were saved for the
denomination.

The last named fact applies with far more force to the
effects of another noteworthy event marking the period
of adolescence.   It was the originating of the Americanization movement already mentioned.

§6. THE AMERICANIZATION MOVEMENT

A couple of times we noted the intention of the church
leaders to cling to the name and language of Holland.
They forgot that the God of nations has His hand in the
amalgamation of various peoples to form new nations.
So it had happened in the Netherlands with its originally
so widely different elements: Friesians, Saxons, Franks,
and Celts. So it was in England. So it happens in the
United States. Consequently the sons and daughters of
the pioneers of 1857, as well as many of the younger
people of the Masonic Movement churches of 1881, cared
for the English language of our nation far more than for
the Holland tongue of their ancestors. In Grand Rapids,
where our people daily mixed with others, far more than in
smaller places or in country surroundings, a demand for
religious worship in English made itself heard at the
opening of the decade here discussed. A separate English-
speaking organization was asked for, since the fact was
realized that a slow process of Americanizing the entire
congregation was out of question because newcomers,
continually arriving, were unable to use the language of
the land in their worship, while the young American-born
element did not understand the Dutch. The swarming
method of the bees appeared to be the best mode of procedure, for the time and the place. Men like the Revs. P.
Schut and R. T. Kuiper and Profs. Boer and Hemkes, promoted the movement as necessary to retain the coming
generations. Others, especially the Revs. Vos and Hulst,
opposed it as "dangerous", and ascribed worldly motives
to it. Even its best champions failed to point out the fact
that Americanization was much more than a measure of
self-preservation, but rather a patriotic duty toward the
unification of the nation, and opening avenues for the
propagation of our principles as a leaven and a salt—a
God-given duty for us with our Calvinistic heritage. But

notwithstanding this failure to realize the full significance
of the movement, and in the face of all opposition and
dilatory tactics, the first English-speaking Christian Reformed Church was organized, November, 1887—the
LaGrave Avenue church of Grand Rapids. Only eighteen
communicant members joined at the start. In 1893 the
second English-speaking church in the West was organized, the Broadway congregation of Grand Rapids. For
several years they were the only churches of their kind in
the denomination, outside of those of the Hackensack
Classis. Both had their "period of struggle". But the
movement they headed could not be stopped, and its development would surprise many, as the next Chapter
shows.

§7.   GROWTH IN ACTIVITIES FOR THE KINGDOM OF GOD— THE PRESS AND SOCIETY-LIFE

Passing by growth as seen in the work of the Training
of ministers, and the advance in missionary activity, because discussed in separate Chapters (VI and VII), it be-
hooves us to chronicle here that the period under discussion reminds of that of the adolescence of human beings
because of great *activity*—as young people delight in taking up all kinds of things, and show a remarkable spirit of
capability for teamwork. Not alone was *De Wachter* at
the beginning of this period changed from being a semi-
monthly to a weekly, but in 1894 considerably enlarged at
the beginning of the editorial career of Rev. A. Keizer,
until 1918 its editor-in-chief. In 1880 the first issue appeared of the *Jaarboekje* or Yearbook for the denomination, edited and owned by the Revs. J. Noordewier and
G. K. Hemkes. A year later, the Church published its first
collection of *General Rules* (Algemeene Bepalingen), ap-
pended to the Church Order of Dordrecht. Several pastors published catechism books, notably the Revs. H. Van-

der Werp, L. J. Hulst, K. Kuiper, and J. M. Remein, even as the Rev. J. I. Fles already in 1878 had laid one on the press. The Rev. R. T. Kuiper, as stated in §2, published two books on conditions in America, both ecclesiastical and social. In 1897 a monthly, under the leadership of the Rev. F. M. Ten Hoor, started its career, *De Gereformeerde Amerikaan,* published by H. Holkeboer, Holland, Mich., Two months before its first number appeared, another monthly had been launched at Orange City, Iowa, *De Heidenwereld,* a missionary magazine under the auspices of men belonging to both the Reformed and the Christian Reformed Churches, the first concrete proof of the possibility of coöperation of brethren separated ecclesiastically for well-nigh forty long years.

The press, however, was not furnishing the only evidence of the stirring of new life, the formation of new ideals, the preparing of ambitious programs, from the side of a few leaders. Everywhere religious activity manifested itself.

That was also evident regarding the *Sunday school.* During the period of struggle it had been looked at askance as an innovation, a dangerous competitor of catechism classes, a Trojan horse, carrying traitors inside, etc. The churches of the West, which continued their connection with the Reformed Church, soon made earnest work of developing the institution, Van Raalte's church organizing a Sabbath school as early as 1851. (*The Banner,* February 8, 1917.) But in 1873 a change set in also in the Christian Reformed Church, when the General Meeting strongly urged that every congregation should maintain a Sabbath school. No doubt the Rev. D. J. Vander Werp was back of this resolution. Four years later Prof. G. E. Boer broke a lance for it in *De Wachter* which he edited at the time. And particularly after the union with the congregations which had left the Reformed body as the result of the Anti-Masonic agitation, a new era began.

Men like N. Silvius and H. Bosch, ably pleaded for the newcomer. And so did Mr. J. Veltkamp, a veteran of the Christian School movement (Chapter IX, §5); while the Rev. R. T. Kuiper in the *Tijdwoord,* strongly advocated the Sabbath school as indispensible on account of the condition of Church, School, and Society. In 1888 the denominational organ began publishing comments on the International lesson, which led to the publication of the *Sabbathschool Bode* (Messenger), by James Tanis, of Paterson, continued till 1920, as a useful weekly for the organization mentioned in its title. In 1898 the Hackensack Classis undertook the publication of *Christian Reformed S. S. Lesson Helps,* continued till 1917, and rendering as good a service to the English Sunday schools as the *Bode* did to the Dutch. In 1900 there were nearly one hundred Sabbath schools in as many churches, so that over two-thirds had introduced the newcomer—the whole number of congregations then being 144.

And not alone Sunday schools sprang into being during the period of growth—also a number of Young People's Societies and Young Men's and Young Ladies' Societies. The annual feasts of these organizations were events of considerable importance to the young folk, including recitations, songs, a main address, usually by the pastor or some other speaker of prominence,—and welcome refreshments and some other songs and recitations as the postlude.

In 1900 we find seven missionary societies recorded, and nearly forty singing clubs. Grand Rapids at the time boasted of an "Alliance of Reformed Societies", (see Chapter V, §3). In 1896 we already find evidence of a similar "Bond" of missionary organizations, in northwestern Iowa. This was composed of Christian Reformed societies. But in a Holland Reformed "Jongelingsbond" in the same district, which in 1899 celebrated its third annual

meeting, we find both Reformed and Christian Reformed
Young Men's Associations coöperating.

It was indeed a time of young manhood's hustle and
bustle, dreaming and daring.   Particularly in Iowa
churches sprang up to the right and to the left, so that the
Iowa Classis, which in 1880 had enrolled seven weak and
struggling churches, with only about a thousand souls all
told, served by four pastors, had by 1900 become "two
hosts", the parent body and "East Friesland" together totaling forty-seven churches, with more than nine thousand
souls, and thirty preachers of the Word.   The denominational banner was unfurled in the far Northwest, at Oak
Harbor, Wash. (1893) ; in the distant Southwest, at Nederland, Texas, 1898.   At Winnepeg, Canada, far up North,
work was begun in 1898, and already five years before that
a church was organized at Maxwell City, in New Mexico,
to the South.   In the East an opening was attempted in the
State of Maryland.   Colorado, too, was penetrated in 1892
when two churches were organized, Rilland and Bethel,
the fruit of an ill-fated colonizing attempt, under Netherland auspices, which failed the next year.   But what if
all these attempts were not successful and lasting,as we shall
see in Chapter VII, §1?   They at least stood for ambitious
planning and energetic daring.

So was the discussion going on in those days about
starting *foreign mission work* in nearby Cuba or distant
Persia, and about helping Reformed people across the tropic
of Capricorn, in Argentina.   Nor was there only planning
and dreaming.   Work was actually begun among the Indians of the Southwest, Chapter VII, §2.   And when the
Old Reformed brethren of Bentheim and East Friesland
asked for aid to maintain their recently opened Theological School, help was readily granted to the institution
which, up to 1921, when it was closed, was a blessing to
both the denominations involved.

Ambitious planning and daring? The fact that at the
Synod of 1898 it was resolved to organize a Society to support a regular *College,* and that steps were actually taken
to bring this about—who shall deny that this spelled enterprise of a splendid sort, even though failure marked
the attempt, as Chaper VI shows? Surely, we have reasons
abundant to characterize 1880—1900 as the period of
adolescent aspirations and undertakings, even though less
favorable manifestations of such a period were not lacking, as we shall see next.

§8.   ADOLESCENCE'S "STORM AND STRESS".   DOCTRINAL
CONTROVERSIES

We noted in our simile that young manhood has its
times of turmoil and confusion, seasons of "storm and
stress", as well as a display of growth and activity. Such
applies in a measure to the Christian Reformed Church in
the period covered. Or, to use a different figure of speech,
just as a growing tree as it shoots up and forms its crown
has some of its lower boughs drop off while its trunk is in
formation—so it was the case with the rapidly-growing
Christian Reformed Church. Already as early as 1870, in
Grand Rapids, Mich., a number of families separated
themselves from the Spring Street church to form a new
organization on North Division Avenue under the Rev. C.
Kloppenburg. Six years later another contingent, mostly
of Zeeland origin, severed connections to organize the
Turner Avenue (Grand Rapids), congregation. The people
of these churches were ultra-conservative as to customs,
and stressed the hidden things of God, His decrees, as well
as man's impotence, more than a well-balanced conception of these truths permits. A man somewhat of the
type just described was the Rev. E. L. Meinders named in
Chapter III, §2. He was highly respected at first. When
Rev. G. E. Boer was elected as theological professor, Rev.

Meinders received six votes. At first he praised the work
of the new professor. But soon afterward he began to in-
cessantly criticize him as well as the Revs. Hulst, Fles,
Heyns, H. Vander Werp, and several others, accusing
them of doctrinal unsoundness. His high Calvinism became apparent more and more, as well as his ultra-con-
servatism. Finally matters came to a head at the Synod of
1886 when a declaration was made stating that Rev. Meinders and the South Holland, Ill. church he served, had
withdrawn by majority vote from the Christian Reformed
Church. The main ground for their action was doubt
about the Christian Reformed Churches, both in the Netherlands and here, actually being the historical continua-
tions of the Netherlands Reformed Church of 1618-'19.
Rev. Meinders lived long enough to regret his act. His
people, except a few, in course of time returned to the
Church of their fathers—due largely to the tact of the Rev.
R. T. Kuiper, who ended his ministry among the South
Holland people. Other secessions took place during this
period in Kalamazoo and Muskegon, due largely to personal factors.

Dutch people, like the Scotch, have been called "born
theologians". Many at least are fond of doctrinal disputa-
tions, and some of these had something to do with the
"storm and stress", or at least turmoil and agitation which
at times marked the epoch, as shown by articles in *De
Wachter* and one or two separate publications. Many of
the pioneers of the denomination accepted the stern type
of Calvinism for which their respected leader, the Rev. S.
Van Velzen, had stood in the Netherlands, with emphasis
on God's sovereignty, rather than on His Fatherhood; on
His decrees more than on the gospel offer. That the Covenant of Grace embraced the elect and them only, was commonly believed. Only to the chosen ones grace was sealed
in Baptism. Human spiritual inability was at times
stressed in such a way as to destroy, in effect, human ac-

countability. The border line of Fatalism was approached by some, if not actually crossed. But during the first decade of the period here described, the pendulum swung in an opposite direction—in fact it started to do so already a few years before 1880. Under the leadership of Professors Boer and Hemkes, and the Revs. L. J. Hulst and R. T. Kuiper, infra-lapsarism became the received doctrine, rather than the supra-lapsarism of Rev. Meinders. The Covenant of Grace as embracing believers and their children, like it was established with Abraham and his seed, became the popular conception rather than the one named above, held by the Rev. K. Vanden Bosch and others of his day. That Baptism sealed God's grace objectively, in promise, rather than subjectively, that is, in actual possession, was the teaching of Prof. Boer and others, even as these views were held by most ministers of the second generation of leaders in the Christian Reformed Church of the Netherlands, to which Revs. Boer, Hemkes, and Kuiper, and to some extent the Rev. Hulst also, belonged. Later on, as we shall see, under the leadership of Dr. A. Kuyper, there was an other swinging of the pendulum. (Chapter V, §6.) Dr. G. Vos was the first professor of the Theological School who favored supra-lapsarism, a view of predestination to some extent defended by Dr. A. Kuyper. Opposition to this, led by Rev. Hulst, not alone had something to do with Dr Vos's acceptance of a call to Princeton Seminary (1893), but led to considerable discussion in the columns of *De Wachter* and *De Gereformeerde Amerikaan.* The settling of the agitation involved in this belongs to the next Chapter, §6.

Causing less public disturbance, but nevertheless at times seriously agitating some circles, was a swinging of the pendulum as to the type of preaching. During the period of struggle the emotional, experiential type of religion was loved by the people, and fostered by the pulpit. Mysticism and Labadism were not entirely lacking among the pioneers of 1857, and Covenant relationship was often lost sight of by unduly pushing to the foreground the secret will of God's decree. Such was the case also among the people of the Dutch Secession. But just like in the Netherlands, under the second generation already alluded to, there was a swinging from the emotional toward the more intellectual, from the emphasis on the will of God's decree to His revealed will, so in America, causing occasional complaint, and at times, in some instances, strained relationships.

§9. THE BROADENING HORIZON OF YOUTH

Adolescence is marked by a widening of outlook. Such also applies here. The change of name from the reactionary "True" to that of Holland Christian Reformed, and the dropping of "Holland", agreed on in 1890, with the union with Hackensack's Classis (cf. Chapter III, §1), is an evidence of a giving up of the narrowness and exclusiveness of former days. The legal incorporation of the local congregation something which had been an issue leading to separation in the Netherlands, was advocated and effected without protest, in 1881. In fact, the Grand Rapids congregation was incorporated already before 1861. Prohibition was favored by some as early as 1887, and the Rev. R. T. Kuiper even voiced the sentiment that it did not matter if the bread of the Communion Table were leavened or unleavened, the Communion wine red or white, fermented or unfermented. The Synod of 1884 rescinded a former resolution prohibiting the elders from reading a sermon from the pulpit platform—a hotly-debated matter across the Ocean at one time. The formerly so burning questions of the second holidays and of fire insurance were, in 1886, declared to be adiaphorous matters—left to the conscience of the individuals. There were still signs indicative of a surviving of the old spirit of exclusiveness. But in many

ways there was a *development* as to the conception of
things, a broadening out of views as well as of policies,
under the leadership of men influenced by Dr. Vos, and
particularly by Dr. A. Kuyper and Dr. H. Bavinck—and
these men not alone among the American-trained ministry, but also among laymen of more recent immigration,
profoundly affected by the writings of these Dutch leaders
and by the reformatory movement of the Doleantie by
which, in 1886, a strong element, loyal to Dr. Kuyper and
his presentation of the truth, were forced out of the Established Church.   We shall notice more of this influence in
§6 of our next chapter.   During the period of 1880—1900
the Church Order and Liturgy remained unchanged. Catechetical preaching and teaching were maintained as well
as the Psalter as chief manual of praise, even though for a
time some pleaded for hymns.   A concession of the Synod
of 1883, allowing the use of German hymns in the German
work, was made only under protest and rescinded in 1888.
The education of the ministry and membership remained
object of zealous care as other Chapters show.   Taking
all in all, the adolescent period seemed to hold the promise of vigorous early manhood.   Alas! that that period
also, as we shall see in Chapter V, should be marked and
marred by conflicts.   Nearly every human being must face
them at times.   So would the Church here described.

TEST QUESTIONS

1. How many and which were the Classes organized in the
    period from 1880—1900?
2. Name four of the leading men of this period.
3. Describe the history of the Masonic Movement.
4. What can you say about the German element?
5. What can you say about the Americanization Movement?
6. Which great motive was not recognized in this Americani-
    zation Movement?
7. Give the history of the rise of the Sunday school among us.
8. Which change was evident as to theological doctrinal
    thinking?
9. Which type of religion came to the foreground from 1880
    to 1900?

CHAPTER V

THE CHRISTIAN REFORMED CHURCH DURING ITS PERIOD
OF EARLY MANHOOD'S VIGOR AND STRIFE, 1900—1920

Introductory: 1920 marking a transition. §1. Vigor displayed in
church extension. §2. A Strengthened Ministry. §3. Increasing Strength of the American Element: Publications in English.
§4. Financial and Personal Offerings Increased. §5. New Connections Made and Correspondence Defined. §6. Influence of
Doctors Kuyper and Bavinck, Utrecht Conclusions, Creed Revision. §7. Strife Among the Brethren: Neo-Calvinism, the
Baptism Membership Question, Hackensack's Defection, the
Labor Union Problem, the "Maranatha" Case. Significance of
the Settling of these Issues. §8. The Denominational Calling
Defined. §9. As Others See Us.

INTRODUCTORY: 1920 MARKING A TRANSITION?

IN THE MAIN, the history covered in this Chapter ter-
minates with 1920. It seemed wise to us to do so since
we did not wish to discuss issues still pending, particularly
the one on Common Grace, and those involved in the case
of Prof. Dr. R. Janssen. We are standing in too close
proximity to such matters to judge them objectively and
in all their bearings. Moreover, we deemed it wise not to
go beyond 1920 because it looks to us that we are at the
beginning of a new period in the history of our Church.
The present years are those of transition. The great
World War shook the whole of humanity. The Church, a
part of this humanity, could not escape the upsetting of
things and the changing of thoughts involved in this.
Moreover, Protestant North America, to confine ourselves
to that, is rapidly changing. The acceptance and application of the hypothesis of Evolution has brought forward
"Old foes with new faces": Rationalism, including Higher
Criticism as it undermines Bible authority, Materialism,

and Worldliness. These foes from without are also threat-
ening us more and more, since the former barriers of
language isolation and lack of means to obtain culture are
practically removed. Besides these there are indications,
or at least charges made, that our differences are no longer
as before, intra-confessional, but much deeper and
broader. One noteworthy publication, *The Foe Within
the Gate,* evidences this in its very title. At the Synod of
1920 the significant terms "progressives" and "conserva-
tives" were used repeatedly and without being challenged.
There has been a marked difference in the spirit of some
articles printed in *Religion and Culture* (see §3 below), as
compared with others in *The Witness.*

We do not view the future without apprehension as we
note statements volunteered in some periodicals about
Psalms vs. Hymns, calls for a change in Catechism preaching, a questioning of the value of creedal statements, etc.
Moreover, such books as Dr. James Orr's *The Progress
of Dogma,* and the agitation in the Netherland Churches
about the "extension of the Confession", will not fail to
bring up new issues among us. What has been called "the
urgent need of a theology which expresses the *social* as-
pects of Christ's Gospel with the same emphasis as the New
Testament does"......"the need of the modern church,
requiring in addition to the well-tested *theological* fundamentals, the formulation and authoritative adoption of
ethical and *social* dogmas", (Vollmer, *New Testament Sociology,* pp. 269 ff.), that, too, will not leave the Christian
Reformed Church in America untouched.

And so, not to mention more "signs of the times", we
seem to be on the border-line of a new epoch, and one that
will confront us with new *difficulties.*

In the *Calvinist* of September 15, 1917, the Rev. W.
Groen wrote about "The Difficulties that the Christian Reformed Church must Overcome in Solving its Problem
of Americanization". He asked: "Can these churches re-

tain their distinctive features and flourish as the influence of the religious and church life of the Netherlands becomes weaker, and our people are assimiliated by the growing American nation?" The first difficulty, he stated, was the lack of a single vivid historical background. Three movements are involved in the growth of the denomination: of 1857, of 1881, and the influence from the Netherlands since 1890. "The last has an overwhelming influence. However, the break with the Netherlands must come sooner or later, and as a result there will arise the question: Can the Church be self-sustaining after such a break, or shall this prove fatal? The answer depends upon whether or not these churches can reconstruct their historical background and create for themselves a definite task for the future".

The second difficulty, it was asserted by Rev. Groen, would be that of applying a strict discipline even over the industrial lives of the membership—in view of the spirit of American economic principles, and the third one proceeded, it was said from American religious life, which cares, as a rule, little for purity of faith and doctrinal distinctions.

No doubt, there are "breakers ahead". May the God of our Fathers, the God of ages past, be our hope for years to come! In dependence on Him, we trust that the strength of our principles will not fail to make itself felt. There were tests endured with encouraging results in the matters related in §6, as we shall mention at its end. While not without fears for our part of God's Zion, we are hopefully facing the future. Let us pray and plead much, as Habakkuk (3: 2) that Jehovah may maintain and revive His work in the midst of the years. That we should name this Chapter that of "Early Manhood" will, we think, be justified by history. For one thing, as such a period is marked by a cessation of external growth, it is notable that the opening years of the third decade of the twentieth century are already showing that the ratio of our numerical increase is not what it was in former decades.

§1.   VIGOR IN CHURCH EXTENSION

Early Manhood stands for strength rather than for growth physically, for calm accomplishment rather than idealistic dreaming, although not all idealism is lost; for contact with outsiders, for development and fixing of principles, and if need be for facing issues, even though this involves unpleasant conflict. These things, to some extent, apply to the history of the Christian Reformed Church from 1900 to 1920.

Growth in uumbers was not as marked from 1900 onward as from 1880—1900, due in part to the practical cessation of immigration during the great World War. Still, the increase from 144 churches in 1900, to 245 at the end of 1920, and from 53,794 souls, to nearly 95,995, during the same period, was encouraging. Moreover, the fact that the number of classical organizations had increased from nine in 1900, to thirteen by 1912, showed a closer knitting, a better articulating of the body ecclesiastical. The old Classis of Iowa was, in September, 1904, divided into two bodies: Classis Pella and Classis Orange City. March, 1910, the Classis of Pacific was formed as an offshoot of the Orange City organization, and two years later (March, 1912), the Sioux Center Classis was organized as a second offshoot. Vigor was displayed, moreover, in the way of permanent *church extension*. While, as stated in Chapter IV, §7, the far-flung battle line had crossed the Canadian border northward, reached Colorado, Texas and New Mexico southward, Maryland in the East, and the Pacific coast in the extreme northwest of the United States, this did not prove lasting. Various causes led to a practical retreat. But it was only a temporary setback that was suffered. In 1900 permanent work was begun in Lynden, Washington. Oak Harbor, on Whitby Island, Washington, was revived the next year. In 1908 a church was organized in Winnipeg, Manitoba. Two years later, in Canada's far northwest, Edmonton came into being. During 1909 a promising work was begun in California, at Redlands, and the outlook for growth in that beautiful State is encouraging. In Colorado's capital permanent work was started in 1907. Montana had become the home of a strong church, Manhattan, already in 1903. Help was extended even to the struggling Argentina churches, help hitherto confined to financial assistance, because insurmountable obstacles prevented the going thither of a clergyman, as the Synod of 1904 had resolved upon. (See Chapter VI, §7.) The upper peninsula of Michigan also was invaded, Rudyard dating from 1901. Indeed, it had become a "far-flung battle line", and American publications began to note that there was such a denomination as the Christian Reformed Church.

§2. A STRENGTHENED MINISTRY

Numerically, this is true first of all. The ninety-eight preachers of 1900 had, by the end of 1920, become a force of one hundred eighty-six ministers. But, secondly, and that is what we had in mind particularly, the ministerial force was strengthened in this period because a better education was furnished, as shown by the constantly improved curriculum, Chapter VI, §3 and §4. An increasing number obtained the A.B. degree. Several took a postgraduate course in Princeton Seminary. A limited number obtained doctor's degrees at the Free University of Amsterdam and at other institutions of higher learning. Publications of various sorts indicated mental vigor that commanded respect from outsiders.

§3. INCREASING STRENGTH OF THE AMERICAN
ELEMENT. PUBLICATIONS

As we noted in Chapter IV, §6, in 1900 only two American-speaking congregations existed, apart from those of
the Hackensack Classis. But soon a change occurred. Not
alone were a number of churches of this kind organized in
Michigan, in the heart of the old "Colony", but as early as
1903 Chicago saw the birth of Second Englewood, the vanguard of the Classis of Illinois. In 1920 the Mississippi
was crossed by the movement, Austinville dating from
1920, and even in faraway Washington, Second Lynden
came to birth in the same year. In the Hudson Classis the
English movement grew more slowly. While several
churches conducted some services in the language of the
land prior to the date, in Paterson the "Bethel" congregation did not originate earlier than December, 1921, beyond
the time limit of this Chapter.

That the American element increased strongly was also
shown by the growth of *The Banner*. Started in 1866 by
the Rev. J. Y. De Baun as a 16-page monthly, called *The
Banner of Truth,* the official organ of the True Reformed
Dutch Church, it was, in December, 1903, transferred to
Michigan, in charge of "The Banner of Truth Publishing
Co.," with the Rev. J. Noordewier as president, and the Rev.
H. Beets as editor-in-chief, assisted by various brethren.
Already in December, 1906, the new Company was able
to make the paper a weekly. In 1914 it was sold to the de-
nomination to take its place next to *De Wachter* as de-
nominational organ, its subscription list in 1920 number-
ing 5,300 subscribers.

During the fall of the preceding year the *Yearbook for*
1914 marked the first one of a series of annuals for denominational purposes in the language of the land. In 1914 a
metrical version of the Psalms, for use in the American
churches, was approved of by the Synod, even as an offi-

cial translation into English of the Standards and Liturgy and Church Order had been prepared, matters discussed in detail in Chapters VIII and X.

That English was increasingly used in the Seminary as medium of instruction and exclusively in "Calvin College", marked progress in Americanization, as well as the introduction of a series of Catechism books in English, by the Revs. H. Beets and M. J. Bosma (Chapter IX, §4). The appearance of the *Instructor* for the Sabbath School (1915), as well as the cessation of the publication of its Dutch predecessor, the *Sabbathschool Bode* (1920), were other evidences of the linguistic change going on.

The Michigan Annual Sabbath School Convention, dating from 1895, at first conducting its exercises exclusively in Dutch, had at its meeting in 1920 not a single subject handled in the language of the fathers. That the Christian Schools had discarded the Holland language as medium of instruction in nearly every instance during the second decade of the twentieth century, is shown in Chapter VI, §6, which also mentions publications advocating the cause.

While, strictly speaking, stepping over the boundary line of the period covered by this Chapter, we add here that the monthly organ of the students of the Theological School and Calvin College, the *Calvin College Chimes* (dating from 1906), while at first publishing a considerable number of articles in the speech of the fathers, is increasingly employing the American language, while the *Grundy College Messenger,* from its first issue (November 1921) onward, used the English exclusively. This decrease of Dutch and the increase of English likewise appears in other publications circulating among our people. *De Heidenwereld* also introduced an English department in 1920.

The Witness, which made its bow to the public in December, 1921, as "A monthly published in the interest of the Reformed faith", was bi-lingual from the start. *Religion and Culture,* however, at first, from May 1918, a quarterly, and since June 1921 a monthly periodical, publishes nothing but English articles, although quotations in the tongue of the fathers liberally sprinkle some of its contributions.

We should not fail to name here, although not confined to our denomination, but, like *De Heidenwereld,* meant for both the Reformed and Christian Reformed Churches, *The Young Calvinist,* formerly the "Clarion Series". Since January 1920 it appears monthly as the official organ of the American Federation of Reformed Young Men's Societies. This Federation, organized in September, 1919, in 1923 enrolled thirty Societies located in seven different States of our Union. "Its purpose is to aid the young men of our churches in the many difficulties that present themselves, especially in connection with the Americanization process. For that reason the Federation tries to organize Young Men's Societies wherever possible. These Young Men's Societies it aims to organize into strong local leagues. The ideal is to have every young man affiliated with a group, and all these groups united in a strong national organization. Realizing the difficulty of continuing to preserve the interest of our young men in the distinctive Reformed principles, the Federation is ever working toward that ideal". (President R. Postma quoted in *The Banner,* April 12, 1923.)

§4. FINANCIAL AND PERSONAL OFFERINGS INCREASED

At first most of the people belonging to the Christian Reformed Church possessed but slender means. "Not many noble, not many rich" applied to our pioneers in America as well as to the early christians in Corinth. But in the course of time, Dutch energy and thrift revealed itself encouragingly as shown also in congregational and denominational property holdings. The government census of religious bodies for 1906 stated that there were 181 church edifices belonging to the churches of the denomination, with a seating capacity of 62,334. Church property was valued at $903,600, against which there appeared an indebtedness of $216,287, and 136 parsonages, valued at $290,250. Thirteen organizations were using halls. As compared to the report for 1890 these figures showed an increase of 75 organizations, 14,199 communicants, and $475,100 in the value of church property. But in the census report of 1916 a splendid and somewhat uniform increase was registered. There were then reported 233 church edifices, valued at the sum of $1,658,308, an increase of 83 per cent since 1906. The indebtedness in 1916 resting on the church buildings was $486,408. The 184 parsonages, about which data were sent in, were valued at $619,095, an increase of 113 per cent above 1906. The average salary for pastors was given in 1916 as $1,073, whereas at first the amounts usually were from $300 to $500, plus use of the parsonages. Contributions for missions and benevolences in the last named year were reported as $159,400, an increase of $29,739 since 1906, or 22 per cent higher than the preceding decade. It was also stated in the 1916 report that church expenditures as given by 221 organizations, covering running expenses, improvements, and benevolences, amounted to $715,193—a creditable showing indeed.

It goes without saying that parsonages as well as church edifices had become considerably better as the years rolled by. It is true, the Van Raalte church building, erected in 1856, was a noble type of a house of worship, but nearly all of the older structures used for church services were far less stately. In fact, some of them were not much better in appearance than barns. Slowly on, however, a change for the better set in. The edifice of the first church of Grand Rapids, erected in 1870, located on

Spring Street (now Commerce Avenue), was a solid brick structure, with a good sized steeple to adorn it. The first American-speaking church in Grand Rapids, in 1887 reared a church edifice which betokened dignity, and during the opening years of the twentieth century dozens of congregations in Michigan and in the East, and a few in the West, built fine brick houses of worship as well as comfortable pastor's homes. Different *church funds* also showed a laudable increase of the spirit of generous giving, particularly the *Emeritus Fund*. Dating from 1874 it was but a struggling "martyr", trying to keep the wolf from the door of aged and indigent pastors and pastors' widows and orphans, depending as it was on "collections" twice a year. But in 1904 it was placed on an assessment basis, and since then has nobly acted its part in caring for the retired veterans of the cross and the bereaved families of departed ministers. The same spirit of increased offering for denominational funds was shown in the receipts of *Church Help,* a treasury created in 1892 to aid new congregations to obtain church property. Its first committee, organized in 1894, was composed of the Revs. E. Breen, J. Manni, and H. Bode. In 1920 it was reported that over $38,000 was owed to the fund by the various churches which had been aided—a comparatively small amount. However, if this little tree is properly taken care of it will prove some day that "tall oaks from little acorns grow".

But far more uplifting and encouraging than this increase in gifts of money is the increase in *Personal Offerings.* And by this we mean the giving of one's self in dedication to Kingdom work. While many denominations in our land utter bitter complaints about a falling off in numbers of students for the ministry at home and for mission work abroad, the opposite was the case among us. Whereas during 1900 only 17 students were reported enrolled in the Seminary department of the Theological School and 55 in its Preparatory Department — the

School catalog for 1920—1921 gave as summary of enrollment 44 in the Seminary, 122 in the College, and 131 in the Preparatory School. While not all in the College and Preparatory departments were, of course, looking forward to the ministry, the great majority did. And whereas in former days but very few thought definitely of missionary work, by 1920 there were at least 40 "volunteers"—see Chapter VII, §10.

§5. NEW CONNECTIONS MADE. ECCLESIASTICAL
CORRESPONDENCE DEFINED

Manhood stands, as we said, for forming new connections. That also applies to *affiliations with other denominations*. We have already related that the Anti-Masonic Movement entailed an improved relationship with the Church in the Netherlands. Our pastors visiting the Netherlands were welcomed in Reformed pulpits of the old Home, and in the New World certificates of membership coming from the Reformed churches of Holland were accepted at face value. Still, this relationship was undefined. Such was also the case with the "correspondence" carried on from the first with the Reformed (Dopper) Church of South Africa and the Old Reformed churches of Germany. And with none of the American sister denominations a regular correspondence was carried on. But the Synod of 1900 ushered in a new epoch by defining what this Correspondence was to include and with which churches it was to be carried on. It was proposed to have the delegates not simply bear "fraternal greetings" to the major church courts, as customary in the American Church world, but to have advisory vote in all matters pertaining to the general interests of the denominations concerned. Watching that there was to be no departure from Reformed principles touching doctrine, worship, or discipline was stated to be a mutual obligation. In the case of a proposed revision of Confession and Liturgy in so far as doctrines were involved, mutual consent, conformable to the Word of God, was declared needful. This was assented to by the General Synod of the Reformed Churches in the Netherlands. But the Christian Reformed Church of that country, composed of those who had refused to enter the union of 1892, was unwilling to begin such relationship, and the Reformed Church of America also declined to make such arrangements. The exchange of greetings by fraternal delegates at General Synods and no more, constitute the official connection between the so closely related bodies of Dutch stock in the New World. Proposals of "Church Comity" in home mission fields were not accepted hitherto.

Ecclesiastical correspondence, consisting of exchange of greetings, is carried on with several other American denominations, namely, the United Presbyterian Church, the Synod and the General Synod of the Reformed Presbyterians and the Associate Presbyterian Church. The joining of the *Federal Council of the Churches of Christ,* resolved in 1918, was confirmed by the Synod of 1922.

"The Federal Council of the Churches of Christ in America, organized in 1908, is an agency for Christian cooperation. Thirty Protestant Evangelical bodies are joined in its fellowship, activities and support. Through the Council these communions are enabled to unite in concrete service to the community, the nation and the world.

"The Council gives the churches coöperating a united voice on questions of international relationship, world peace, disarmament, and the crusade for a warless world. It promotes fellowship with churches of other lands, and seeks the world-wide realization of Christian ideals.

"The Council provides means for a united impact of the coöperating bodies on questions of vital importance, such as united evangelism, social service, better race relations, international justice and good-will, works of mercy, Christian education, and the promotion of a better type of citizenship.

"The Council, through the city and state Federations, furnishes a means of bringing the combined power of the local Protestant churches to bear upon community problems which concern them all. This coöperation results in increased efficiency in coöperative evangelism, social service, comity, Christian education, religious service in public institutions, church publicity, and social and civic betterment". (Cf. *The Banner*, January 18, and February 15, 1923.)

The *Home Missions Council* of the evangelical denominations of North America, and the *Foreign Missions Conference* were joined, the former in 1912, and the latter in 1918. Both are organizations composed of delegates of mission boards of evangelical denominations of America to deliberate and plan regarding common problems and tasks. They have no legislative authority, hence the names indicative of their nature: council, conference. They are, however, of great importance in shaping policies and are practically indispensible in view of the common tasks and the national and international relationships involved in world-wide work of missions. Not one denomination, single-handedly, but the whole Church, can bring the whole gospel to the whole world. That is the great reason for coöperation. Unless it means surrendering precious principles, such fellowshipping in the common Kingdom task is a necessity and a duty as well as a privilege.

§6. INFLUENCE OF DOCTORS KUYPER AND BAVINCK, UTRECHT CONCLUSIONS, CREED REVISION

In Chapter IV, §8, we noted that Dr. G. Vos favored supra-lapsarism whose relative truth had been defended by Dr. A. Kuyper, although he also accepted the truth involved in infra-lapsarism. In fact, neither he nor Dr. H.

Bavinck considered this deep problem solved satisfac-
torily. (*Heraut,* No. 1484.)   Both of the men named have
exerted considerable influence on our Church-life, as already remarked in §9 of Chapter IV.   Particularly is this
true of Dr. Abraham Kuyper, born in 1837, founder of the
Free University, at one time prime minister of the Netherlands, a man of wonderful intellect, and boundless energy.
At first, while Dr. Kuyper still belonged to the Established
Church, he was looked at somewhat askance by the older
leaders of the Christian Reformed Church of Holland, as
well as by some of the older preachers of the American
Christian Reformed Church, notably by the Rev. L. J.
Hulst (see §7 below).   But Dr. Vos with his broader vision,
introduced him to his students as a man of genius, who
was not alone endeavoring to reform the old Church of
the Netherlands but rejuvenating theology as well.   Later,
when the reading of Dr. Kuyper's weekly, *De Heraut,* became more common than before, and men of a later immigration arrived who were enthusiastic followers of the
Dutch leader, his influence grew apace among us.   It is
still too early to adequately estimate Dr. Kuyper's influence in the New World.   In the Old World he was the man
who fulfilled what John Robinson had told the Pilgrims
on the way to New England what was going to occur:
new light breaking forth from the Word of God.

As Daniel Webster said of Alexander Hamilton: "He
smote the rock of the national resources, and abundant
streams of revenue gushed forth; he touched the dead
corpse of Public Credit and it sprung upon its feet"—so we
may say as to Dr. Kuyper's work.   With the Moses' staff of
his genius he touched the Reformed theology, left in a
petrified condition, and it displayed unsuspected vigor,
and he developed Calvinism from a system of theological
tenets, to a world-embracing life system—a "Wereld-beschouwing", as the Dutch phrase has it.

The claim may well be made that Dr. Kuyper unfolded a christian system of thought which made it possible that all the five faculties of a university could coöperate in the domain of science, to give unto God all the glory, and to unify our thinking. He developed christian philanthropy, pointing out the way to the deaconate to exalt Christ as the Consoler. He awakened the Reformed people from the slumber of anabaptistic indifference regarding public affairs, showing that christians, while pilgrims here below, as soldiers of Christ have a calling with reference to the life of the nation. He was the man of the antithesis, revealed in the domain of the Church, the State, science and social life.

In this paragraph a second Dutch leader of importance should be named, DR. HERMAN BAVINCK. Born in 1854, of Bentheimer descent, a son of the Dutch Secession, this gifted man was trained in part at the famous university of Leyden. As professor, at first of the Kampen Theological School, and later as Dr. Kuyper's successor in the chair of dogmatics of the Free University, Dr. Bavinck wielded a powerful influence through his masterful *Reformed Dogmatics,* giving a scholarly presentation, rejuvenation, and affirmation of the truths of Christianity according to the Reformed Standards. His utterances on Common Grace, and those of Dr. Kuyper on it, originated later discussion among us on the subject, but excluded here for the reason given in the introductory paragraph.

The Rev. J. C. Rullmann, well known Dutch Church historian, at our request, thus formulated the significance of both of these men: "Dr. Kuyper has brought Calvinism in its national and international significance to evaluation and influence. Dr. H. Bavinck showed us the significance of the new culture for christendom. The first named was the man of the antithesis, the last named of the synthesis, but both were deeply convinced of the tremendously big task which the Reformed churches in the Netherlands have before them in the future. For, with whatever gigantic courage they devoted themselves to their task, they were the first ones to acknowledge that they left much of it undone, and reminded of the word of à Lasco, the organizer of the Holland Refugee Church in London, that the development of succeeding centuries was not to be stopped, owing to the increased light which God might bring forth through following generations."

In a Church History of this nature, we cannot go into details as to the program and achievements of these great men, giants in their days. We must of necessity confine ourselves to what most directly touched our life as a denomination, and that is in the sphere of theology.

Dr. A. Kuyper whom many honored with something akin to "hero worship", advanced certain peculiar views about the great doctrine of Justification, claiming that there is not alone a justification of a sinner in time, when he in faith embraces Christ and His merits, something taught plainly in the Confession of Faith, but also, in God's counsel from all eternity. Moreover, Dr. Kuyper claimed that regeneration took place immediately, through the workings of the Holy Spirit, whereas others had taught that the Word of God was in all cases instrumental in this inner change of a sinner. A fourth point he taught, in connection with his views on Baptism, was that the seed of the Covenant, according to the promise of God, is to be considered born again and sanctified in Christ until the contrary fact is shown, later on in life.

These views led to much agitation in the Netherland Church, echoed in church papers among us. But in Holland certain "Conclusions" were adopted by the General Synod of Utrecht, held in 1905. They occupied a mediating viewpoint of the matters involved, and had a quieting effect. Such was also the case in the Christian Reformed Church in America which had been stirred considerably about them, and which formally adopted these "Conclusions" in 1908. The discussion carried on, as well as the act of the Synods involved, had brought out that the Reformed conception of God's truth was broad enough to permit the "expansion" of the Creed of the Church, thus recognizing the fact that Calvinism is not a petrofact, incapable of growth, but a living organism. (Cf. James Orr, *The Progress of Dogma,* Lecture X.)

On the whole the adoption of the "Conclusions", as already remarked, had a quieting and settling effect on the life of the Church, particularly regarding the Baptism question, alluded to in Chapter V, § 8. Considerable of a clarifying and satisfying view of this subject is due, we believe, to the publishing (in 1916), of *Heilig Zaad,* a treatise on Baptism, by Dr. J. Van Lonkhuyzen, an able and zealous disciple of Dr. A. Kuyper, who particularly in his Chicago weekly, *Onze Toekomst,* constantly pleads for acceptance of the life- and world-view of his revered teacher, as well as for the principles of Church polity advocated by another strong man of the Free University, Dr. F. L. Rutgers.

In line with the teachings of Kuyper, Bavinck and Rutgers, doctrinal development was shown in what may be called a revision of the Creed. Article XXXVI of the Netherland Confession of Faith (see Chapter VIII, §2 of this History), declared civil government or the magistracy, "not only to have regard unto, and watch for the welfare of the civil state; but also that they protect the sacred ministry; and thus remove and prevent all idolatry and false worship; that the kingdom of antichrist may be thus destroyed and the kingdom of Christ promoted. They must therefore countenance the preaching of the gospel everywhere, that God may be honored and worshipped by every one, as he commands in his Word."

The Synod of 1910 declared that "This phrase, touching the office of the magistracy in its relation to the Church, proceeds on the principle of the Established

Church, which was first applied by Constantine and afterwards also in many Protestant countries. History, however, does not support the principle of State domination over the Church, but rather the separation of Church and State. Moreover, it is contrary to the New Dispensation that authority be vested in the State to arbitrarily reform the Church, and to deny the Church the right of independently conducting its own affairs as a distinct territory alongside the State. The New Testament does not subject the Christian Church to the authority of the State that it should be governed by political measures, but to our Lord and King only as an independent territory alongside and altogether independent of the State, that it may be governed and edified by its office-bearers and with spiritual weapons only. Practically all Reformed Churches have repudiated the idea of the Established Church, and are advocating the autonomy of the churches and personal liberty of conscience in matters pertaining to the service of God.

"The Christian Reformed Church in America, being in full accord with this view, feels constrained to declare that it does not conceive of the office of the magistracy in this sense, that it be in duty bound to also exercise political authority in the sphere of religion, by establishing and maintaining a State Church, advancing and supporting the same as the only true Church, and to oppose, to persecute and to destroy by means of the sword all the other Churches as being false religions; and to also declare that it does positively hold that, within its own secular sphere, the magistracy has a divine duty towards the first table of the Law as well as towards the second; and furthermore that both State and Church as institutions of God and Christ have mutual rights and duties appointed them from on high, and therefore have a very sacred reciprocal obligation to meet through the Holy Spirit, who proceeds from Father and Son. They may not, however, encroach upon each other's territory. The Church has rights of sovereignty in its own sphere as well as the State."

The Christian Reformed Church, therefore, unequivocally announced that it stood for a free Church in a free State—a thoroughly American principle.

§7. STRIFE AMONG BRETHREN: NEO-CALVINISM, THE
BAPTIZED MEMBERSHIP QUESTION, HACKENSACK'S
DEFECTION, THE LABOR UNION PROBLEM,
THE "MARANATHA" CASE

"Neo-Calvinism". It could hardly be expected that no voices would be raised among us in protest against at least some of Dr. Kuyper's views. In a book, *"Oud- en Nieuw Calvinisme,* by Rev. L. J. Hulst and Prof. G. K. Hemkes (1913), it was asserted that Dr. Kuyper had "changed the accent (klemtoon) regarding different matters, among them the conception of theology as a science, common grace, the fundamental conception of Calvinism, Justification, the Covenant of Grace, and Regeneration. This, it was claimed, had serious consequences for the administration of the Word and the Sacraments, and for the Church as to its purpose and ministry.

But the publication of the volume of the two venerable men who wrote it, caused no marked disturbance. Discussion of the matter in the columns of the religious monthly *De Gereformeerde Amerikaan,* a discussion opened in 1905, had in its day, made a much deeper impression and caused considerable more agitation in the press as well as in various congregational circles.

More serious in outward consequences than all this discussion of "Neo-Calvinism", was another matter causing "strife among the Brethren". We refer to agitation leading to legislation and secession on the subject of certain rights of adult baptized members, a matter which for brevity's sake we call:

The *Baptism Membership* Question. From the beginning of the Dutch Secession it had been allowed by the Rev. De Cock and others to have parents who themselves had not yet made confession of faith, but were walking in the footsteps of the flock, present their infants to Baptism. But just like the "Half-way Covenant" in New England led to undesirable results, so with this "Baptized Member System", as it came to be called. Large numbers of parents delayed taking vows of membership to gain admission to the Communion Table, but never hesitated to approach the Baptism Font with their little ones. They allowed themselves, in the opening words of the Form of Baptism, to be addressed as "Beloved in the Lord Jesus Christ", declaring their children to be "sanctified" in Him, but at all other times professed the contrary, or at least did not accept the inferences of what was declared about and by them at Baptism. And especially in some congregations the percentage of regular membership was far below what it should be, compared to the number of souls or families. No wonder that men of vision became alarmed, lest the Church should degenerate into a "moral society" instead of remaining a Church. Already at the Synod of 1880 the South Holland consistory registered an objection to having baptized members answer the questions of the Form of Baptism at the administration of the Sacrament. After considerable agitation the Synod of 1894 declared that the Baptized Membership System was a departure from the Word of God and old Reformed ways. Persistent refusal to partake of Communion was later on declared to lead inevitably to excommunication. The right to have baptized members present their children to baptism was denied in principle in 1894, and gradually put into practice. But in some circles it took a long time before all consistories fell in line. Especially in Muskegon it caused much agitation, leading to secession in 1907. But the Synod of 1904 emphasized anew that the principle should be maintained, everywhere. And while not without its drawbacks in practical life, the results are proving the wisdom of insisting on keeping the use of Baptism and Communion on parity. For one thing, the new ruling perceptibly raised the ratio of confessing members. In 1890 about one-third of the persons belonging to the various churches were confessing members (3.3), while the figures of the Yearbook for 1922 showed that about one-half of the total number had made confession of faith (2.2). By ways of contrast, to show what unlimited baptized membership leads to, the *Mitarbeiter* of the Reformed Church in America (November, 1919), stated that of the thirty-nine East Friesian congregations of that community, there were eleven which numbered more families than confessing members.

Hackensack's Defection. As stated in Chapter IV, §5, the Hackensack Classis, when in 1890, it voted for union, made some reservations. It had been resolved, namely, "that in this organic union our internal government, forms of church worship, and our corporate name shall not be interfered with, in any way, by either Church. That we be entitled to representation, that the organic name shall be Christian Reformed Church, and that this shall be the basis of union". Numerically the Hackensack Classis was weak, only numbering 507 families, a total of 2,000 souls in its 13 congregations, shepherded by seven pastors. And it was weak as to true unity in a doctrinal sense. Not long after 1890 charges of heresy were made against one of the pastors, and his Arminianism was evident. There was also weakness as to church discipline. While Free Masons remained barred, according to a resolution of 1831, members of so-called minor secret societies were tolerated as church members. These things led to much unpleasantness, and finally to open rupture. The majority of Classis claimed that the union of 1890 was conditional, and asserted that the conditions, named above, had repeatedly been violated—that the language barrier had prevented intelligent action at Synod, that new tests of membership (referring to the exclusion of members of minor orders), had proven an injury to the congregations and a source of unrest, and that there was difference in practice respecting the Confession. It was charged: "Far too many (of the Christian Reformed Church) are satisfied with an objective confession, through fear of Labadism". "For these and other reasons we desire to return to our former fraternal relation". What those "other reasons" were has never officially been declared.

But not all of the Classis of Hackensack consented to sever the ties with the denomination. Under the leadership of the Revs. J. A. Westervelt, J. Dolfin, and J. F. Van Houten, the stronger churches remained loyal and, as stated in another connection, they helped to stop undesirable "leaks". As to the feeble remnant of the Hackensack Classis, since 1908, when it isolated itself, some of the congregations have joined other denominations. The others, at Leonia and in New York City, are in a dying condition.

It was regrettable that the brethren involved practically became defenders of the minor Secret Orders. But the denomination was in no mood to tolerate this. The principle had been accepted: fellowship in Secret Orders is incompatible with membership in our churches, and it was maintained even at the cost of losing the coöperation of brethren accepting the same fundamentals.

The Labor Union Problem. The age-long struggle between capital and labor resulted everywhere in civilized lands in the organization of *unions* of workingmen, sometimes called Trade Unions. Their aim was combination, to present a united front to capital (which often was combined for its purposes), in order to protect labor and to promote the interests of the working class. In America the formative period of unionism lasted from about 1740 to 1840; quiet growth, not free from Socialism, occurred up to 1865, when a period of active effort began. The Knights of Labor, dating from 1869, at first a secret labor union, aimed to bring all workingmen into one great organization without reference to the trade unions to which they belonged. In 1886 they numbered half a million of members. Disastrous strikes under their auspices caused reaction. Since 1886 the American Federation of Labor came upon the foreground. Its principles were opposed to those of the Knights of Labor in that it recognized the full autonomy of each trade to regulate its own internal affairs.

It was during the ascendency of the Knights of Labor that the attention of our denomination was first drawn officially to Unionism. At first, 1881, workingmen's unions were condemned out and out as unchristian. Two years later it was mentioned that some unions of employers also merited rebuke. The Synod of 1904 quite properly distingunished between *degenerated* unions, whose principles and activities are plainly contrary to Holy Writ, and association with which is incompatible with membership in the Christian Reformed Church, and *neutral* unions. About the latter the Synod of 1916 stated there were not enough data on hand to show that membership in the church was incompatible with membership in them, "unless it can be shown that a certain union gives constitutional warrant to a certain sin or sins, or reveals in its regular activities that it champions sins."

It had already been decided in 1892 that each union was to be judged on its own merits.

The 1916 Synod stated that if any of our people are forced to belong to a so-called neutral union in order to obtain a livelihood, they are to witness for Christ by word and deed, in the midst of these unions, and if hindered in this, to break with them.

Already in 1892 it was attempted in Grand Rapids to form a workingmen's union in a christian spirit, on the model of the "Patrimonium" labor society in the Netherlands, but without lasting success.

The Synod of 1904 urged our men to form Christian labor unions, and the one of 1916 advised that in places where separate christian unions were desirable, they were to coöperate as much as possible with other unions in order to obtain or maintain social justice.

This long story shows that there was indeed a wrestling with a perplexing problem to find a christian solution. As Prof. Heyns expresses it: "Since it is undeniable that capital has dealth unfairly with labor, especially because it pays the workingman what it must and not what it should; since it forsakes him in his old age, and the State, the police and the press usually care less for his interests than for those of capital, it cannot in itself be condemned that the laborer by means of joint action tries to protect and to strengthen himself—unless, of course, he employs forbidden means and himself oversteps the boundaries of justice and fairness. Consequently the attitude of the Church regarding unions is entirely different from that regarding Secret Orders." (Cf. Chapter IX, §6.)

The "Maranatha" Case. The orthodox American church world, especially as represented by the Moody Schools of our land, in the opening years of the twentieth century, was led to champion Pre-millennialism—a view of the "last things" which in many respects was the old Chiliasm in a new dress. In the year 1917 the Rev. H. Bultema issued a book entitled *Maranatha,* in which he made a serious attempt to graft Pre-millennialism into the stock of Reformed theology. *The Banner* of June 14, 1917, predicted that the book would arouse considerable criticism. Pre-millennial views, never popular in Calvinistic circles, had been condemned already by the Christian Reformed Synod of Franeker in 1863. In 1883, when the Rev. J. I. Fles was admitted to the denomination, he had to retract certain views connected with Chiliasm, expressed in his aforementioned Catechism (*Leer des Heils*). Drs. A. Kuyper and H. Bavinck had condemned Chiliasm repeatedly as Judaistic. The fact that two resurrections were taught, separated by the 1,000 years of the Millennium, two or three different Comings of the Lord, and at least as many Judgments, as well as the teaching that bloody sacrifices would once more be offered in Jerusalem's Temple, as "memorials looking back to the cross"— all these and other things, had caused large numbers to reject the system taught in Rev. Bultema's book. Particularly two teachings were singled out as contrary to the Confession of the denomination, namely, the one about the *essential* difference between the New Testament Church and Israel, and the other about the Kingship of Christ. The Synod of 1918, before which the case was laid, accepted the view that according to the Standards of the Church there was not the least doubt about the two things under dispute:

(1) "The Unity of the Church of all ages, Israel not excluded. The Church of all ages is essentially one".

(2) "The Kingship of Christ. Christ is not alone the Head of His Church in an organic sense, but also emphatically King of His Church in the juridical sense of the expression."

The consistory of the First Church of Muskegon was charged to take the matter up with its pastor. But it refused to do so. Intervention from the side of the Muskegon Classis at length in 1919, led to a decision involving deposition, something which the consistory was unwilling to execute. Legal battles about the church property brought victory to that part of the congregation which accepted the Synod's interpretation of the Standards, and the old organization, dating from 1867, was continued. In Grand Rapids, Grand Haven, Holland, Moline, and Chicago, the "Berean Reformed", as the new group named itself, obtained a foothold.   September 15, 1920, representatives of these bodies met to form a new denomination.   Charges were published against the Christian Reformed Churches embracing such serious things as that the Word was no longer preached in purity, and that office-bearers in Muskegon had been deposed and others threatened with discipline, contrary to the Word. A third charge was that the Sacraments were no longer administered according to the institution of Christ. The use of the individual communion cup was condemned, the tolerance of Higher Criticism was asserted, as well as the holding of the view of presupposed regeneration and striving after human greatness and unity (*De Bereër,* July 21, 1920).   The Church did not consider it worth while to refute these wild charges, though many regretted keenly that the breach had been made. But the keen edge of that regret has largely been worn off by this time, because different things, happening in the camp of the "Bereans" and like-minded people, are plainly indicative of the fact that Pre-millennial premises almost inevitably lead to developments out of line with sound Calvinistic principles.   (Cf. *The Banner,* April 7, 1921.)

The *Significance* of the settling of the above named cases is more important than such may appear at first sight.   It is noteworthy as showing the trend of church life, the driving force of principle.

That the Neo-Calvinism controversy led to no split proves that the Reformed Creed is sufficiently elastic to permit what in the introductory paragraph of this Chapter were called intra-confessional differences, i.e., those which leave the fundamentals untouched.

The settling of the Baptized Membership question evidenced the desire to maintain the motto of the fathers: *"Ecclesia reformata semper est reformanda",* that is, the Church meriting the name "Reformed" must ever be reforming.   In this case there was imminent danger of the

Church of God degenerating into a "moral society", the mistake made by the Pilgrim Fathers of New England, with their "Half-way Covenant".

The resistance regarding "Hackensack's Defection" indicated determined opposition to "lower the bars" as to secret oath-bound societies (see Chapter IX, §6), while, the stand about unions shows an attempt to be fair in recognizing the rightful place of coöperation in the proper form, in justice to labor. Finally, the action in the "Maranatha" case proved an awakeness to the fact that the underlying principle of the Pre-millennial view, a literal interpretation of prophecy, is subversive to the Christian Creed as built up by the struggling Church throughout the ages, and dividing what God united in His counsel: His one people, of the Old as well as of the New Testament dispensation, His one Vineyard although in charge of different keepers; His one Olive Tree.

§8. THE DENOMINATIONAL CALLING STATED

To vigorous manhood belongs the mapping out of a life-task. This tendency appeared also during the period of the history of the Church here described. While during its years of struggle and its adolescent period signs were not wanting of some degree of introspection to ascertain what was the plan of God in bringing our people to these shores, and what His purpose was in enabling them to form a separate regiment of God's army—things of this sort were evidently not very clear to most of our forebears.

But at the opening of the period here outlined, we notice several attempts at reaching a clear conception of the denominational task. Since, as we stated in Chapter II, §9, the pluriformity of the Church entails some kind of a distinctive *mission* and specific contribution, we shall try to define it here before taking up the various detailed activities of the Church which, to some extent, are or at least should be, attempts to carry out that calling.

It should be needless to remind ourselves of the fact that as a part of the Church universal, it is the task of the Christian Reformed denomination to devote itself, in common with the other manifestations of the body of Christ, God's royal priesthood: to show forth the excellencies of Him who calls His people out of darkness into His marvelous light (1 Peter 2: 9). The Church is not simply to be a gathering of believers, looking to Christ for salvation, but a mother of believers as well, a prophetic witness for Christ and His Word, a priestly dispenser of charity, and royally striving that Christ everywhere may be crowned king of all domains of life.

That attempts have been made and are being made to do its share of that great work, is evident not alone from what we already named in previous Chapters, but especially from the next Chapter on the educational institutions of the Church, and Chapter VII on missions. But besides this, there were, as we stated, endeavors made to *formulate* the special mission of the denomination, and to define the contribution it could be expected to make as such.

The Rev. E. Breen, a man of vision and loyalty, who died in 1921, after thirty-two years of consecrated ministerial service, was one of the first to voice what others had sensed before him. He stated to the Synod of 1906 that God's purpose in bringing us here was that, with our peculiar Dutch character and our Calvinistic principles, we were to be a blessing to the religious and moral life of our nation.

Particularly the Rev. J. Groen, in his semi-centennial oration (*Gedenkboek,* p. 213 ff.), outlined "Our Calling and Ideals for the Future." They were determined, he said, first, by our being a Church, a part of the one, visible, instituted, militant Church; second, by our national descent;

third, by our Reformed principles; fourth, by our history, and last by the special religious needs of our country at the present time. Theologically we were to maintain and develop our Reformed principles, without schismatically condemning everything outside of us. We were to labor with might and main to extend our Church, striving to bring about union with others, especially with brethren of Dutch blood and Reformed origin. The administration of the Word and the Sacraments was to be emphasized instead of losing ourselves in all kinds of "institutional" church work. But in all domains of life we should allow the light of the Word to fall, and particularly the cause of missions, according to our principles, should never be forgotten. "Churches upholding such things, our country needs, as the hope of the nation. . . . And although our Church is young, small, and weak, our principles are old, tried, and strong, and in every way up-to-date. Through God we shall do valiantly. If we remain faithful to the principles we inherited from our fathers, in the face of both liberalism and narrow sectarianism, if we labor diligently and persistently to defend and develop Calvinism,. . . . then we shall not alone be a blessing to ourselves, to our children, to our people of Dutch descent, but to this entire great, growing nation which already was a rich blessing to the world, and will be still more, if it maintains righteousness which exalts a people".

In a similar spirit wrote Prof. F. M. Ten Hoor in *De Gereformeerde Amerikaan,* and B. K. Kuiper in *Ons Opmaken en Bouwen.*

That such visions were seen and voiced indeed proves the arrival of manhood's period. How much of this has been realized as to education and missions, the two following Chapters show.

§9. AS OTHERS SEE US

Coming to the close of the history of the denomination as a whole, and before taking up other matters, we may well pause a moment to face the questions put at the close of Chapter I: "Would these pioneers and their posterity reach these objectives, (as to education and mission work), and remain loyal to the principles of the Secession people?" God knows, and history shows how far below the ideal we still are, as God's Church in its militant state in a fallen world ever will be. But that at least something of the ideals has been realized and principles are still adhered to, is indicated by the testimony of three outsiders—writers who have not been afraid of criticizing us at times. Dr. H. E. Dosker, in his *Church History,* published in 1901, spoke of the Christian Reformed Church as "boundlessly zealous, thoroughly conservative, and a very active factor in the development of the western portion of Reformed Church-life". In the edition of 1913, he substituted "Calvinistic" for conservative, but repeated the rest of the laudatory phrases unchanged. *The Leader* of July 3, 1918, testified about our people: "They have zeal, conviction, solidarity, a definite group-consciousness, leadership, and as a leaven working where the meal is, they may count for more than in the past". And even the author of *Landmarks of the Reformed Fathers,* who so bitterly attacked our pioneers and their work, as Chapter II showed, speaks of the Christian Reformed Church of today as "far superior to what the "True Church", as she once called herself, was in 1870. She is no longer seceded from all other Protestant denominations; and her active churches, her many excellent pastors and teachers, her piety and great sacrifice for the cause of Christ, entitle her to a place among the churches of the Reformation". *Soli Deo Gloria.*

TEST QUESTIONS

1. What can you say about the church extension from 1900 to 1920?
2. What is meant by a "strengthened ministry"?
3. In which states did the American element grow the most?
4. What can you say about the increase in financial and personal offerings for the Kingdom?
5. Which "new connections" were made during this period?
6. What can you say about the influence of Drs. A. Kuyper and H. Bavinck, the points involved in the "Utrecht Conclusions", and the changing of Art. 36 of the Confession?
7. What do you know of the "Baptized Membership question", and why did Synod take a decided stand on it?
8. What do you know about the Labor Union Problem?
9. Which two points were the main bone of contention in the "Maranatha" case?
10. What did the Revs. Breen and Groen state about our calling?

WORKS OF REFERENCE

"Gedenkboek", Rev. J. Groen on "Onze Roeping en Idealen", page 213 ff, and G. Kuiper, "The Mission of Our Church from a Member's Point of View", page 239 ff. Prof. F. M. Ten Hoor, articles on "Amerikanisatie" in "De Gereformeerde Amerikaan", particularly Vol. XIII.

B. K. Kuiper, "Ons Opmaken en Bouwen", in English in "The Banner" of 1911—1914, especially "Our Task", "The Banner, May 8, 1913—June 11, 1914.

"Unionism and Unions", by a Comm. of the Chr. Ref. Church. Published by order of Synod, 1902.

CHAPTER VI

INSTITUTIONS OF HIGHER LEARNING: THE THEOLOGICAL
SCHOOL AND KINDRED INSTITUTIONS; THE
CHRISTIAN PRIMARY SCHOOL

INTRODUCTORY

WHY SHOULD a denomination open and support a
School devoted to the training of its ministry? It is
a costly undertaking. It takes men away from the regular
work of the pastorate. It demands that those who feel
called to serve in the Gospel spend precious years of preparation. When God really calls men to His work, as
Elisha of old was called, why not depend upon the immediate illuminating work of the Holy Spirit to equip one for
service? So many have spoken in the past, and even in
the present there are churches which look with disdain
upon "servants of the letter", prepared in what have de-
risively been called "preachers' factories". That nevertheless the great Churches of Christendom insist on a
regular educational training has some good reasons back
of it. Not that it is denied that a God of free and sovereign grace is not able to call a man immediately from
his secular work and make him serve acceptably in His
vineyard. There are exceptions to every rule. Some men
are auto-didact—that is, self-taught so to speak, because
of unusual talent. But the rule is—preparation for life-
work by means of regular instruction. The Church of
God *needs* well-equipped men. The Church, through its

ministers, is the chosen instrument to have God's Kingdom come. An instrument must be well-made. The minister is the sower of God's truth. Sowing requires preparation. To the Church have been committed the oracles of God. To explain them needs a well-trained mind. The Church is set for the defense of the Gospel. That also demands education. It is called a pillar of truth. That also presupposes the right presentation, so that even those who run may read the proclamation affixed to that pillar.

Because of these and still other reasons which could be named, the Church of our Fathers across the sea insisted on a well-trained ministry. This was maintained over against the Anabaptists of the Reformation period, who despised human learning, ostensibly depending on the immediate illuminating work of the Holy Spirit, and over against Roman Catholicism which had exalted the sacrament above the Word. While the Roman Church throughout centuries could boast of eminent scholars, the rank and file of its clergy during the Middle Ages and later, were but poorly educated. For that matter, one needed not to be learned to read certain forms and to perform stated ceremonies. A little Latin sufficed. But the Reformed principle demanded that the pastor should first of all be a *minister* of the Word, able to intelligently expound the Holy Scriptures and to refute those who proposed heresies contrary to the Bible. To train such a ministry required educational activity, even as our Lord Himself, for the space of three years, had trained His disciples to become His apostles. Paul, himself a splendidly educated man, had enjoined Timothy: "The things which thou hast heard from me among many witnesses, the same commit thou to faithful men, who shall be able to teach others also". In harmony with this apostolic injunction, in the course of time, Theological Schools had been opened in Alexandria, and Antioch, and other places around the Mediterranean, during the early Christian cen-

turies.   During the Middle Ages theology was taught as
part of the curriculum of the Universities of the Old
World.   And one of the first things the founders of the
Dutch Republic did was to open higher institutions of
learning at Leyden and elsewhere.   Scarcely had the Secession of Holland started when its ministers, university
men themselves, began to train some of their most promising followers, for the work of the ministry.   At first this
took place in various provinces, but in 1854 it was amal-
gamated and centered in the Theological School opened
that year in the city of Kampen.

§1.   THE THEOLOGICAL SCHOOL DURING THE PERIOD OF STRUGGLE

Since the ministers of the Netherland Church frequently were loath to come to America to help the "Seceders", the question of educating their own clergy came
up very early during the separate denominational life of
our pioneers.   We first find it mentioned in 1861.   Lack of
means, however, stood in the way of doing anything
definite.   But during July, 1863, at the motion of the Rev.
K. Vanden Bosch, it was decided to take the matter up.
The Rev. W. H. Van Leeuwen consented to do the teaching.   Monthly collections were to be taken for the cause—
the beginning of the "Ex Bonis Publicis Fund"—which,
as a rule, loaned $200 per year to the indigent students.
This at first was a general denominational treasury.   Its
old name, "out of the Public Funds", referred to church
property which had been sequestrated by the Dutch government.   Of course, the title is a misnomer in America.
"Student Fund" or "Students' Aid Fund" would be a far
better name. Since 1888 the various Classes maintain their
own funds. The Rev. Van Leeuwen trained only one of the
early ministers, the Rev. J. Schepers already named in
Chapter III, §4, while the Rev. J. Noordewier was prepared

for the ministry by the Rev. R. Duiker, at one time pastor of the First Church of Grand Rapids. All the other men ordained in America during the first part of the period of struggle were educated by the Rev. D. J. Vander Werp while pastor at Graafschap, 1864—1872, and at Muskegon from 1872—1876. (See Chapter III, §4.) The study of this able and consecrated man served as class-room. Twice a week he instructed in the "Kern" or "Marrow of Divinity", by Rev. A. Francken (Chapter I, §6), and in various other branches of theology, history, and literature, notably in the Dutch language. The younger "Nazarites" were also taught the rudiments of Latin, Greek, and Hebrew. Since 1871 the course of the students who took up the "ancient languages" was six years; that of the others four. It was during the year just named that an extraordinary step was taken. Mr. Wolter Hellenthal, born in 1849 at Fillmore, Mich., had, with the consent of the "True" Church to which he belonged, finished five years of work at Hope College, of the Reformed Church in America. He was a young man of unusual promise, and at the expense of the Student Fund was sent to complete his studies at the Kampen School. Alas, already a few weeks after his arrival in the Netherlands, he died of smallpox, October, 1871. We presume that this disappointing experience deterred our pioneers from sending others across the ocean and was considered a hint of divine Providence indicating that training at home was the most natural as well as the less expensive mode of procedure in the case. As to expense, this was preventing the opening of a Theological School in the sense of having a man devote himself entirely to the work of teaching, although Rev. Vander Werp brought this up repeatedly. Like Moses, however, while he caught the vision of the Promised Land, he did not enter it. This privilege was accorded to his Joshua, the REV. G. E. BOER, who abundanlty deserves honorable mention here. Born in 1832, a graduate of the Kampen Theological School, he in 1873, while pastor at Niezijl, received a call from the First Church (Spring Street) of Grand Rapids, then the only church of the denomination in the city. After acceptance, a period of great mental distress and spiritual struggle was passed through, caused by fear that he had made a mistake. How strangely we at times misjudge Divine Providence! In America God would make his life that of extensive usefulness, whereas his stay in Holland might have meant no wider service than that of a country pastor.

From the very beginning of his arrival here the Rev. Boer became a leader in his denomination. His fraternal relationship to Holland brethren of the Reformed Church shocked some of the more exclusive "True" people. But his zeal for missions, for christian primary instruction, for the christian society work of the younger element, and his advocacy of the Sunday school, brought a new spirit into the life of the church, not alone in Grand Rapids, but throughout the denomination. He was able to spread his progressive ideas the more since he in 1875 was placed in charge of *De Wachter,* and of the instruction of the four students, then in training for the ministry, the fatal illness of the Rev. Vander Werp (cancer), leading to this transfer of Elijah's mantle to Elisha. The next year Rev. Boer was chosen as the first "docent" or professor, especially charged with the work of preparing men for the sacred office. His salary was $1,300; his seminary a room of the second floor of the Christian School on Williams Street, now the property of the Salvation Army, and the number of students was very limited at first. But there was boundless zeal, splendid bodily vigor (an important factor in human success), a proper measure of self-confidence, and daily trust in Him who assures of strength according to our days. Prof. Boer rendered yeoman's service. He trained men remarkably well-equipped for actual service, considering the limited curriculum and few years, at the most six, which each man spent at school. His praise ought to be in our churches as long as they endure, even though it was only the period of struggling at the time, and the day of small things.

§2. THE THEOLOGICAL SCHOOL FROM 1880—1900

But a new day dawned as the period of adolescent growth opened. In 1880 recognition of the institution by the State of Michigan was mentioned, and the Curatorium, hitherto numbering four regular members and some trustees, was enlarged by the appointment of a delegate from each Classis to assist at the examinations.

The course of studies was augmented when the REV. G. K. HEMKES, in 1882, began his labors at the Theological School. Born in 1838, and having received a liberal education in Holland, he had come to America in 1877 as pastor of the Vriesland church. As writer, while still in Europe, and later in America, as editor of *De Wachter* and author of several books, particularly on *Adventism* and on the Christian Reformed Church (*Rechtsbestaan*), he wielded a facile pen. He proved to be a valuable co-worker with Prof. Boer. Prof. Hemkes continued in the professorate till 1908. He died in 1920, sixteen years after his tried yoke-fellow, Prof. Boer, had suddenly been called to his reward.

But while both of the men named rendered splendid service, such was especially the case with DR. GEERHARDUS VOS, who served the Theological School as professor from 1885 till 1893, an altogether too brief period, but one of great value to the institution. His work brought not alone the English language to prominence in the School, but particularly a broadening, renovating and deepening of the courses of instruction. Those who were fortunate enough to sit at his feet will ever be grateful to this splendid scholar whose departure for Princeton Seminary, already alluded to in a previous Chapter, was keenly regretted.

Before Dr. Vos bade farewell to the Grand Rapids institution, new quarters for it had been erected, at the corner of Madison Avenue and Franklin Street, dedicated in 1892, a fine edifice. The funds for it were obtained largely through the efforts of the Rev. J. Noordewier, who went up and down the denominational territory for this purpose.

Three years later it was shown that English was indeed rapidly obtaining a place of prominence, since in 1896 the first Catalogue of the institution was published in the American language. In the issue of this Annual for 1899 – 1900 it was stated that the Theological department was in charge of three professors, the Rev. G. E. Boer, teaching hermeneutics, Biblical history and natural theology; Rev. G. K. Hemkes, professor of Biblical languages and literature, church history and christian ethics; and Rev. H. Beuker, professor of archæology, exegesis, dogmatics, homiletics, church government, symbolics, liturgies, poimenics, and catechetics. These men also instructed in the Literary Department, which since 1894 had two men on its staff for this special work, Profs. A. J. Rooks and K. Schoolland. Alas, already in the spring of 1900 PROF. H. BEUKER died suddenly. He also had proven to be a man of God, not alone in the Netherlands, where he held prominent pastorates, and occupied a leading place in the councils of the Christian Reformed Church, and as editor of *De Vrije Kerk,* but here also as professor, since 1894. He had also been one of the founders of *De Gereformeerde Amerikaan,* referred to in another connection.

The adolescent growth of the period applied to the School, not alone as to faculty and curriculum, but also as to numbers of students. While in 1880 there was a total enrollment of 10, in 1900 there were 72 students. From 1877 to 1900, inclusive, ninety-four clergymen had gone forth from the institution to proclaim the Gospel of free grace.

§3. THE SCHOOL FROM 1900—1923. "CALVIN COLLEGE"

That the new era of the young manhood can be dated from the beginning of the twentieth century is evident also in the history of the School here described.   The Catalogue for 1899—1900 still spoke of "The Christian Reformed Theological Seminary" as "an Institution of Learning, designed with the aid of Almighty God, to form men for the gospel ministry. Hence, the School, in both departments, has been organized with direct reference to this end.... The regular course involves seven years; four years are devoted to the Preparatory studies and three years to the Theological work. In the Literary Department, a thorough classical and historical course is afforded. The Holland language is the principal language of the Church which the School represents; and, consequently, no pains are spared to make the students well-versed in it. Besides, English, the language of the country, and German, the language of a large field in the West, find prominent places in the curriculum."

But a different note is struck in the Catalogue for 1900—1901. While it is stated that the Theological School had as its primary object the training of men for the gospel ministry, "in the Preparatory Department instruction is also given in those additional branches which are needed for university and college entrance, and for obtaining various teachers' certificates". Three courses were offered: a Theological, a Classical, and a Scientific Course. For the first time we find an article on *"Our Fundamental Principle"*. Manhood's definition of principle manifests itself. Listen to the ringing sentences: "We take pride in declaring emphatically.... that in our Theological School, consciously and from firm conviction, the Reformed Theology is zealously championed, strongly defended, and consequently represented according to ability. This is deemed necessary especially in this country, where, owing to lack of principle, subjective ideas and changing views abound. Furthermore, we are of the opinion that these same principles, which in the wide domain of the general sciences are characterized by the term *Calvinism*, give to the educational work and scholarship of the School its meaning and force not only, but also its very reason of existence."

It was a resolution of the 1900 Synod which had opened the School for students aiming at other vocations than the ministry, and the Annual for 1902—1903 displays the fact that women had been enrolled as well as men. Again we find the scope of the institution enlarged as the Catalogue for 1906—1907 announces itself as the "Yearbook of the *John Calvin Junior-College* and Theological School", called, "Institutions of the Christian Reformed Church". We read: "According to the constitution all instruction given must be in harmony with 'Reformed Principles.' The various branches of study, therefore, are considered from the standpoint of faith and in the light of Calvinism as a life- and world-view. Herein lies the distinctive character of our College". Of the six years' course offered in what was formerly called the Literary Department, the first four years were in a general way the equivalent of a high school or academy, and the last two, making the Junior College, were the Freshmen and Sophomore classes of a complete College.

The name "John Calvin Junior College" persists to appear on the title-pages of the "Yearbooks" until the Annual for 1908—1909 speaks of "Calvin College", the Synod of the first named year having determined to take steps looking toward the establishment of a four-year College course, by 1910. But it proved to be easier to "take steps" than to reach the goal. It took additional men as well as greatly increased laboratories and more roomy quarters as well. Happily, the last named desideratum was obtained when in September, 1917, a splendid structure could be dedicated on the twelve-acre campus in the southeastern part of Grand Rapids, a building erected at a cost of $150,000, an imposing edifice, constructed of re-inforced concrete, and brick veneer, thoroughly modern, provided with the best equipment for lighting, heating, and ventilation. The teachers' staff had meanwhile been increased so that the Yearbook for 1923 could give a College faculty of twenty, headed by the Rev. John J. Hie-menga, A.M., B.D., as president. The appointment of a president as the permanent head of the College, instead of having a "rector" in annual rotation, had been advo-cated repeatedly in *The Banner*, but it was not until 1919 that the office was created. The president's duties were outlined as those of the executive officer of Calvin College, propagating our principles, promoting the School's finan-cial interests, representing it in all its external relations, furthering the educational and spiritual welfare of the student-body, and shaping the educational policy of the institution. In the "Educational Program" which Presi-dent Hiemenga published (*The Banner*, Nov. 13, 1919), he stated that his ideals were the opening of a Christian High School in Grand Rapids under separate auspices. "Cal-vin" was to be the center of the higher education of insti-tions of learning among our people, offering a full Sem-inary, Preparatory, Classical, Modern Classical and Nor-mal Course. With respect to the development of the Col-lege, he stated in 1922 that this should be guided by three considerations. The first is to follow the historical line pointed out by our churches since 1900, that is, that Calvin College should, in course of time, become the property of a society for higher education, aiming ultimately at a "Calvin University". Secondly, the peculiar Calvinistic characteristics, convictions, and responsibility should ever be kept in mind in the instruction given, permeating it, so that we may be a salt and a leaven to our nation. Thirdly, in view of our peculiar times and special needs, our education should emphasize natural science, particularly biology, to combat the tremendous influence of present-day theories of evolution, in fundamental opposition to our life- and world-view, and furthermore philosophy, sociology, history, education, and missions. Progress in the direction given, is made right along under President Hiemenga's leadership. Early in 1923 he could report that Calvin College was not only offering a complete two years' Normal Course, but that the Michigan authorities had assured him that those who completed that course would receive State life certificates. A campaign for some $100,000 for a dormitory was begun publicly at about the same time the above announcement was made and was successful. A campaign for a million dollars for educational purposes, approved of by the 1920 Synod, has, however, been suspended till more prosperous times arrive. Well- earned tribute should be brought here to the Rev. J. Vander Mey, who since 1913 acts as Educational Secretary, traveling everywhere to obtain funds for "Calvin". Up to 1922 he had collected in cash and pledges, for College and Seminary, about a quarter of a million of dollars. Such figures, obtained mostly in small sums, speak volumes in praise of this brother who shows a happy combination of christian consecration and Friesian persistence.

§4. THE SEMINARY

By this we understand at present the theological department of the Grand Rapids institution, whose history we are tracing here. Its progress has not kept pace with the development of Calvin College, which, as our readers saw, is the outgrowth of the Literary Department of the old Theological School. There was some growth in the Seminary, however. In 1900, as we noted at the beginning of this Chapter, there were only three men who were teaching specifically theological branches. They were:

Rev. Geert E. Boer, Professor of Hermeneutics, Natural Theology, Biblical History, etc.; Rev. Geert K. Hemkes, Professor of Biblical Languages and Literature, Church History, etc.; Rev. Foppe M. Ten Hoor, Professor of Dogmatics, Exegesis, etc. The Synod of 1902, however, created a fourth chair, occupied by Dr. R. Janssen, Professor of Exegetical Theology; while Rev. W. Heyns was chosen as Professor of Practical Theology. Prof. Boer was placed in charge of the Library and Archives. But it was not till 1914 that a fifth Professorate was created. The faculty then was composed of Rev. Gerrit K. Hemkes, Professor Emeritus of Church History; Rev. Foppe M. Ten Hoor, Professor of Systematic Theology; Rev. William Heyns, Professor of Practical Theology; Rev. Louis Berkhof, B.D., Professor of Exegetical Theology, New Testament; Rev. Samuel Volbeda, Th.D., Professor of Historical Theology; Ralph Janssen, Ph.D., Theol. Doct's., Professor of Exegetical Theology, Old Testament.

With Calvin College having all in all a faculty of some twenty persons, it seems out of proportion that the Seminary should have to content itself with a staff of only five professors. This paucity in number of teachers is still more unsatisfactory when we compare it with the teaching staff of other Seminaries in our land, enrolling about the same number of students. The United Presbyterian Seminary at Pittsburgh, Pa., for instance, reports a faculty of eleven members. The Louisville, Ky., Presbyterian Seminary, has eight professors, and the Western Theological Seminary, Presbyterian, eleven.

The Library situation also is unfavorable compared to what other Seminaries in our country have. The Western Theological Seminary at Holland, Mich., has as many as 11,500 volumes in its Library, while Hope College, nearby, possesses 23,000 bound volumes. But our Seminary and College combined, in 1923, reported only 7,600 volumes.

There is outlook, however, that the condition will be improved slowly on.

The increase of the courses in the Seminary has not kept pace with the increase in various branches of study in Calvin College. There is notably a lack of instruction in apologetics; the history, science, principles, and methods of missions; the history of religion; comparative religion; and the study of the English Bible, while sociology and religious education are also absent from the curriculum, althought taught in practically every other Presbyterian and Reformed Seminary in our country.

The Seminary is also in need of a building of its own. At the present time it is practically dwelling as a sojourner in the edifice which has been fitted up for College purposes. No doubt the appointment of a president who would devote himself entirely to the institution would be instrumental toward greatly improving the situation. Our people love our Seminary and will be glad to come to its aid if appealed to properly, so that it may be brought and kept up-to-date as to branches and methods of study, while at the same time remaining loyal to the great doctrines of the Reformed Church, equipping men as efficiently as possible, to preach an unchangeable Gospel to an ever-changing age.

§5. KINDRED EDUCATIONAL INSTITUTIONS

We speak of *issus de Calvin,* that is, Calvin's offspring in a spiritual sense, people perpetuating and developing his principles. Calvin College in Grand Rapids also has its scions in the educational world, not alone in its graduates, but in the shape of institutions patterned after it, imbued with the same motives, holding up before the world the same high ideals. None of these, however, is officially connected with the denomination. They are all supported by independent societies whose membership is open to people of the Calvinistic persuasion other than Christian Reformed. But since the membership of these organizations, their faculties and students, are still so overwhelmingly belonging to the denomination whose history is discussed here, some space ought to be given them.

The oldest of these kindred institutions is *Grundy College,* in Grundy Center, Iowa, largely the fruit of the prayer, the planning and the persistence of one consecrated man, the Rev. Dr. W. Bode. Decades ago, the Rev. C. Bode and others had been pleading for a School to provide for the educational needs of the German element of the Christian Reformed Church (Chapter IV, §4). At God's own good time Rev. Bode's eldest son was allowed to rear the structure his father had longed to see erected. October 4, 1916, Grundy College was opened. Its first faculty was composed of the Revs. W. Bode, J. Timmermann, D. H. Kromminga, A. Clevering, L. King, and M. Schulte. The enrollment in 1922, of nearly one hundred students, speaks of growing initial success. Grundy College's education is based on Reformed principles, and aims to educate ministers, teachers, and others.

Western Academy, opened September, 1919, is building on the same platform. Located at Hull, Iowa, its first faculty was composed of Garrett Heyns, A.M., as principal and Herman Wyngaarden, A.B. Annual income, $12,000; number of students approximately 100. It is aimed to develop a thorough course of normal training for the benefit of prospective teachers in the Christian Primary Schools, and in general to provide a secondary education that stands second to none.

Within three years four *Christian High Schools* were opened in as many cities. The *Chicago* Christian High School is the oldest of these, dating from September, 1918, and located in Englewood. First faculty Mr. M. Fakkema and Miss C. Rooks.   Income, $9,000.   Enrollment, 1922, 116.

The *Paterson* Christian High School followed, opening its doors, September, 1919.   First faculty, J. B. Schoolland and G. Bos.   Annual income, $5,000.   Students enrolled, 25.

The *Grand Rapids* Christian High School dates from September, 1920.   Its home is the former Theological School building, corner of Madison Avenue and Franklin Street, purchased for $20,000.   Its first faculty numbered ten teachers, under F. J. Driessens as principal.   The enrollment, March, 1922, was 360.   Annual income, $45,000.

The *Holland* Christian High School is as old as its Grand Rapids sister institution.   Its first faculty was composed of Principal H. Dekker, and E. Wolters and J. Jellema.   All of these institutions aim at secondary education: "based on the Word of God, as interpreted by the doctrinal standards of the Reformed Churches".

A *Missionary Training School* was opened in February, 1921, in Chicago, Ill., at first teaching only evening classes, the faculty composed of Revs. E. J. Tuuk and P. D. Van Vliet, and the Messrs. M. Fakkema and J. Vande Water. Its principal purpose at present is the training of layworkers for City Mission activity.

A *Normal School,* opened in Grand Rapids in 1919, enjoyed only a brief existence of two years, under the principalship of B. K. Kuiper, but its ideals, though dormant for the time being, are sure to be realized sooner or later.

§6.   THE CHRISTIAN PRIMARY SCHOOL

Not alone secondary and higher education was the object of the fostering care of the Christian Reformed Church—also primary school instruction.   As we noted in Chapter I, §8, one of the objectives of our pioneers for coming to America was the education of their children in Christian schools, "a privilege that we lack here [in the

Netherlands] since in the public schools a general moral instruction is given which may offend neither Jew nor Romanist, while free schools are barred". True to this ideal, in the Scholte Colony in Iowa, we find already during the early months after Pella's founding, Mr. James Muntingh converting his log house into a school-room, and here, for three years, teaching reading, writing, and arithmetic, to children by day, and to others at night, and by candle-light. He taught both Dutch and English. Isaac Overkamp was the first teacher of the township school, a highly praised instructor.

Due to Rev. Van Raalte's urging among the Pella brethren, a school of the Dutch Reformed Church of Pella was established in 1861, the first corps of teachers being headed by Isaac Overkamp. But alas, by February, 1867, the school had ceased to exist, and for the space of forty-five years the idea remained abandoned in so far as Pella was concerned.

In Roseland, Ill., a Christian School was maintained from 1849, and during many years, by Peter De Jong, well-known leader of the pioneer band there, as we related in Chapter I, §8. De Jong was born near Schoorl, in North Holland, and died in Roseland at a ripe old age.

In Michigan, also mainly through Van Raalte's initiative, christian education was stressed at first. When Dr. Wyckoff (Chapter II, §4), visited the Hollanders there in 1849, he noted that "the Colony is paying as much attention as possible to schools and Christian education. They have a Dutch school and an English one in the city (Holland); at Zeeland a Dutch school, and will soon have an English school and all the rest will follow". Repeatedly Rev. Van Raalte pleaded for the cause. Valuable service was rendered by pioneer teachers such as H. Doesburg, of Holland; A. J. Hillebrands, of Groningen; H. De Bruin, of Zeeland; Mr. Berkenpas, of Vriesland; Mr. Nieuwendorp, of Drenthe; and Mrs. Rev. Nykerk, of Overisel. But Dr.

Wyckoff's prediction was not fulfilled. While those who retained their connection with the Reformed Church have displayed commendable zeal as to Christian secondary and higher education, they sadly lost sight of their ideals concerning primary schools. Not so, however, those who withdrew in 1857. The Grand Rapids Church maintained a Christian school from the very beginning of its existence, and the Graafschap consistory as early as April 20, 1857, took the matter up. By 1875 Christian schools existed not alone in the two places just named, but also in Muskegon, Grand Haven, Kalamazoo, and South Holland, with other places contemplating to take steps in the direction of carrying out the declaration of the General Meeting of 1870, stating as the conviction of the assembly "that the school is the nursery of and for the Church, and that every congregation was called to open a free school". The Holland language, naturally, was stressed at first, though there are evidences that the English was not entirely neglected, and as early as 1864 we find a classical discussion about the possibility of introducing orthodox English books in the district schools.

The publisher of *De Wachter,* C. Vorst, in 1862, was the first one to print four "school booklets" in the Dutch language, an undertaking in which the Classis backed him officially.

Nor was the fostering care confined to what we mentioned hitherto. As early as February, 1861, the looking around for persons of talent and promise to be trained for teaching, was named as well as doing this regarding suitable persons for ministerial education. It was even decided, in 1871, to take up the matter of educating men to become school teachers, and to look for a suitable person to provide the normal training involved. Nothing came of this, however, and in loyalty to truth it should be stated here that the "Dutch Schools" at the time were far from ideal institutions of learning. The discipline often was wretched, the equipment poor, the buildings inadequate, the salaries discouragingly low, and the moral support of some of the parents far from satisfactory. All honor to the pioneer teachers who, notwithstanding so many handicaps and discouragements, devoted some of the best years of their life to the primary schools. We should never forget such men as A. Pleune, J. Gezon, G. Van Oyen, P. Monningh, E. Luininga, T. M. Vanden Bosch and others who served acceptably and self-denyingly during the period of struggle.

We may distinguish *four periods* in the history of the Christian Primary School in our circles.

During the first, 1857—1880, the teaching of Dutch was emphasized. During the second, 1880—1890, the Christian character of the School received stress, especially through the pleading of men like J. Veltkamp, B. J. Bennink, H. Jacobsma, J. B. Hoekstra, and others. During the years 1890—1900 the English was accorded a place next to the Dutch, and from the beginning of the twentieth century we may date approximately the fourth period, wherein the language of our country has become the medium of instruction in all our Christian Schools, the Dutch usually being taught only as a branch. Meanwhile, toward the close of the nineteenth century, under the advocacy of P. R. Holtman and others, a change took place as to the *auspices* under which the primary schools labored. Up to that time they were under congregational control. Since then they have been maintained in nearly all cases by "Societies" of Christian parents and others, on the principle that education in its various stages is primarily the duty of parents as such rather than that of the church or the state. (See Chapter IX, §5, for detailed discussion.)

In 1898 Synod issued an urgent appeal, written by the persistent and able champion of the cause, the Rev. K. Kuiper, and stating that positive Christian instruction was involved in the Bible command about the training of children in the fear of the Lord, as well as in the promise made by parents at the baptism of their children.   Furthermore, no separation should be permitted between the civil, social, and the religious life in the matter of education.   The revised *Church Order* (see Chapter X, §5)' had the matter of Christian education embodied in its Article 21: "The consistories shall see to it that there are good Christian Schools where [in which?] the parents have their children instructed according to the demands of the Covenant".   Under the impetus of this denominational encouragement, spurred on by the success of the Christian School movement in the Netherlands, as well as under the inspiration and conviction of the principle expressed above, and under the leadership of strong men, many of them reared in the Christian Schools themselves, either in Holland or in America, the free Primary School movement has made much progress in every way, and is able in more than one place to successfully compete with public institutions.   A battle to obtain a fair portion of the public money set aside for the education of the citizens of our land, looks to us as a part of a future program, to be drawn up courageously.   But even without this support, the cause in recent years has grown by leaps and bounds. That esteemed veteran teacher and leader in the cause, B. J. Bennink. is our authority for the statement that in 1922 there were 75 Free Christian Primary Schools of our people in at least 15 States of our Union, besides Canada, enrolling 11,000 pupils, taught by 300 teachers, at an annual expense of $275,000.   The societies in the different centers form "Alliances".   In 1921 a "National Union of the Christian Schools" was formed, to promote the welfare of Christian instruction in general by means of the training of teachers, the publication of propaganda literature, the raising of the standard of instruction, the protection of the economical interests of the teachers, the extension of a helping hand and the supervision of schools. March, 1922, the first number of the organ of this Union appeared, the *Christian School Magazine,* with Garrett Heyns, of Hull, Iowa, as editor-in-chief.

In Los Angeles, Calif., our people are coöperating with a Society for Christian Instruction, composed of christians of all evangelical beliefs, who endorse the following statement of principles:

(1) The Bible is the infallible Word of God.

(2) God as the Creator of the universe, and His unfailing providence over the same.

(3) The deity of our Lord Jesus Christ, His virgin birth, His substitutionary atonement by His death on the cross, His bodily resurrection, and ascension, and His personal return.

(4) The personality of the Holy Spirit, His ministry of regenerating men, and of sanctifying, comforting, and guiding Christians in accordance with the Scriptures.

(5) The creation of man in the image of God, his fall through disobedience, and his opportunity for salvation and eternal life through justification by faith in Christ.

(6) The supreme Christian task is to preach the Gospel as a witness to the world, and to build up those who accept Christ as personal Saviour "unto the measure of the stature of the fulness of Christ." (Ephesians 4: 13.)

(7) Ethics for every phase of life, including Christian stewardship, as based on the Word of God.

No doubt the future will reveal that the perpetuation and extension of the Christian School movement will demand an increasing coöperation on the broader basis of principles above outlined. (See Chapter IX, §5 about the principles underlying the Christian School movement.)

TEST QUESTIONS

1. Why does the Church of God demand a well-trained ministry?
2. How was the ministry trained during the early centuries of the Christian Church and later?
3. What can you tell about our early training under the Rev. D. J. Vander Werp?
4. What can you say about the persons and work of Professors G. E. Boer, G. K. Hemkes, G. Vos, and H. Beuker?
5. What progress is shown by the Catalogs of the School from 1900—1922?
6. What are the functions of the president of Calvin College?
7. What can you state about the Seminary as a separate institution?
8. Tell what you know about Grundy College, the Western Academy, and the Christian High Schools opened in recent years.
9. What do you know about the Christian Primary Schools during the period of Struggle—up to 1880?
10. What can you tell about the movement since the twentieth century began?

WORKS OF REFERENCE

Dr. H. H. Kuyper, "De Opleiding tot den Dienst des Woords, bij de Gereformeerden".

J. Vander Zee, "The Hollanders of Iowa".

M. C. T. I. Lectures, 1914, (Michigan Christian Teachers' Institute).

Prof. L. Berkhof, Education, pp. 111—125, in "Subjects and Outlines".

CHAPTER VII

MISSIONARY ACTIVITIES OF THE CHRISTIAN REFORMED CHURCH

INTRODUCTORY: THE WHY OF MISSIONS

B Y MISSIONS we understand the organized efforts to christianize people living outside of the Covenant of grace or in practical estrangement from it. In American denominational usage the term has also come to include church extension work, the "gathering of churches", such as takes place in new settlements of our people and elsewhere. The work of missions is based on the will of God as expressed in His decree, His command, and His promise. His decree includes the redemption of a multitude which no man can number, out of every nation and of all tribes and peoples and tongues, Rev. 7:9. The missionary command is principally the one of Matthew 28:19, 20: "Go ye therefore and make disciples of all the nations, baptizing them in the name of the Father, and of the Son, and of the Holy Spirit, teaching them to observe all things whatsoever I commanded you". The promises in which God has expressed His holy will about missions are numberless, among them such as Psalm 22:27: "All the ends of the earth shall remember and turn unto Jehovah; and all the kindreds of the nations shall worship before thee". Malachi 1:11: "From the rising of the sun even unto the going down of the same, My Name shall be great among the Gentiles".

The Lord of the harvest sends forth laborers into His harvest by means of local churches (Acts 13: 1), or groups of churches (Acts 15: 22-25; 2 Cor. 8: 19, 23). Missionaries are ministers of the Word, aided by all kinds of "helps" (1 Cor. 12: 28), for medical, educational, and other philanthropic purposes, which "helps" are to serve as handmaidens in the work of evangelization, the chief part of true missionary activity. The *object* of missions is threefold: the conversion of sinners, the planting of churches, and the glorifying of God (Eph. 1: 10; 3: 10, 11; Rom. 11: 32). *Incentives* to missionary activity are and should be: (1) Loving obedience to carry out the command of our Savior, that God's will may be done in earth as it is in heaven, His decree executed and His promises fulfilled; (2) the inexpressibly great and urgent need of perishing multitudes; (3) the strategic opportunity of the present, with open doors everywhere; (4) the very nature of christian life, also that of the church, namely, to grow; (5) the impulse of christian love: to give, rather than to receive; (6) the reflex blessing for the church as well as for the consecrated worker, shown by history; (7) the privilege of serving as an instrument in bringing to Christ the reward of His suffering (John 4: 35; Isaiah 53: 10, 11). Compare special reasons under Home, Indian and Jewish Mission work, §1, §2, and §3.

§1. HOME MISSION WORK

The denominational Home Mission work in the sense of Church extension activity was carried on during the early years of the history of the denomination, by the various ministers. Especially the Rev. K. Vanden Bosch is entitled to credit. He traveled not alone in Michigan, but organized a church in Milwaukee at an early date and was active in Illinois and Iowa as well as in New Jersey. The Rev. D. J. Vander Werp also nobly took his part in going up and down our land, in days when traveling meant exposure and fatigue as well as loss of valuable time. But necessity compelled them to be in journeyings often, to gather scattered fellow-believers of Dutch and East Friesian and Bentheim stock. It was realized soon, however, that such work could not very well be carried on by men in the regular pastorate. Therefore we find as early as 1864 the need expressed of a "classical minister". But either men or means, or both, were lacking until 1879 when the candidate T. M. VANDEN BOSCH became itinerant minister for Home Missions. The incumbent had taught school in Kalamazoo before he took a short course in the Grand Rapids Theological School. He was a lover of missions, though, as we shall see later, not as stable as he might have been. His work led to the appointment of a Home Mission Committee (1880), with K. Vanden Bosch, kinsman of the new missionary, as president, Rev. G. Broene as treasurer, and Rev. E. L. Meinders as secretary, an organization later known as "Board" and functioning till 1907, when the work, formerly denominational, was placed under classical auspices. Since then a general treasury committee merely functions to receive and distribute the funds offered by the various congregations. Rev. T. M. Vanden Bosch labored East and West as well as in Michigan, and his resignation in 1882 was accepted with regret.

For the space of four years no successor was obtained and no doubt serious losses as to church extension would have occurred if it had not been for devoted ministers like the Bode and Broene brothers, already named, and the Revs. R. T. Kuiper, Meinders, and others, among them theological students. These men traveled up and down the Dakotas, Minnesota, and Kansas as well as in Iowa, "gathering churches". In Northern Michigan several new churches were organized during a panic under President Cleveland's administration. Finally, in 1886, candidate

M. J. MARCUSSE succeeded Rev. Vanden Bosch. The new worker labored with success, organizing eleven congregations during his missionary activity, which terminated in 1888. This encouraged the Synod of the year last named to call a second worker into the field, the REV. M. VAN VESSEM, who brought the message far and near, in three languages, the German of his mother, the Dutch of his father, and the English of his native land—America. The two years of his missionary service abounded with laudable activity. A third worker who rendered splendid service in the Home Mission field was the REV. E. BREEN, who labored very successfully, although only for about the space of one year, and so much zeal for the work was aroused that the 1892 Synod empowered the Missionary Committee to engage as many workers as its funds allowed. Soon we see three new men working in the Home Mission fields. The Rev. J. Noordewier combined activity in that line with collecting funds for the new school building. The Rev. H. Bode labored especially among the Germans, and moreover, was laudably active in caring for the people brought to Colorado through a colonization effort made by an Immigration Society with headquarters at Utrecht in the Netherlands.

A very glowing but misleading publicity brought some 300 Dutch people, nearly all of the Reformed faith, to the San Luis valley in Colorado. They had looked for an "Italy in western North America", with a soil like that of the Netherlands. Houses were said to be ready to receive them. Instead, when the vanguard, about 200 people, arrived on the spot, seven miles from Alamosa, December 1, 1892, they found what was practically a wilderness, abounding with sandy soil, covered with sage brush, chico, and rabbit brush, and with primitive places of shelter. At times sickness and the death of several children, as well as the cold, drove the immigrants practically to desperation. The Utrecht company was unable to pay the second installment on the land option. A "Farmers' Committee, composed of L. Verburg, D. Sjaardema, J. Zwier, F. Zylstra, and A. J. Van Lummel, took matters into its hands. But it was unable to effect a lasting improvement. Some made a contract for land belonging to the Empire Land and Canal Company and in this "Holland Colony" a congregation was organized during February, 1893. Others went to Crook, in the Platte valley, in northwestern Colorado. Both settlements soon proved to be failures.

But, as stated, the Rev. H. Bode and others were active in bringing many of the deluded colonists to various congregations, notably in Iowa, where they strengthened church-life considerably. Three of the sons of the Colorado victims later entered our ministry, namely, the Revs. F. and W. Stuart, and D. Zwier. While the Colorado undertaking was a failure, it brought a blessing in disguise to the Christian Reformed Church, owing to missionary effort.

The Rev. J. A. Westervelt was the first home missionary of the denomination laboring exclusively in English-speaking circles, 1892—1893, a work which since then has, alas, been practically at a standstill. When the missionary workers named hitherto retired from the work, assuming pastorates, new forces were obtained. In 1895 the candidates J. W. Brink and J. Smitter were ordained to serve as home missionaries. At the Synod of 1896 it was reported by the Committee that its workers had labored in thirty places, and that since the Synod of 1894 not less than fourteen congregations had been organized. Expansion territorially, too, was in evidence. Before the end of the nineteenth century churches had been organized literally from coast to coast. (See Chapter V, §1.)

A happy broadening of missionary vision was evident in the decision of the Synod of 1898 to begin labors among the "Americans"—as soon as work among our people allowed this, "that influence might be exerted among the American people". The idea of the leaven and the salt was gaining ground. And that this leaven and salt might be as good as possible, in other words, that the workers might be equipped properly, was no doubt back of the resolution of 1902 that missionary branches of study should be taught in the Theological School.

Space fails us to give even the names of the men who labored in the mission field under the auspices of the General Board of Home Missions, which, as already told, ceased to function in 1907, when Classical Home Mission Committees took over the actual work, each within its own territory. But those who labored in this field deserve the lasting gratitude of the denomination. And among those entitled to thankful appreciation are not alone the workers especially set aside for the task, but also the pastors of certain centers who labored just as diligently in the "gathering of churches", such as the Rev. J. Manni around Pella, Iowa, and the Rev. E. Breen around Orange City, in the same State. If we, like Roosevelt, can speak of the "Winning of the West", it is due, under God, to teamwork of all kinds of laborers, and to their vision of the worthwhileness of carrying our principles into "regions beyond".

As to outstanding figures among the noble band of our Home Missionaries, we mention particularly the Rev. J. R. Brink from 1905 to 1907, and again since 1913, a worker with unusual success in his labors of gathering and strengthening churches. There would not be the girdle of congregations now encircling Grand Rapids and Kalamazoo, if it had not been, under God, for his wise planning, statesmanlike guidance and persistent effort.

Home mission work is very important. There are not alone the reasons for it given in the introductory paragraph, but additional ones of the greatest import. We have, for instance, our Savior's example—going up and down His own country doing good, teaching, and healing. We have His special command to be His witnesses, in the order given: "in Jerusalem, and in all Judea, and in Samaria, and....unto the uttermost part of the earth"—a charge clearly bringing out that our first duty is gospelizing those nearest to us. Home mission work is the foundation; foreign work the superstructure.

Home mission work also is a patriotic duty—and a christian is a patriot. The Bible states that righteousness exalts a nation. True righteousness is imparted by means of christian efforts to seek for the lost sheep, to teach the ignorant, and to furnish church homes to the immigrants and others who never enjoyed church privileges. Especially in view of the fact that more than half of our nation's population is outside of the visible church, and over twenty-six million children and young people without Sunday school privileges, the urgent need of mission work to "leaven the nation" and to keep it from decay is evident.

Finally, home mission work brings the most encouraging *returns*. It supplies and strengthens the home base. Many servants of God, at home or abroad, have been brought into the church by means of mission work among the unchurched. There are several instances of that in the Christian Reformed ministry. Moreover, institutions of learning have quite a number of students enrolled from territory opened by the home missionary. Careful computation brought out the fact that at least four-fifths of the congregations of evangelical churches of our country are of home mission origin, and fully one-half of the amount contributed for home mission work comes from churches once depending on home missionary funds. And as to assets regarding intercessory prayers, from the lips and hearts of those whom the Lord through His servants found as "strangers, wandering from the fold of God", no one can estimate their value.

> "Our country's voice is pleading,
>   Ye men of God, arise,
> His Providence is leading,
>   The land before you lies;
> Day-gleams are o'er it brightening,
>   And promise clothes the soil,
> Wide fields for harvest whitening
> Invite the reaper's toil."

§2. INDIAN MISSION WORK

From the very beginning of the history of the denomination there were a few individuals who loved the cause of missions. This is evident from the fact that already in 1857, at the second classical meeting, it was resolved to hold monthly prayer-meetings for the extension of God's Kingdom, with a special offering for the purpose of distributing Bibles. Two years later offerings for a Missionary Society were recommended. To S. Lukas of Graafschap belongs the honor of having anew stirred up the churches when interest had begun to wane in the course of the year. The money collected during these missionary meetings was at first sent to South Africa where the Rev. D. Postma was laboring, in the Transvaal, and also to the Netherlands to aid the new missionary work of the church of the fathers. In 1878 a pentecostal collection was resolved upon as a standing rule, and the Rev. J. Noordewier was appointed treasurer of the fund. Nothing, however, was done during the period of struggle in the line of direct mission work among the heathen.

Let no one despise the churches of that time for this. It was a period of root formation rather than that of fruit-bearing. For that matter, the modern missionary movement was still in its early stages among Dutch people everywhere, and besides that, there were many needs at home while dollars were scarce and members few. Moreover, in Grand Rapids and Vriesland the men and women of 1857 left all behind of the church property for which they had toiled and paid, as well as those who retained their connection with the Reformed Church, and never was a voice raised to re-imburse them. All the other congregations, except Graafschap and Noordeloos, had to rear their parsonages and churches without any help whatever from outsiders or from any denominational fund. As we think of what these pioneers did single-handedly in building their structures for religious purposes, and sending for their pastors from abroad, we rather wonder at the spirit of self-sacrifice some must have displayed. Our emulation much rather than our scorn is called for. And as soon as the hands of our pioneers were free, comparatively speaking, they engaged in the task of extending a helping hand to people living outside of the Covenant of Grace. The Synod of 1888 started a new epoch in this regard. It resolved to appoint a special committee for this work. Its five charter members were the Revs. R. T. Kuiper, E. Bos, and T. M. Vanden Bosch, and the elders J. W. Garvelink and J. Gelock.

That Synod also agreed by majority vote to commence mission work among the Indians of our land, because it was felt that a special debt of honor was due the aborigines of our country, a people "scattered and peeled", that we might become settled and enriched. The force of "beginning at Jerusalem" was felt as a special argument applying to the Indians, and enforced by the thought that the white man had dispossessed him of so much, that only spiritual wealth could be a substitute for.

October 23, 1889, was the eventful day of the installation of the first Christian Reformed missionary to the pagans. It was the Rev. T. M. Vanden Bosch who, as we saw, had also been the first Home Missionary. He gave himself, when he found that no one else among our ministry was obtainable for the work. He went out courageously to the Rosebud Agency in Dakota to labor among the Sioux Indians. But the people of the Western prairies were not like those of the Isles of the Sea, "awaiting his doctrine". The missionary lacked all special training for his work. He did not realize that infinite patience is needed for gospel work among our aborigines, because the Indian, taught by "centuries of dishonor", does not confide in the white man's message till he has time to learn to trust the messenger. Discouraged and disillusioned Rev. Vanden Bosch retired from the work during the fall of 1890. The Church was shocked from center to circumference by this apparent failure of a much-prayed-for work, perhaps unaware of the historical fact that other denominations went through similar discouraging experiences in founding new missions.

For a time there was a standstill in the activity among the heathen, although there was progress at the "Home Base". Local missionary societies began to study the subject. Articles in the Church weekly spread information. Gifts for the work slowly on increased and two young men were in training for the work. The Synod of 1896 reaffirmed the action taken eight years previous, and after a trip of investigation the Navajo field in New Mexico was selected. On the 10th day of October, 1896, the pioneer missionaries arrived at Gallup, N. M., being the Rev. and Mrs. H. Fryling and Mr. and Mrs. Andrew Vander Wagen. A few days later work was begun at *Fort Defiance,* where the Government maintained a Boarding School for young Navajos, and where a building had been purchased from the Methodist Episcopal Church. Fruits were not entirely lacking at this place, but antagonism displayed by the Roman Church led to the giving up of that post in 1904. Meanwhile, in 1897, the Pueblo of the *Zuni* Indians, forty-five miles south of Gallup, New Mexico, had been selected as a second post. Mr. Vander Wagen was stationed there until 1906, when he was succeeded by the Rev. Fryling. During the year just named a little Chapel had been erected, facing the Zuni village. Later on a little Day School was opened in the Chapel and, moreover, from the beginning of the opening of the Black Rock Zuni Government Boarding School about four miles distant, the work among the children of that institution was placed in charge of our workers. In 1915 Mr. M. Vander Beek became assistant to Rev Fryling to engage in work especially among the young men and according to Y. M. C. A. methods, a work continued with encouraging success by Mr. B. Sprik, 1921. Among the women of the village, work is carried on by a matron.

In 1898 labors among the Navajo Indians were begun at *Tohatchi,* then known as Little Water where the Government had opened a Boarding School. Mr. James E. De Groot was the first missionary in charge, to be succeeded by the Rev. L. P. Brink who rendered valuable service from 1900 to 1913. Dr. L. S. Huizenga and others also labored at this post. Since 1915 Mr. M. Bouma has been doing good work at Tohatchi. *Rehoboth* was opened in 1903 as a Boarding School under our own auspices. The disheartening experience in Fort Defiance had led to see the desirability of having a Boarding School of our own, away from the Indian Reservation although near enough to be in constant contact with the people among whom the work is carried on. Six children were received there by Miss Nellie Noordhof in December, 1903. In 1910 a hospital, enlarged during 1921, was added. Since 1912 the Rev. J. W. Brink is pastor in charge aided by a splendid corps of workers, who labor in the school as well as in the hospital. During the year 1910 work was begun at Two Grey Hills at present known as *Toadlena.* Baptists had labored there since 1907. Here an Indian Boarding School is maintained by the Government. Rev. L. P. Brink,

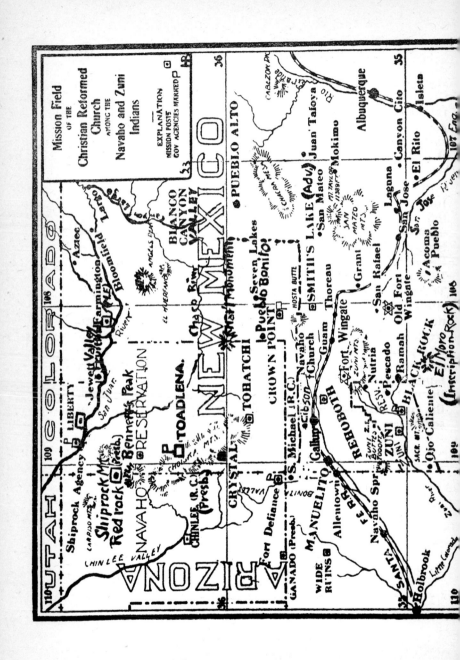

stationed there since 1914, works diligently at this place. *Crown Point,* opened in 1913 when the Government founded its post and school there, has seen remarkable gospel fruit under the ministry of the Rev. Jacob Bolt, since 1915 stationed there, ably seconded by his wife. Within two years fifty-seven received Holy Baptism at this post.

In the fall of 1921, when the quarter-centennial of the Indian Mission work was celebrated, it could be reported that not less than 202 adult Indians had been baptized by our workers during that period. The urgent need of the Navajo field is the service of devoted camp-workers like Brother W. Mierop, who has been in the service at first at Two Grey Hills, and since 1920 is stationed at Rehoboth. The need is also felt of obtaining consecrated converts for studying in a *Training School.* Throughout the history of missions, while evangelizing has been done by foreign workers, the real work of christianizing has been carried on by native converts. Our Navajo field is a very extensive one. It is as large as a whole province of the Netherlands. Several problems are connected with it, one of them, that of the material prosperity of the converts, when the new religion places them on a new intellectual and social level.

> "Grant, Lord, that we repay our debt,
>   In regions solitary yet,
>   Within our spreading land;
>   Where pagan tribes, away from Home,
>   In heathen darkness blindly roam,
>   Needing our helping hand."

> "Lord God, so full of wondrous love,
>   Grant us Thy spirit from above;
>   To move each Christian heart.
>   Till heralds shall Thy truth proclaim;
>   Till temples rise to praise Thy Name
>   Throughout our desert West".

§3. JEWISH MISSIONS

The Jew also should be the object of missionary care. Estranged from the living God of the Bible, rejecting God's Son, trying to build up a righteousness of his own, or in blatant unbelief denying God altogether, such is the condition of the fifteen millions of descendants of Abraham. They sorely need the helping hand of Christian love in the Master's Name. Jewish mission work is the duty of the Church because the Lord Jesus told His apostles they were to begin their labors at Jerusalem, Luke 24: 47. There apostles set the example in this part of Kingdom activity. God's decree also embraces a number of Jews, Romans 11: 25-28. Moreover, we owe a debt to this people. "Our Lord has sprung out of Judah", Hebrews 7: 14. The first heralds of the Cross were Jews. The oracles of God were committed to them, Romans 3: 2, and they took scrupulous care of them. "Christians", so-called, have at times terribly wronged them. And notwithstanding the cruelty they endured, Jews have rendered many good services both to the old country whence our fathers came—their haven of refuge in a time of storm—and to the New World, now the habitation of over three millions of them.

Yet, strange to say, the Church has been very slow in discharging its debt to the children of Abraham according to the flesh. So it was also with the Christian Reformed Church. During its period of struggle only now and then a voice was raised to advocate Jewish mission labors. But in 1892 the Synod decided to ask for funds to further the work, and for a number of years the Rev. J. I. Fles, himself of Jewish stock, pleaded touchingly for the cause by means of word and pen. The first Jewish Mission Committee was composed of the Revs. Fles and W. Heyns and elder S. S. Postma. During the first few years various mission work, carried on under different auspices, was supported, notably that of the Chicago Hebrew Mission. But the new century brought expression of the desire to undertake work denominationally and according to our confession, whereas most of the Jewish mission activities had been carried on by independent societies, without specifically Reformed tenets. The desire was fulfilled in 1913, when the Paterson Hebrew Mission, which three years before had been started as "interdenominational work", passed over into the hands of a Committee representing the Christian Reformed Church. In 1915 a permanent home was purchased for it, 48 North Main Street, Paterson, N. J. The work carried on includes gospel meetings, out-of-doors, weather permitting, and indoors right along, Sunday school and weekday classes, distribution of tracts and Scripture portions, house-to-house visiting, and since 1917, dispensary work. A reading-room also helps in calling attention to the things of God's Kingdom, that the Jew may find his Messiah—the great purpose of the undertaking. Workers have come and gone. Consecrated women labor here as well as men. The Missionary-in-charge is Herman H. Schultz.

The *Chicago Jewish Mission* originated in the decision of the Synod of 1918. Its first missionary was the Rev. J. H. Beld, 1919—1921, ably assisted by his wife and others. Its home is the old church property of First Chicago, at 1324 W. 14th Street, in the heart of a ghetto district. The work carried on is along the lines mentioned above. The Missionary-in-charge is J. Rottenberg, of Jewish stock, and aided by other workers.

§4. WORK AMONG IMMIGRANTS AND SAILORS

Contributions for Immigrant work in New York harbor were given as early as 1867. Naturally the work appealed to the Pilgrims of the West and their scions and followers, themselves once strangers knocking at our gates. But it was not until 1910 that work under specifically denominational auspices was begun, at the suggestion of the Hackensack Classis. Brethren belonging to this body and others, appointed by the Hudson Classis, are in charge. Mr. M. Bouma (see §2) began his labors as superintendent in February, 1910, to be succeeded by the Rev. H. Dekker, 1913—1916. Rev. T. Jongbloed served from 1919 to May, 1922. The Missionary-in-charge, since May, 1922, is M. J. Broekhuizen. At first located on Hudson Street, in Hoboken, N. J., new and far more commodious quarters were secured two years later, at 332 River Street, Hoboken, N. J., where the "Holland Immigration Bureau" renders splendid aid to the Holland immigrants as they pass through the great eastern gateway of our country. Work is also carried on in behalf of Dutch sailors who spend some time on our shore, providing a reading-room as well as opportunity to write letters home. The institution has kept many a seafaring man from ways of sin, and continually points him to the great Pilot, whose name is Jesus. (Cf. *The Banner,* March 1, 1923, ff.)

§5.   EVANGELIZATION AND MORMON WORK

A distinct branch of mission work is what has been called "Inner Mission". It reaches out particularly to those within our own borders who live in entire or partial estrangement from the Covenant of Grace. It consists in combining, by systematic endeavor, works of Christian philanthropy with evangelical effort in behalf of the physical and particularly the spiritual welfare of the needy classes. The name, "Rescue Mission Work", has at times been given to this part of Kingdom activity. It is being carried on in several places, such as Grand Rapids, Muskegon, Holland, and Paterson, usually through Sunday school work. But to the Chicago churches belongs the honor of having initiated a far more comprehensive work in the "Helping Hand Gospel Mission", 850 West Madison

Street, Chicago, Ill., where labors of this kind were begun during the winter of 1912—1913. In 1914 the Rev. P. J. Hoekenga was the first minister who gave himself energetically to this branch of activity, succeeded later by the Rev. A. J. Rus. The Missionary-in-charge is Mr. J. Vande Water, who began his labors as assistant in 1915, and proves himself to be the man for the place, ably assisted by others, among them A. Huisjen. Various other stations are operated in Chicago and environs. Mr. E. J. Ellens is in charge of similar work with headquarters at Hammond, Indiana.

Work among the *Mormons,* the deluded followers of John Smith, has also been undertaken by the Christian Reformed Church, although, alas, not as permanent and fruitful as the above named activities. Already in 1863 some Holland people had gone to Utah. The census of 1920 speaks of as many as 56,429 people of Dutch birth in that state. In 1896 Rev. Vanden Heuvel pleaded for starting work among the Utah Hollanders. And praiseworthy efforts, inspired by the Rev. I. Van Dellen, were made later on by the corporteur, Brother W. Van Westenbrugge and the Rev. W. De Groot, the former beginning his work in 1911, and the latter in 1913. They tried earnestly to prevail upon our people to give up Mormonism. But the results were discouraging, due in part to organized opposition from the side of the Mormon hierarchy. While a few were persuaded to renew allegiance to the doctrine of their fathers, the work was given up in course of time, or at least remains suspended, until now.

§6. THE CHURCHES IN THE ARGENTINE REPUBLIC

From 1889 to 1891 some two or three thousand Dutch people, many of them belonging to the Reformed Churches of the Netherlands, migrated to the Argentine Republic, drawn thither by glittering promises of material prosperity. Some forty families settled at Micaela Cascalares. The financial crisis of 1890 brought great misery. A number of the people then went to Tres Arroyos, twenty-five kilometer distant. Others went to Rosario and Buenos Aires. In Buenos Aires C. Van Nieuwenhuizen at first served as teaching elder. In 1900 a church was organized there. A. Struis, who at first had been teaching elder at Rosario (since 1897), served the Buenos Aires church as pastor from 1901 to 1905. At first his church was crowded. There was a flourishing Sunday school, Singing Society, and Women's Society. But Rev. Struis was not able to hold his audience. Many young people severed connections with the church. Some went into the world, others joined the Baptist and Methodist Churches. Struis resigned. He was succeeded in 1910 by the Rev. A. C. Sonneveldt who served till 1914. Four years later H. H. Hoogendorp took his place, serving till 1923.

In Tres Arroyos, where T. Visbeek had done much to gather the remnant into a church, organized in 1908, Rev. A. Rolloos served at first, succeeded in 1913 by Rev. S. Rijper, who in 1920 returned to Holland.

Meanwhile some Boers from South Africa, as well as a number of Hollanders, had settled in Chubut, some 1,000 miles south of Buenos Aires. Revs. L. P. Vorster and A. J. Jacobs, from South Africa, worked here successively until Rev. Sonneveldt came from Buenos Aires to shepherd the two congregations in that faraway country.

Rev. J. Van Lonkhuizen, D.D., did much in 1908 to place the work in the Argentine Republic on a Reformed basis.

Since a number of years the Christian Reformed Church in North America supports the work of these struggling churches to the amount of about $2,500 every two years. The Argentine congregations form a Classis, connected with the Provincial Synod of South Holland (South), of the Reformed Churches of the Netherlands.

Arrangements are pending to furnish American manpower to the Argentine churches as well as money.

As to the numbers of our people in Argentina, it was reported in 1923 that the Chubut churches had some 800 persons on their rolls, while the Buenos Aires congregation numbers 100 souls, and Rosario 60. Tres Arroyos reported 21 confessing members and 41 members by baptism. San Cayetano, considered a branch of Tres Arroyos, numbers 41 souls.

What vast distances are involved in the work in Argentina may be inferred from the fact that Chubut is six days' sailing from Buenos Aires, while Rosario and Tres Arroyos are respectively 8 and 16 hours per train away from the Argentine capital. Our people are placed in very unfavorable surroundings spiritually. It is to be hoped that other believers from the Netherlands will join them, to strengthen that what otherwise seems likely, in course of time, to die. Plans to bring more immigrants are on foot owing to the zeal of the Rev. Sonneveldt.

§7. THE CHINA MISSION

Since a number of years voices were pleading for beginning mission work in some country outside of our national boundaries. Cuba was mentioned during the years following the Spanish-American War. Persia was championed by some as a desirable field. Others called attention to the Dutch East India islands of Bali and New Guinea. A few spoke of the crying need of China, or mentioned the Sudan. Many factors were at work to stir up the people of the denomination to carry the Gospel to "regions beyond". A missionary department in *De Wachter*, opened February 20, 1901, occasional poems on the subject, the work of many misionary societies, the missionary appeal which many a teacher in our Christian Schools wove into the teaching, increasing acquaintance with the abundant missionary material published in English and to some extent in Dutch—the broadening horizon of our young people as better schooling was obtained—all this, as well as more preaching on missions than before, and more consecrating of children to the cause by devoted fathers and mothers—helped to swell the chorus of the voices pleading for work overseas.

The rest of the story of the China work and the plans for its future we asked Dr. L. S. Huizenga to tell us.

He informs us: "The result of all these factors", named above, "led to the overtures of several Classes to the Synod of 1918 to open a foreign field. A committee appointed by a previous Synod, 1914, brought no unanimous report and led to little advancement. The Synod of 1918 appointed a committee with instructions that only showed to what high pitch enthusiasm had developed. The committee was instructed to visit and investigate in person Central Africa and China, a tremendous territory with no less than one-third of the world's inhabitants, and to report two years later. Whether the Synod fully realized what it asked of its committee will never be known. Probably not fully weighing the costs, nevertheless fully determined to do the best they could, the Synodical Committee started on their task.

It was made impossible for the committee to visit the field, but investigations were conducted at home in the cosmopolitan city of New York. Here men from both fields were met and conferences attended, giving opportunity to study the fields in detail for several months. Hereupon the committee conducted an active campaign in the whole denomination, seeking to make their findings known to the churches. A report of seventy pages was prepared for the Synod, and a sum of about $75,000 was collected for the opening of the new field. The aim of the financial part of the campaign was only $50,000, showing how willing the people were to give to the cause.

Pioneer Workers

The Synod of 1920 met shortly after this campaign was finished. It also proved to be ready for action. It chose China[1] and appointed Dr. Lee S. Huizenga and Rev. J. C. De Korne its first foreign missionaries. Rev. H. A. Dykstra was added to these two men after a couple of weeks, and within four months this small group set sail for China. The LaGrave Avenue Church of Grand Rapids, Mich., called Dr. Huizenga as their missonary pastor and he was installed on October 10th, 1920. Rev. J. C. De Korne accepted the call of the churches of Zeeland and was installed as their representative in a foreign field on September 21, 1920. Rev. H. A. Dykstra received a call from the three West Side churches in Grand Rapids, Mich., and was ordained to the holy ministry on September 22, 1920.

Three Years of Pioneering

On October 30, 1920, our pioneer group of missionaries met in a small upper room in Federal Hotel, San Francisco, with Rev. P. J. Hoekenga and a few of his parishioners. Rev. J. J. Hiemenga, President of Calvin College, had also made a special effort to come, arriving just in time for our last farewell prayer meeting. We shall never

---

[1] Reasons given by Synod for choosing China:

(1) The rich language and literature of the Chinese.

(2) Healthy climate (this was not based on trustworthy information we are afraid).

(3) Travel and telegraph is convenient. (This all depends upon the location chosen.)

(4) Strategic importance.

(5) Education of children. (This is a poor argument, as the education of the children in China requires much sacrifice on the part of the missionaries, probably as much as in Africa. This all depends upon the location chosen.)

(6) People are conservative, intellectual, and hence fit our people's type of character more than the African, who is emotional.

forget the interest these men showed and the deep emotion that filled their hearts as they entrusted us to the hands of Him who never faileth.

A few minutes later the steamship *China* started on her journey across the Pacific waters. Thirty years had she carried missionaries to the East. On this trip the number of missionaries was greater than that of men from other walks of life.

Our pioneer company consisted of three ordained men with their wives and children. Alphabetically arranged they were as follows: Rev. and Mrs. J. C. De Korne and two children, Baldwin and Melvin; Rev. and Mrs. H. A. Dykstra, Rev. L. S. Huizenga and three children, Ann, Myrtle, and Eunice. The oldest in the company was in his fortieth year and the youngest only two months. One had eleven years of experience in medical mission work and pastoral duties, the others with less experience, were filled to the brim with enthusiasm. The adults were ready to make sacrifices, the children had no say in the matter. The necessity was forced upon them. Qualified to preach the Gospel and to heal the sick the pioneer company longed for the day when they could settle in what they might call their own field, and might begin to realize their ambitions. Still three years of pioneering preceded this time.

A few historical data in connection with this period will be helpful. Passing by some smaller details, such as the study of various fields in China, conferences with China's foremost missionary experts, studying Pekinese in Shanghai, living at the Missionary Home longer probably than any other three families from any Mission, getting acquainted with Chinese life, getting tastes of China's extreme cold and torrid heat, trying to solve the mysterious money exchange, let us go into more detail concerning a few outstanding experiences.

In the first place we want to speak of our investigating tours. The last to leave the steamship *China* on its arrival in Shanghai, on November 23, 1920, was the oldest member of the group; the first to go to the neighborhood of our new field were the two younger men, Rev. J. C. De Korne going by one route, Rev. H. A. Dykstra by another. They were followed in a few days by Dr. L. S. Huizenga. Each traveled by a different route through Kiangsu province, thus seeing much of the field and work of the Southern Presbyterian mission, but neither of them seeing the field to which the Lord finally led the Church.

The next trip was even more interesting. It took the men away from their families for seven weeks. They left on H. M. S. *Dunera* on February 9, 1921, and returned on March 31, 1921, traveling 2,700 miles by ocean vessels, by palatial river steamers, by Chinese Junk, by rail, by coolie chair, by Chinese houseboat and every other imaginable method. This trip taught us a great deal of what can be done by well-planned mission work in a few years; it showed also, in contrast, some of the bandit outrages and desolations wrought by them.

Although the old Chinese junk, filled with dry bones and rocking on the sea like a drunken man, nauseated the company, yet the whole field and especially the beautiful piece of mission work of Rev. C. E. Patton so inspired, that the men were ready to recommend it to our Church. We expected to take over this field from the Northern Presbyterians, but when all was done and said, they decided to attempt manning the stations left vacant by Rev. C. E. Patton's departure, by other men and not to give it to the Christian Reformed Church. To this day we are afraid it was because we were too Reformed for them.

A still later trip, which took the men through the length and breadth of our present Jukao field, proved of the greatest value. It led the missionaries to advise the Synod as follows:

"We recommend this field (Jukao) to our Synod because:

a) The fields proposed by Synod, Fukien, Honan, Yunnan did not prove favorable.

b) It is virgin territory.

c) It is in the most populous province of China.

d) It is favorable for coöperation with the Southern Presbyterian Church.

e) The strategic value of the field in its proximity to Shanghai, is evident.

f) The prosperity of the people.

g) It is inexpensive as to travel to and from the homeland.

h) It is sufficiently large and can be extended northward *ad libitum.*

The study of the language was next undertaken.

All Boards allow their new missionaries to spend the first two years largely in language study. If possible, one year is spent at a language school. Since there are many dialects in China, language schools have been erected in various places. For our Jukao field the Nanking Language School is best adapted, although the Peking Language School can be used also.

Being the pioneer group, we could not begin language study until we had located our field.

Our field having been settled upon by Synod in June, 1920, Rev. and Mrs. J. C. De Korne and Rev. and Mrs. H. A. Dykstra left in October, 1920, for Nanking to study Mandarin, and Dr. and Mrs. L. S. Huizenga followed them in January, 1921. During the fall of 1922 all went to Taichow, Kiangsu, to continue language study with private teachers except Mrs. Huizenga and her children. Within two years of entering upon intensive study of the language, both Revs. De Korne and Dykstra had already delivered their first gospel message in the Chinese language to a Chinese audience. An interesting account of the first sermons is given by Rev. J. C. De Korne as follows:

".......During the afternoon of that same day there was a gathering of believers in our little chapel in Jukao. Only the baptized Christians and those known to be inquirers were admitted. Thus only about twenty-five people were present.......Little gatherings like this have been held for several months. The believers and inquirers had been brought together by our alert evangelist, Mr. Ching. But what to me was the important feature of this particular Sunday afternoon was the fact that this service was led by our own brother Dykstra. It was the first time that he or any member of our mission in China had preached a full sermon in Chinese. The work has been going on for some time through our native evangelist, but this service marked the beginning of the preaching of one of our own men. Only one who has struggled with this difficult language can appreciate what that service meant to us. He took as his text a clause from Acts 4: 13: 'They took knowledge of them that they had been with Jesus'. In clear, intelligible Chinese he told this handful of believers and inquirers that following Jesus would bring them power, but that it would also bring them persecution.......Brief mention will suffice for the next service of this eventful day. I fear I might overestimate its significance, since I had the privilege of delivering the principal address. It was the first time I had delivered a prepared speech in a chapel, and since it was our own chapel, in our own Jukao, it meant much to me. It was an evangelistic service, and the chapel was thrown open to all who cared to come. The building holds less than a hundred people, but it was well-filled. I tried to tell them

simply about Jesus as my friend and as the friend of all
sinners....... That night, as brother Dykstra and I talked
over the events of the day, we both felt thankful for the
day's experiences. We had long looked forward to the
day when we could begin to preach; here, at last, was a
beginning of it. Well, within two years from the time that
we were able to begin language study in earnest we began
our work. For that, too, we thanked God and took
courage."

PRACTICAL MISSION WORK

From the very beginning we sought to do some practical mission work. We all spoke in English to the Chinese and asked some older missionary to interpret our
messages.

Early in 1921 Dr. Lee S. Huizenga was requested to
take up the medical work in Kashing for one year. The
Huizenga's were in Kashing until January 1st, 1922, when
they removed to Nanking to join the other families. Here
the doctor served the University Hospital half days for
nine months and studied the language the other half days.
October 1st, 1922, he took up the work in Taichow Hospital until June 23, 1923, when he left for Peking to spend
three months with the Peking Union Medical College.

Revs. De Korne and Dykstra gave valuable service in
famine relief work during the spring of 1921, and the following year teaching classes of Chinese young men while
at Nanking and Taichow. In Taichow Rev. J. C. De Korne
began speaking to the Chinese on the streets one afternoon
a week. Many tracts were also distributed by the missionaries to the Chinese.

FIRST REAL ESTATE IN CHINA

The 17th of November, 1922, marks the time of the beginning of our mission work in China upon the territory
approved of by Synod. Upon the above date the small

chapel at Jukao was officially taken over by our mission from the Southern Presbyterian mission at Taichow. An appropriate service that evening marked our inauguration in the work. The following things were taken over by us at the value indicated, figured in United States money:

16 benches ....U. S. Gold	$ 5.67
6 bamboo chairs .... " "	1.50
2 large tables .... " "	3.00
2 stone jars .... " "	1.50
2 lamps .... " "	2.75
1 organ .... " "	2.50
1 hand bell .... " "	.50
1 pulpit .... " "	.25
2 iron pans .... " "	.50
Total................... " "	$18.17

The total of U. S. $18.17 certainly was not a huge sum start out work on. We rented our first chapel at $36.00 (Am.) a year, and paid our first native evangelist $8.00 (Am.) a month for salary. Such were the beginnings in Jukao in real mission work. The chapel at present is open every evening in the week except Saturday, and classes for inquirers and members are held during the week.

The first piece of land was purchased in February, 1923. It is a small tract of land outside of the city, large enough for the homes of two missionary families. A second piece of land was bought in May following, and will be used for a residence of the missionary physician. It is inside the city in order that the physician may be nearer the hospital. In August a third piece of land, with Chinese buildings in good state of repairs, were bought for a beginning of a hospital. To this will have to be added later on. All land is bought to use for an unlimited time according to the treaties made between China and the United States.

The first single woman evangelist to come to China was Miss Willemina Kalsbeek, arriving in Shanghai De-

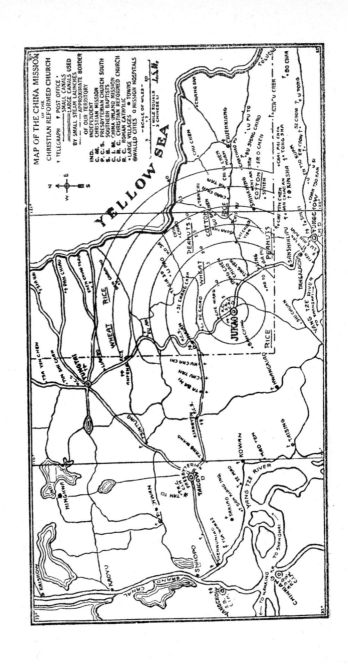

cember 31st, 1922, and she proceeded at once to Nanking for language study.

Miss Angie Haan was appointed nurse for Jukao on July 19, 1923, and sailed on the Japanese steamer *Tenyo Mauro*. She arrived in Shanghai October 15th, 1923, to go at once to Nanking for her first year language study.

Miss Kalsbeek's salary has been pledged by the West Side churches of Grand Rapids, four in number now cooperating, and Miss Haan's by the Neland Ave. congregation of Grand Rapids.

This closes the first three years of our missionary pioneering in China. The end of this period sees all three families located in our field in temporary quarters, with hopes of getting in permanent buildings soon, and our reinforcements still in Nanking.

PLANS FOR THE FUTURE

The policy of the present "Mission to China" is to do intensive work and to push the work to the regions beyond as soon as we believe those in the centre from which we proceed have adequately heard the gospel. All stress is to be laid upon Evangelistic work. Medical work and school work are only handmaids to the higher calling of the church to preach the Gospel.

Since the city of Jukao will for some years be our main station, the mission plans to open chapels at each gate on or near the main street. Jukao is a walled city of between 50,000 and 100,000 people. Daily many thousands from outside pass through the city gates. By putting our chapels near each of the four gates, it is possible to be within easy reach of all the people.

Rev. H. A. Dykstra is responsible for our first chapel in Jukao, opened by the Southern Presbyterians a few years ago. It is at the north gate of the city. Rev. J. C. De Korne is responsible for the east gate, where he ex-

pects to rent a building to be used as chapel. The medical
work is to be located at the west gate. Since the medical
work may develop into a rather large hospital, with much
hospital paraphernalia, it was deemed wise to buy a place
for an indefinite number of years, so it would not be necessary to move. The first building of a hospital plant is
now being prepared in a Chinese way to meet patients
during the day, and to be turned into a chapel at night.
Our aim for the near future is to open a 24-bed hospital
together with the clinic. This will probably have to be
enlarged soon.

As to a Chinese staff, each missionary is allowed to
work out his own policy under mission approval. Rev.
Dykstra has already a Chinese missionary helper, Mr. C.
King, and will be adding others as the work increases.
Rev. De Korne likewise expects to put a man in the Jukao
east gate chapel and have others go into the country. The
medical work will require the greatest number of native
helpers, as its method of service varies greatly from the
evangelistic work. From the start one or two Chinese
doctors will be necessary, one probably for surgery and
the other for medicine. Two nurses, graduated from Chinese hospitals, will be put in charge, a male nurse for the
men's work and a female nurse for the female work.
Each of these will have to be assisted by helpers and
orderlies. A laboratory technician will be necessary at
once, and a drug clerk as well. For evangelistic work
with the patients and for chapel work in the evening, an
evangelist and a Bible woman will be necessary.

All the chapels, as well as the clinic, will be open daily.
Bible Study Classes and children's work will be organized
as soon as possible, and country work can be taken up as
rapidly as Chinese or foreign evangelists are available.
Women's work will be taken up by the Bible women as
soon as it can be arranged. Miss W. Kalsbeek will soon
enter upon her task as Evangelist. Miss Elizabeth Byrne,

an English-speaking Chinese woman, trained in a mission school, took up the woman's work in connection with the hospital in October, 1923.

It is our policy to do as much as possible through the Chinese. The time has come for foreigners to do less and for the Chinese christians to do no more. To prepare the Jukao christians for a church organization independent of our church at home is our aim. This is in perfect harmony with the consensus of opinion of the foreign missionary body in China as well as the rapidly growing indigenous Chinese church. In Kiangsu province the Presbyterian church government is already fairly well established. There are several Chinese Presbyterian churches in Kiangsu, forming presbyteries and a Synod. To this already existing Chinese church we expect our christians in Jukao to belong as soon as they have material enough to organize. With the Lord's blessings we hope this organization will take place in the near future.

Our present plans have given little thought of educational missio mwork, partly because the public school system in Jukao is good, and partly because the present force are all evangelists. Coöperation with the Southern Presbyterians in the training of native evangelists may soon come up for more careful consideration.

The Future

How large our missionary plane in China for the next twenty-?five years should be, is still an open question. It is hard to predict the future in China. For the present men can be placed as fast as the Church can send them. At times it seems as though the Chinese church will be sufficiently awakened to her high calling in the next generation to take up the evangelization of her own country. Our field also will be affected by this owing to its proximity to Shanghai, one of China's great centers. At present our missionaries are making a serious study of just how far we should extend our missionary activities in China with this awakened desire on the part of China to be delivered from the foreign swaddling clothes of denominationalism and occidental forms entirely foreign to the Eastern mind, and to develop for herself an oriental type of christian church, conformed both with the eternal principles of God's Word and the Eastern civilization. An unique period it is in China's religious history, well worth much study and prayer both by our force on the field and by the Church at home.

LEE S. HUIZENGA.

§8. THE MISSION BOARD AND THE DIRECTOR OF MISSIONS

An important factor in the work of missions is the Board of Missions, under whose direction the work among the Indians and in China is carried on. At first this body was known as "Committee for Missions to the Heathen", and was composed of the Home Mission Committee and the treasurer for Foreign Missions, (Article 114, Minutes of Synod of 1886), but two years later a separate committee was appointed, consisting of the Revs. R. T. Kuiper, E. Bos, T. M. Vanden Bosch, and the elders J. W. Garveling and J. Gelock. Rules and Regulations governing this body were adopted by the same Synod of 1888. Later each Classis was represented on the Committee, till the Synod of 1910, which reduced the number of delegates to five and elected as such the Revs. M. Van Vessem, J. Groen, H. Beets, H. Walkotten, and J. Dolfin. A new "Mission Order" was adopted in 1912. In 1914 there was a return to the old rule of having each Classis represented on the Board, and such continues till the present.

"Board of Heathen Missions of the Christian Reformed Church" is the legal title of this body whose ever-increasing responsibility entitles it to a large place in the prayerful interest of the Church of God.

Director of Missions. The Mission Board recommended
to the Synod of 1912 the appointment of a "field secretary" te devote himself entirely to the cause of missions,
because the constantly increasing work demanded such a
functionary for its correspondence and financial interests.
But the proposal was defeated at the time. The 1920 Synod,
however, decided to appoint a "Secretary of Missions"
(Zendings-Directeur), to labor under the supervision
of the Board of Missions, of which he shall be a member *ex officio.* His duties were outlined in *"Rules and
Regulations".* Of the Board he is to be secretary. His
duties regarding the missionaries are to visit their fields
from time to time, to counsel with them, and to adjust personal relations between them. Regarding other missionary organizations his duty is to attend the meetings of the
Home Missions Council and Foreign Missions Conference,
(Chapter V, §5), and of such of their respective committees as his work in the interests of our Mission requires,
as well as to place himself in such personal contact with
our own Jewish and Home Mission organizations as will
enable him to properly advocate their interests. Duties
with reference to the denomination were outlined as follows: "To visit as many classical meetings and congregations as his other duties allow; to enlighten and enthuse
the people on the subject of missions in all its branches;
to stimulate prayer for missions; the study of mission literature; to have christian young men and women consecrate themselves to the cause of missions at home and
abroad; to organize, wherever deemed necessary, Missionary Societies and Mission Festivals and Conferences, and
to present the cause of Missions to these meetings. He
shall also write or edit and advance the publication of
such missionary literature as covers the entire field of our
missionary activities at home and abroad. And since the
Church has no general budget for Missions, he is charged
with studying the financial problems of our heathen mis-

sion work and to promote such giving, by individuals and congregations, as will, with God's blessing, provide the means needed for our missionary undertakings". The Rev. H. Beets was chosen for this important task. He began his labors September 27, 1920.

§9.   MEANS TO AROUSE A MISSION SPIRIT

A great aid in the successful performance of the many duties required of the Director of Missions will, no doubt, be the carrying out of the *program* to arouse a mission spirit adopted by the Synod of 1910, advising the churches the following:

To preach missionary sermons from time to time.

To discuss the matter of missions as much as possible in catechetical classes, and by means of quarterly lessons in the Sunday school, as well as through systematic study in the various Societies of the churches. At public meetings the church-members are to be labored with regarding this matter and as much as possible annual mission feasts are to be held. Local churches are to reach after the ideal of sending out and supporting missionaries of their own, with systematic weekly offerings for the cause.

May the offering of sons and daughters for the blessed work not be forgotten. And thanks be to God, there is encouraging progress in this, as the next paragraph plainly shows.

Although there remains much land yet to be possessed, other denominations have successfully employed various *agencies* and *methods* which we may well copy, in so far as harmonizing with our principles. *Personal work* for and by individuals, one winning one, has proved to be a great blessing in many cases, and is a very biblical method of activity. Andrew found Peter, his brother, to point him to Christ and Philip found Nathanael (John 1: 40-45).

The *Sunday School* should have a missionary committee to look for new openings for mission work and to arrange occasional missionary programs. The Sunday School library and that of other organizations should circulate plenty of good missionary literature for old and young. A missionary magazine should be read regularly. There should be *missionary societies* of young men and young women, or young people in joint organizations, as well as women's and men's missionary societies. Such organizations will divide and locate responsibility. They will enlist activity, awaken enthusiasm, promote prayer for and the study of missions, provide opportunity for Christian service, and win recruits for service at home and abroad. The *every member canvass* should not be forgotten to provide the "sinews of war". This has for its object an offering *every week* from every member of the church according to ability, on the basis of Christian stewardship, 1 Cor. 16:2. In many churches this canvass is made annually, by special committees, whose activity is preceded by special preparation and training, with earnest prayer. The duplex envelope system is connected with this plan. It means that each Lord's day, as we bring our offerings to the Lord's house to provide for our own religious needs, we remember the people still estranged from our Lord, but whom we are to love as ourselves. And that love we show by bringing them the Bread of Life —through missions. Well-to-do members should finance "substitutes" in the mission field. Many have found *tithing* a blessed rule for giving, still bringing God's blessing as promised in Malachi 3:10. Have *you* adopted this rule —how much do *you* give for missions each week—do you try to win souls and lives by personal effort—so we may well ask our readers. (Cf. The Mission Budget of our Christian Reformed Church, by the Rev. J. Dolfin, *The Banner,* January 11, 1923.)

§10.   THE STUDENT VOLUNTEER MOVEMENT

This Movement which is not without influence on the missionary activities among our people, is entitled to a place in these pages. It originated at the first international conference of Christian College students held at Mount Hermon, Mass., in 1886, at the invitation of D. L. Moody. Of the 250 delegates who attended, 21 had definitely decided to become foreign missionaries when the conference opened. Before it closed one hundred of those present had recorded as their "purpose, if God permit, to become foreign missionaries". Deputations were sent to various colleges, and since then the Movement spread throughout our land and beyond it. The *purpose* of the Movement is as follows:

(1) To awaken and maintain among all Christian students of the United States and Canada intelligent and active interest in foreign missions.

(2) To enroll a sufficient number of properly qualified student volunteers to meet the successive demands of the various mission boards of North America.

(3) To help all such intending missionaries to prepare for their life-work and to enlist their coöperation in developing the missionary life of home churches.

(4) To lay an equal burden of responsibility on all students who are to remain as ministers and lay-workers at home, that they may actively promote the missionary enterprise by their intelligent advocacy, by their gifts and by their prayers.

Prior to January, 1911, no less than 4,784 volunteers had been sent out as missionaries by over fifty different missionary boards of the United States and Canada. More than two-fifths of the sailed volunteers are women. Systematic and progressive study of missions is regularly promoted by this Movement and various institutions of learning contributed money for missionaries as well as workers.

March 3, 1915, a "Student Volunteer Band" was organized at Calvin College, "with eyes open to the needs of the world, and hearts aglow with the ideal of being sent out into parts where the Shepherd who gave His life for His sheep is yet unknown". Nine students were the charter members of this organization. Some of the members of this constantly growing Band are already abroad. Others are ready to follow. The ideals and vision of this Band are expressed in its motto: "Even unto the ends of the earth".

"Go, heralds of salvation, forth;
    Go, in your heavenly Master's Name;
From East to West, from South to North,
    The glorious gospel wide proclaim.

"Go forth in faith, God's gospel take,
    Till God's great reaping day shall come;
Then they who sowed in tears shall wake
    And hail the joyful harvest home."

"When, Lord, to this our western land
Led by Thy providential hand
        Our wandering fathers came,
        They found peace and prosperity—
Let, in return for this, our youth
Go everywhere to preach Thy truth!
        And all praise be to Thee!"

TEST QUESTIONS

1. What is understood by "Missions", on what is the work based, and what is its object? Which incentives appeal the strongest to you?

2. What can you say about the Home Mission work of the Church as carried on till 1907 under a denominational Board?

3. Why is work among the Indians our duty?

4. Which stations are occupied at present among the Zunies and Navajos?

5. What can you say about our Jewish Mission work?

6. What do you know of the labors among immigrants and sailors and of the evangelization work?

7. What do you know about our China Mission?

8. What is the work of the Mission Board and of the Director of Missions?

9. Which program for arousing a missionary spirit was mapped out by the Synod of 1910? In how far is it carried out in your own congregation?

10. What is meant by the Student Volunteer Movement, and why should you personally not "volunteer" for the work?

WORKS OF REFERENCE

Dr. E. Pfeiffer, "Mission Studies".

Dr. A. DeWitt Mason, "Outlines of Missionary Studies".

Dr. H. Beets, "Triumfen van het Kruis", with introductory chapter on "De Zending in de Heilige Schrift", by Dr. H. Bavinck.

Rev. J. Dolfin, "Bringing the Gospel in Hogan and Pueblo".

Prof. L. Berkhof, "Paul the Missionary".

Smaller books on Navahoes and Zunies by Rev. H. Walkotten.

CHAPTER VIII

THE CHRISTIAN REFORMED CREED AND LITURGY

Introductory: Why a Creed? §1. The Heidelberg Catechism. §2. The Netherlands Confession of Faith. §3. The Canons of Dordrecht. §4. The Liturgy in General. §5. The Various "Forms" of the Liturgy. §6. Liturgical Improvement Proposals.

INTRODUCTORY: WHY A CREED?

BY CREED we understand an official statement of belief. In this Chapter, principally devoted to the Creed of the Church as embodied in its doctrinal standards, the prefatory qusetion may well be put:
"Why Should a Church Have a Creed at all?"
The cry of many is: "The Bible, and nothing but it, is our Creed." One group of Christians has adopted the slogan: "No Creed but Christ". Now, as to the first statement about the Bible and nothing but it—as a creed, this is a misleading motto. All true Chrstians hold the Bible to be God's inspired revelation. It is for all who fear God truly "the Book of fundamentals". All essential, creedal statements are supposed to be derived from its sacred pages, built upon its utterances. But the Bible, while very plain as to the essentials of religion, is very deep, as a mine often is, and no wonder. It really is a divine *library* of not less than sixty-six different books. And the bone of contention has always been, *"what saith the Scripture"* on this or that subject? The point of dispute between God's children has never been: is the Bible inspired, fundamental, authoritative. But the difficulty has always come in when people tried to *interpret* its statements and systematize its different utterances. When groups of people claim that they teach nothing but what the Bible teaches, they are not alone unfair in their implication of what

other orthodox churches do, but they mislead as well. Their *interpretation* of the Bible is then flaunted as the only genuine, and identified by them with the Word of God itself—a very presumptuous thing to do. God has given no particular denomination an exclusive patent on divine truth nor a monopoly in infallible Bible interpretation. It requires, in the deepest sense, *"all the saints"* to apprehend what is the breadth and length and height and depth, and to know the love of Christ which passeth knowledge, Eph. 3: 18, 19. And that "all the saints" not simply of one age or of one country, but of all ages and of all lands and races. So wonderfully rich is the truth of God in Christ.

The slogan, "No Creed but Christ" also is misleading, whatsoever way it is taken. Christ Himself involves a "creed", about His deity, His relation to the Trinity, His human nature, atonement, resurrection, etc. And none of those important things can be separated from other correlated facts embodied in precious doctrines. Christology is not the whole of theology nor can it stand apart. God's truths are a chain of many links; we cannot separate them at will. Moreover, in groups of churches claiming to have no creed, there is, after all, something of the sort, a "consensus" of opinions of the founders and leaders, an "unwritten creed", a traditional one—something at times harmful in its effects because an unscrupulous or fanatical majority can twist and whip such an unwritten creed in a very tyrannical way.

The Christian Reformed Church has a *written* creed. And it has good *reasons* for this. The first reason is because its standards form something of a *compendium* or digest of the great truths of the Bible, a *resumé* of its leading contents. The Bible, as already mentioned, is very large and many-sided. Our minds cannot comprehend and systematize all of its utterances. Therefore we consider our creed a bird's-eye view of the great doctrines of grace, furnishing us something of an *"analogy of faith"*, a standard to measure opinions by as these are being formulated during the course of the years. Such a resumé has been made from the earliest times, so that we are following a good precedent. Hebrews 8: 1 speaks of a "summing up", (Dutch, "hoofdsom") of the things covered by the writer, and in Ephesians 4: 5 Paul gives a resumé of the great truths he stood for: one Lord, one faith, one baptism, and one God and Father of all. In line with this Bible precedent in the course of time the *Apostles' Creed* grew up, completed in its present form about 500, and the other *ecumenical creeds,* part of the common heritage of the one Catholic Church of God of which the Christian Reformed Church is a branch. Ecumenical signifies general, that is, pertaining to the entire Christian Church. The *Nicene Creed* is the first and oldest of these ecumenical creeds, thus called after Nicea in Asia Minor, where a great Council was held in 325. This Creed refutes the Arians who denied the deity of Christ. At the Nicene Council great influence was exerted by a young deacon from Alexandria, ATHANASIUS, after whom a second ecumenical creed is named, one devoted mainly to an exposition and defense of the holy Trinity. A third ecumenical creed of considerable importance is the one formulated in 451, at Chalcedon, after which city in Asia Minor it is called. It defines the relation between the natures of our Lord.

The second reason for having a written Creed is that it may serve as a *bond of union* and fellowship of likeminded followers of Christ. For that reason the Dutch fathers often called their standards "formulas of unity", while others spoke of "articles of concord". A third reason for the formulation of Confessions has at times been the need of furnishing outsiders, particularly governments, with official statements of what was really believed by the group of believers, in the face of calumny which provoked persecution, or to prove that all could not be charged with the extreme views possibly held by a few. The fourth reason for having a written creed has resulted from activity of people inside the Church, propagating views undermining fundamentals or drawing pernicious inferences, so that re-statements were needed, or more careful defining and elaborating. This last reason accounts particularly for the formulation of the Canons of Dordrecht, §3 below. The third reason had considerable to do with the writing of the Confession of Faith, §1, and the second and first apply to some extent to the publication of the Heidelberg Catechism, §2.

Finally, a written creed renders service as a *standard of orthodoxy* for preachers and teachers of a given denomination. For that reason a *"formula of subscription"* has been provided by the Church of the Fathers, see Article 53 of the Church Order, to be subscribed to solemnly. It expresses belief in the articles and points of doctrine of the standards as fully agreeing with the Word of God, the teaching and defense of them, and the rejecting of errors militating against these doctrines. In case difficulties or different sentiments regarding them should arise in the mind, these are not to be proposed, taught or defended in public until first revealed and submitted to the consistory, Classis or Synod.

A creed, therefore, instead of deserving to be decried as a mere human invention, a galling chain of the mind, etc., ought to be *valued* highly. Not, of course, that it should be considered the equal of the Bible, or a substitute for it. The Word of God is both the source and the foundation of the Creed: Appeal from the latter to the former is permissible and may at times be a matter of duty. The Scriptures alone are infallible; Standards bear the earmark of human limitations. Additions to them are needed from time to time, as new treasures are dug up in the mine of the Word, or, to quote Robinson once more, as new light "breaks forth" from its pages. The creed is not or should not be a petrofact but a living, growing organism. Re-statement as well as enlargement of the creed may even be necessary. But—and that is very important, revision should always follow the *historical line of development* revealed by the Holy Spirit in and through the Church as centuries rolled onward. It should never be revolutionary, overthrowing the old foundations to erect new structures from the bottom up. Such would be a practical denial that God fulfilled His promise of the Spirit's guiding into all truth, according to John 16: 13. "Other foundation can no man lay than that which is laid, which is Jesus Christ", (I Cor. 3: 11); "Being built upon the foundation of the apostles and prophets, Christ Jesus Himself being the chief corner-stone" (Eph. 2: 20.)

§1. THE HEIDELBERG CATECHISM

The first of our doctrinal standards, as printed in our Psalters, is *"The Catechism, or Method of Instruction in the Christian religion* as the same is taught in the Reformed Churches and Schools in Holland and in America." This is a very highly-valued work wherever Reformed people of Dutch stock are found. Yet it is not of Holland, but of German origin. Its birthplace is the city of Heidelberg in the Palatinate, after which famous town it is known the world over. There its first edition appeared in the year 1563. Its third edition, the one in common use, dates from the same year.

Authors of this Catechism were two young German divines, well-acquainted with the Reformed churches of their day, not alone of their native land, but also of Switzerland and France. Both suffered persecution for the sake of their Reformed faith.

Zacharius Ursinus was the chief one of the Catechism

authors. Born at Breslau, 1534, a student at various universities, acquainted with the reformers Melanchthon, Calvin and others, he was professor at Heidelberg from 1561 to 1576. He died in 1583. He was a man of profound learning, with a rare gift of teaching and of fervent piety. Ursinus was aided in his work of writing the Catechism by CASPER OLEVIANUS, born at Treves, 1536. He had studied the ancient languages at Paris and other places, and theology at Geneva and Zurich, these last being great centers of Reformed learning at the time. At Heidelberg, since 1560, he taught theology there and preached at court. He, like Ursinus, left Heidelberg in 1576, and died in 1585. Olevianus was inferior to Ursinus in learning, but his superior in preaching and in church government.

Others of less renown aided these men, even as they built their Catechism of material found in other books of the kind. But the names of these two godly men, Ursinus and Olevianus, are inseparably bound up with our Catechism as well as the name of a third man, the one at whose court Olevianus preached. We refer to the elector or ruler of the Palatinate of which Heidelberg was the capital, FREDERICK THE PIOUS (1515—1576), one of the noblest characters of history, and as his popular name indicates, a man of godliness. He had Ursinus and Olevianus draw up the book to instruct the people of his domain in the fundamentals of the christian religion as he had embraced them in their Reformed presentation as distinct from the Lutheran.

The Heidelberg Catechism from the very beginning became a very popular work. Next to the Bible, the *Imitation of Christ* by Thomas à Kempis, and Bunyan's *Pilgrim's Progress,* no book, it has been stated, has been more frequently translated and more widely distributed and used. It has been generally acknowledged as a masterpiece in its line, unsurpassed for depth, comfort, and beauty, representing Christianity in its evangelical, practical, cheering aspect, not as a commanding law, intellectual scheme, system of outward observance, but as God's great gift to man, as a source of peace and comfort in life and in death.   Its first question and answer is the whole gospel in a nutshell.   Blessed are all who truly know its precious meaning.

The Heidelberg Catechism, following the order of Paul's epistle to the Romans, is divided into three main parts.   After the first two introductory questions, we find Questions 3—11 setting forth how great our sins and miseries are (Lord's Days II—IV).   The second part, Questions 12—85, treats of our redemption (Lord's Days V—XXXI), and the concluding portion, Questions 86—129, (Lord's Days XXXII—LII), is devoted to the gratitude the redeemed are to show.   The second part is by far the largest, and contains an explanation of the Apostle's Creed under the three heads of God the Father, the Son, and the Holy Ghost.   The doctrine of the sacraments, a much-discussed subject in Reformation days, has several Questions devoted to it.   The third part expounds the Ten Commandments of Exodus 20 as a rule of obedience, as well as the Lord's Prayer.   An epitome of the Decalogue as a means of teaching us how great our sins and miseries are, is found in the first part of the Catechism.   This three-fold division corresponds to the order of religious life in practical experience, and to the three leading ideas of repentance, faith, and love.   Several of its answers are acknowledged gems, such as the definition of faith, providence, the significance of the name "christian", the benefit of the ascension, justification by faith, and others.   The length of some answers as well as the extensive treatment of the sacraments have been considered faults to be remedied, the former leading to various attempts at abbreviating, particularly in the case of the *"Compendium"*, of the REV. H. FAUKELIUS, dating from 1608, a very popular abridgment of the Catechism whose use was permitted

by the Synod of Dordt, 1618-1619. Since centuries it has
been printed along with the standards. See Chapter IX, §4.

In the Church of our Fathers the Heidelberg Catechism
soon found a hearty welcome after Dathenus had translated it and published it, in 1566, in connection with his
Psalter, see §5. An English edition appeared in 1591. In
1764 the Rev. L. De Ronde's English translation was published in New York, and three years later its revised edition, under the auspices of the Collegiate Reformed church
of New York. This translation was gone over and revised
by a committee of the Christian Reformed Synod, and
finally approved in 1912.

The Netherland Reformed churches from the beginning adopted the Heidelberg Catechism as an authoritative standard, requiring subscription to it as well as exposition of it, and from them the book has come down to us,
as one of the three *formulas of unity,* expounded regularly
in the form of sermons, see Chapter IX, §3.

§2.   THE NETHERLANDS CONFESSION OF FAITH

The second one of the three standards of the Christian
Reformed Church, printed as a rule back of the Catechism, but antedating it by a few years, is the Netherland
Confession of Faith, frequently known as the Belgic Confession, a name connected with its origin in the Southern
Netherlands. Its author was a Belgian, Guy de Bray
(Guido de Bres), born at Mons (Bergen) in Hainault, 1522.
De Bray had been converted to the Reformed faith about
the year 1547 and became a fervent preacher of the "new"
religion, driven from place to place. In the year 1567 he
was apprehended by the Spaniards then persecuting the
believers in the Netherlands and thrown into a miserable
dungeon. But the faith he displayed in his captivity was
as remarkable as that shown while at liberty. To a visitor
he remarked that the noise made by his chains was like

sweet music in his ears, because he bore them for the sake of the Word of God. He died bravely as a martyr, May 31, 1567, being hung at Valenciennes.

Already as early as 1559 de Bray had made a draft of several articles of the Reformed religion. He consulted several leading men in the final preparation of the Confession, which somewhat follows that of the French Confession of Faith of which Calvin was the chief author. Published in the French language in 1561, the next year a Dutch translation of it appeared, approved by the Synod of the Hague in 1583, and later somewhat revised by the Dordrecht Synod of 1618-1619. From the very beginning this Confession was accepted by the Church of our Fathers as an adequate and satisfactory exposition of the chief doctrines of grace, and subscription to it was required from the preachers and teachers of the Reformed Churches.

From our ancestors this standard has come down to us, and except for a slight change in the closing sentences of Article 36 (Chapter V, §6), it is held by the Christian Reformed Church as an authoritative confessional writing. Its thirty-seven articles may be subdivided into *six groups*. The first group covers the doctrine of God and His works, including articles on the Bible, Articles 1—13. The doctrine of man, including the Election dogma, forms the second group, Articles 14—17. The third group, Articles 18—21, covers the doctrine of Christ; the fourth, Articles 22—26, treats of the doctrine of salvation: faith, justification, sanctification, and good works, the abolishing of the ceremonial law and Christ's intercession. The fifth group discusses the Church and its sacraments and the views held concerning the magistrates, (Articles 27—36), while the last chapter contains a brief but impressive discussion of the doctrines of the last things, under the heading, "The Last Judgment". As to the English translation of this—what we wrote under the heading on the Catechism applies also

to the Belgic Confession.   While not as popular as the Heidelberg standard, the Confession is a noble document,
and its careful study repays any one who devotes prayerful attention to its contents.

§3.   THE CANONS OF DORDRECHT

This is the third one of the standards of the Christian
Reformed Church.   It is the youngest of the three.   While
the Heidelberg Catechism was born in a time of struggle
with Rome and Lutheranism, and the Belgic Confession
during the bloody days of persecution, in mortal combat
with the Roman Church, aided by Spanish oppressors,
while anabaptist perversion of truth greatly endangered
the movement of the Reformed Reformation, the Canons
of Dordt were formulated during days of great internal
strife.   In the opening years of the seventeenth century, in
fact already during the closing decade of its predecessor,
certain views had been advocated by men of the Reformed
Church who were led by JAMES ARMINIUS, who from 1602
to 1609 was professor of theology at the University of
Leyden, and after whom his partisans have been called
Arminians.   In the year 1610 certain of the Arminian
leaders formulated a series of articles called the "Remon-
strantie" (Remonstrance).   The "Remonstrance" showed
that its signers departed from the received Reformed doctrines on five important points.   They believed that God's
decree of Election (Article XVI of the Confession), was
based on foreseen faith, that the Atonement was general,
that man accepts the Gospel according to his own arbitrary choice, that God's grace is resistible, and that a believer may fall from grace.   After much agitation and civil
strife a Synod was convened to settle the matter.   Representatives of Reformed Churches abroad were delegated
as well as leading ministers and professors of the Netherland Church.   Sessions were begun November 13, 1618, in

the city of Dordrecht, after which this national, and in fact to some extent, Ecumenical Synod, was named. During the middle of January, 1619, the "Canons" were finished and the foreign delegates left, but the Dutch representatives held twenty-seven more sessions to revise the Confession of Faith and the Catechism, as well as the *Church Order* (Chapter X, §5). Canon signifies a "rule". Five of these were formulated, covering the points of the Remonstrance already named.

The first head of doctrine contained in the first "Canon" is about "Divine Predestination", showing that Election is not based on foreseen faith, but on God's sovereign choice.

The second Canon on "The Death of Christ and the Redemption of Men thereby", teaches that the Atonement is not general, as the Arminians taught, but limited. While the atoning merits of Christ were in value abundantly *sufficient* to expiate the sins of the whole world, it was the sovereign purpose of God the Father that the quickening and saving *efficacy* of Christ's death should extend only to the elect, men out of every people, tribe, nation, and language. The third and fourth heads of doctrine or Canons are combined in one chapter on "the Corruption of Man, his Conversion to God, and the Manner thereof." It is shown from Holy Writ that man has not the "free will" of arbitrary choice attributed to him by the Arminians, since he is dead in trespasses and sins. In Conversion the grace of God triumphs effectively over all opposition, the efficacy of the regenerating Spirit pervading the inmost recesses of the man, opening the closed and softening the hardened heart, infusing new qualities in the will, "Whereupon the will thus renewed, is not only actuated and influenced by God, but in consequence of this influence, becomes itself active. Wherefore also, man is himself rightly said to believe and repent, by virtue of that grace received" The fifth Canon on "the Perseverance of the Saints", shows from the Bible that those truly born of God do not fall from grace utterly, as the Arminians taught, but in the power of God are kept unto salvation. Each of these five Canons is divided into two sets of paragraphs. The first sets forth positively the Reformed conception of the doctrines involved; the second set contains the "Rejections of the Remonstrant Errors."

In the "Conclusion" added to the Canons they are called a "perspicuous, simple and ingenious declaration of the orthodox doctrine", "drawn from the Word of God, agreeable to the Confessions of the Reformed Churches", and the Synod exhorted "all their brethren in the Gospel of Christ to conduct themselves piously and religiously in handling this doctrine, to the glory of the divine Name, to holiness of life and to the consolation of afflicted souls." May we ever be able to hold and uphold the deep truths embodied in these Canons, in the spirit of that exhortation.

§4.   THE LITURGY IN GENERAL

Liturgy pertains to public worship. In the conduct of this certain "forms" or fixed formulas came into use, almost from the earliest years of the history of the Church. During the Middle Ages by the term "Liturgy" was understood the description of the order in which public worship took place. The Roman and Greek Churches made much of all kinds of ceremonial actions, many of them copied from the temple service of the Old Testament. And these ceremonies were all centered round about "Mass" as the chief part of divine services. The Lutherans retained considerable of this old ritual, but the Reformed Reformation broke with it radically. The Word of God was made the center. What precedes the preaching of that Word leads up to that, forming the transition from the earthly to the spiritual. That what follows the presentation of the Word, again forms a transition, namely, from the proclamation of grace to life which is to be sanctified by the Word. The *essence* of public worship is that of a meeting of God with His people. The minister of the Word serves as the intermediary in this. Consequently his function is twofold. As the Lord's spokesman he reads and preaches the Word, administers the sacraments, and blesses the people. He serves as the mouth of the people of God in confessing sin, in imploring His mercies, in praising His Name. In the service of song and in the offering of gifts the congregation of the Lord approaches God directly.

Voices have been raised more than once to allow the Church a larger part in the service, see §6 below.

The *purpose* of public worship is primarily to serve and magnify the Triune Covenant Jehovah, but secondarily the edification of His people, that it may be enabled to know, love and serve God better.

To avoid arbitrariness, to present confusion, to promote harmony and to bring out to some extent the oneness of the Reformed churches, certain *prayers* and *formularies* slowly on came into general use in public worship. The Liturgy of the Church of our fathers, which embodies these, was chiefly born in three cities: Zurich and Geneva in Switzerland, the hearth and home of the Reformed Reformation, and London, at one time the haven of refuge of our persecuted ancestors. Its various parts were collected and arranged by PETRUS DATHENUS, already named in Chapter I, §2. See also Chapter IX, §2. Dathenus' liturgical collection, first published in 1566, contained a number of *Prayers* which have fallen into disuse among us and have not been made a part of our American liturgy. But the *Forms* which Dathenus published have come down to us although not in their original form, and a number of other formularies were added later on as we shall see presently.

§5. THE VARIOUS "FORMS" OF THE LITURGY

The first "Form" printed in our Psalters under the heading "Liturgy" is the one *For the Administration of Baptism.*" It consists of three sections: a general introduction about the three "principal parts of the doctrine of holy Baptism"; then a section devoted "to Infants of Believers", and finally one for administering the sacrament "to Adult Persons". Various forms have been used in the compilation of this important part of our liturgy. But in the main it can be said that Petrus Dathenus arranged the part devoted to Infant Baptism, while that for Adults dates from 1610. The Synod of Dordrecht, 1618-1619, revised this Form to assume the shape it bears today.

In the course of the centuries a number of ministers of the Reformed Church in the Netherlands changed certain parts to harmonize with their own doctrinal views, principally in regard to the Covenant of Grace. A number of preachers in the Christian Reformed Church of Holland as well as in America formerly avoided the use of the prayers which are part of the Form of Infant Baptism. But the Church Order, as well as various synodical deliverances, declare the employment of the Form in its entirety to be obligatory. It is the property of the whole Church, embodying its official doctrines, and no individual minister has the right of altering it to suit his individual views.

This obligatory use, on the same grounds, applies to the second "Form" of our Liturgy, *"For the Administration of the Lord's Supper"*. Dathenus also compiled this, using various older formularies, principally, in this case, that employed in the Palatinate, the home of the Heidelberg Catechism. Both of these time-honored Forms are noble, edifying, and instructive compilations, full of encouragement in the battle of life. Their length, however, has met with objection, particularly that of the Communion formula, the pearl of the collection, which ought to be used in full at each communion service, something which requires too much time.   A simplified edition of the sacramental form for use in the Mission field of the Church, was approved by Synod of 1912.   Let us add here that these formularies are designed for use during *public* worship.   The sacramental service is a part of the divine service whose center, as we saw, is the Word.   The sacraments are God's seal upon the testimony of Holy Writ concerning His Covenant mercies.   Therefore these two ought not to be separated.

The Forms of Baptism and Communion, *sacramental* formularies, are in our Psalter followed by two which are of a *disciplinary* character.   We refer to the *"Form of Excommunication* and the *"Form of Readmitting Excommunicated Persons"*.   Both of these, in their present form, originated in the action of the Synod held in The Hague in 1586.   The former's solemn and biblical declarations ought to fill the heart with terror unto repentance, and the latter should pour the balm of consolation into the contrite soul unto belief in God's restoring mercy. The same Synod of The Hague just named was sponsor to the third pair of Forms—those devoted to *installation* or ordination of the ordinary office-bearers of the Church.   The *"Form of Ordination of the Ministers of God's Word"* is full of solemn Scriptural teaching on the work involved, and the same may be said of its companion, *"Form of Ordination of Elders and Deacons"*.   No office-bearer who carefully and prayerfully studies the contents of these Forms will fail to be benefited immensely by this, and the Church of God will do well from time to time to read these forms, which are not alone setting forth the obligations and responsibilities which the ministers and elders and deacons assume, but also the congregations whose representatives they were chosen to be.

Of far more recent origin than any of the Forms hitherto named, is the fourth pair of forms: those *"For the Installation of Professors of Theology"* and for the *"Ordination of Missionaries"*. The first one has the distinction of having an American minister as its compiler, the Rev. G. D. De Jong, who drew it up in 1894. The Form for the Ordination of Missionaries is of Netherland origin in so far as the introduction is concerned, the concluding charge, and the part devoted to "missionaries to the heathen". Dr. H. Beuker had considerable to do with its compilation, approved by the Chr. Ref. Synod of 's Hertogenbosch, 1875, and the General Synod of the Reformed Churches, 1902. The section devoted to home missionaries is of American origin, first appearing in the Christian Reformed Church Order volume, published in 1905, and edited by Profs. G. K. Hemkes, W. Heyns, and Rev. H. Beets. The last named arranged the addition involved. Both these Forms were approved by the Synod of 1906.

The *"Form for the Confirmation of Marriage Before the Church"* is the closing one of the Christian Reformed Liturgy. It dates from early Reformation days, and appeared already in Dathenus' liturgical Collection of 1566. But if any, then certainly this formulary is the one needing revision. Its very title, speaking of the "confirmation" of matrimony, does not fit American conditions. In the Netherlands the civil magistrates unite people in marriage. The ministers of religion can do no more than "confirming" this—hence the title. But in the United States pastors are authorized by law to solemnize marriages. Moreover, the opening sentence presents a rather gloomy view of life, true enough to fact, but perhaps out of place at a matrimonial feast. But the chief objection may well be considered that the *christian* character of marriage, as described in Ephesians 5, is not sufficiently brought out. Other expressions in the form could well bear wise revision, and there ought to be some modification devised to fit the reading of the form when aged people are united in bonds of matrimony. The length also has met with objection. A movement to improve the liturgy is under way both in the Netherlands, (*The Banner,* February 24, 1921), and in America.

Taking all in all, our Liturgy is composed of noble, edifying and Scriptural formularies, honored by the use of centuries. The Reformed Church has been called *semiliturgical,* standing midway between the extremes of Romanist overdoing and Puritan rigidity. May divine wisdom ever be given to retain this golden mean. The form without the essence is dead and vain worship. On the other hand, God has implanted feelings for harmony, beauty and æsthetics, which should not be killed but cultivated to the praise of Him of whom, through whom and to whom all things are created. Giving the congregation a large share in divine service is also a desideratum in the eyes of many. This and other considerations have led to proposals embodied in the next paragraph.

§6. LITURGICAL IMPROVEMENT PROPOSALS

At the Synod of 1916 the overture was presented: "Synod express the desirability of introducing a uniform order of services in our American-speaking churches, in which the congregation takes a more active part; and exhort these churches to come to an agreement in this matter if possible." This led to proposals laid before the 1920 Synod of the following:

I. ORDER OF WORSHIP FOR THE MORNING SERVICE.

PART   I.   (Organ Prelude.)
                Introductory Service.
                "Votum."
                Salutation.
                Psalm (Psalm 95, 84, etc.)

PART II.   Service of Reconciliation.
Summary of the Law (Matthew 22: 37-40).
Confession of Sin and Penitential Psalm (No. 140: 2).
Absolution.
Apostles' Creed.
Psalm of Praise.

PART III.   Service of Gratitude { Prayer and Benevolence

General Prayer, concluded with "Our Father", etc.
Offertory.
Psalm of Thanksgiving (Psalm 116, etc.).

PART IV.   Service of the Word.
Reading of Scripture.
Preaching.

PART V.   Closing Service.
Prayer of Thanksgiving.
Concluding Psalm or Doxology, or both.
Benediction.

II. ORDER OF WORSHIP FOR SECOND SERVICE.

(Organ Prelude.)

PART I.   Introductory Service.
"Votum."
Salutation.
Psalm.

PART II.   Service of Thanksgiving { Prayer Benevolence and Decalogue

General Prayer, concluded with "Our Father", etc.
Offertory.
Decalogue.
Psalm of Thanksgiving, or Refrain of No. 42.

PART III.   Service of the Word.
Reading of Scripture.
Preaching.

PART IV.   Closing Service.
Prayer of Thanksgiving.
Concluding Psalm or Doxology, or both.
Benediction.

TEST QUESTIONS

1. Give the five reasons for having a Creed in the shape of the doctrinal standards of a Church.
2. What can you say about the origin of the Heidelberg Catechism?
3. What can you tell about the character of this standard?
4. Describe the chief contents of the Belgic Confession.
5. Which five "points", or "heads of doctrine" form the Canons of Dordrecht?   Against which party were they directed?
6. What can you say about the Liturgy in general and the essence and purpose of divine worship involving the use of liturgical forms?
7. What can you say about the two sacramental Forms?
8. Which are the two disciplinary and the four ordination Forms?
9. What can you say about the Marriage Form and possible improvements of it?
10. Which points can you name in favor of the proposed liturgical improvement regarding the "order of worship"?

REFERENCES

Dr. J. I. Good, "The Heidelberg Catechism".
Dr. J. I. Good, "Famous Reformers", Chapter V.
Rev. F. Fortuin, "Drie Formulieren van Eenigheid".
Prof. W. Heyns, "Liturgiek".

CHAPTER IX

DISTINCTIVE PRINCIPLES AND PRACTICES OF THE CHRISTIAN REFORMED CHURCH

Introductory: Why so many different Churches? §1. Calvinism as a distinctive Principle. §2. The Psalter in divine worship. §3. Preaching on the Heidelberg Catechism. §4. Catechetical Instruction. §5. Christian Education: its fundamental principle; reasons for it. §6. The Separated Life: Secret Orders and Worldly Amusements.

INTRODUCTORY: WHY SO MANY DIFFERENT CHURCHES?

TO AN outsider it must be bewildering to see Christendom broken up into so many different organizations! All christians profess belief in the same God, they consider one book God's special revelation, they recite the same Apostles' Creed, and even express to believe: one holy *Catholic* Church. But behold—there are the three great divisions: Roman Catholic, Orthodox Eastern Church, and Protestantism. Moreover, Protestantism was already broken up in the days of the Reformation, so that we speak of the Anabaptist and Lutheran in distinction from the Reformed Reformation.

And even among the Reformed—what divisions! There are the Calvinistic and the Arminian groups, the Presbyterian and the Episcopalian groups, etc. Even the Reformed in America, holding the Heidelberg Catechism as their standard, are divided into several denominations.

Why so many different Churches? And we reply: that on the one hand the differences are not as deep and contradictory as they seem. There are many more essential things on which all true Christians agree than matters on which they differ. And one of the great mistakes of Christendom has been to so overemphasize the differences that the unity was often lost sight of. Did not already

Paul speak of one Lord, one faith, one baptism, as well as
one Spirit and one hope of the calling? (Eph. 4: 4, 5.)   On
the other hand, there are so many differences because
God's truth is so wonderfully rich, so deep, so high, so
broad, that the human mind can not comprehend it all,
nor correlate all of the truth in the same manner.   Moreover, the make-up of the human soul has something to do
with the formation of sects and groups of sects.   We have
already alluded to the differences between three religious
types: action, experiential and intellectual types.   Moreover, *racial* and *national* characteristics are factors in the
differentiations as well as historical development.   While
sin has, alas, a great deal to do with this dividing of Christendom, as well as human limitations, there is discernable
in it the overruling hand of God, who through this vast
diversity of denominations, brings out the wonderful full-
ness of His grace and the riches of His Word, and at the
same time teaches us the Christian grace of forbearance in
love and fraternal coöperation in Kingdom-work.

As we stated in Chapter II, §9, speaking about the
Pluriformity of the Church, each denomination is supposed to be different from others in its mission and its contribution to the Kingdom of God in a wider or narrower
sense, or in both.   But this is determined largely by the
national descent or racial character of each church, and
particularly by that what constantly, though not always
consciously, influences life: underlying *principles* which
control the practice and determine the mission and
contribution.

The following are the *distinctive Principles* and *Practices* of the Christian Reformed Church, not indeed as held
by it exclusively, but emphasized more by us than by other
denominations in our land.   They have been handed
down by the Dutch forebears of our people, or are ours by
logical inference or historical development, or by all of
these factors combined, more or less.

§1. CALVINISM AS A DISTINCTIVE PRINCIPLE

The Christian Reformed Church is distinctively a Calvinistic Church. Such was the case with the Church of the Fathers, Chapter I. The principles of Calvinism permeated its history and enterprises (Chapter II—VII). The Creed and Liturgy are filled with its spirit (Chapter VIII). In its upholding and unfolding its leaders have found its specific task and calling in America—see Chapter V, §8.

But *what is Calvinism*? Dr. A. Kuyper, in his *Stone Lectures,* says that the name Calvinist can be used as a sectarian name, a confessional designation, a denominational title, and a scientific name, and the latter either in an historical, philosophical or political sense. "Historically", we are informed, "the name Calvinism indicates the channel in which the Reformation moved, in so far as it was neither Lutheran, nor Anabaptist, nor Socinian. In the philosophical sense, we understand by it that system of conceptions which, under the influence of the master mind of Calvin raised it to dominance in the several spheres of life. And as a political name, Calvinism indicates that political movement which has guaranteed the liberty of nations in constitutional statesmanship; first in Holland, then in England, and since the close of the eighteenth century in the United States." Speaking of Calvinism in the last named strictly scientific sense, as an independent general tendency, which from a mother-principle of its own, has developed an independent form both for our *life* and for our *thought,* Dr. Kuyper gives the following as its *definition:* "Calvinism is rooted in a form of religion which was peculiarly its own, and from this specific religious consciousness there was developed *first* a peculiar theology, *then* a special Church Order, and *then* a given form for political and social life, for the interpretation of the moral world-order, for the relation between nature and grace, between Christianity and the world, between church and state, and finally for art and science."

Over against Paganism, Islamism, Romanism and Modernism, Dr. Kuyper posits Calvinism as a *life- and world-view*, or in briefer form: a *life-system* (Dutch: wereld-beschouwing).

Which is the determining principle of Calvinism, its *root principle?* Dr. H. E. Dosker states: "the *glory of God* is the center and mainspring of the entire system." Dr. G. P. Fisher: "Calvinism was distinguished by the stress which it laid on the sovereignty of God in the bestowal of grace."

That last is also evidently the conception of Dr. A. Kuyper. "First stands the confession of the absolute sovereignty of the Triune God: for of Him, through Him and unto Him are all things."   "To covet no other existence than for the sake of God, to long for nothing but for the will of God, and to be wholly absorbed in the glory of the name of the Lord, such is the pith and kernel of all true religion."

Dr. B. B. Warfield, speaking of the exact formulation of the *fundamental principle* of Calvinism, defines it as follows: "It lies in a profound apprehension of God in His majesty, with the inevitably accompanying poignant realization of the exact nature of the relation sustained to Him by the creature as such, and particularly by the sinful creature. He who believes in God without reserve, and is determined that God shall be God to him in all his thinking, feeling, willing—in the entire compass of his life—activities, intellectual, moral, spiritual, throughout all his individual, social, religious relation—is a Calvinist." (Schaff-Herzog Enc., s. v. "Calvinism".)

Elsewhere Dr. Warfield stated: "The formative principle of Calvinism is not to be found in its difference from other system, especially the Lutheran, for it has more

points of agreement than difference. No more is to be
found in the so-called 'five points' (see Chapter VIII, §3);
these but lead to the source from which they spring—a
vision of God in His glory. 'Calvinism begins, centers, and
ends with a vision of God in His majesty and the relation
of the sinful creature to Him and with this, an adoring
wonder that God receiveth sinners. It emphasizes (1) the-
ism, which comes to its rights only in a teleology which
recognizes God as the end of all; (2) the religious relation which attains its climax only when God is first;
(3) evangelicalism, which is stable only when it rests all
in God.

"Calvinism differs from theological system not in kind,
but in degree, embodying what all ought to be. Whoever
recognizes God and his own relation to God is, in so far,
a Calvinist. The consequence of Calvinism is a high super-
naturalism—in its view of miracles, of revelation, of the
Bible and of salvation. Calvinism stops nowhere short of
a God-centered world-view—God is all in all. It is the
only system relating the universe to the doctrine of grace
and the glory of God."

Dr. Emil Knodt: "The true world-center has been
recognized and acknowledged the clearest by Calvinism.
It is God's Sovereignty. God is its Alpha and Omega,
the Sovereignty of the Creator, the Sovereignty of the
Judge, the Sovereignty of a gracious King; and this
all comprehended in the Sovereignty of the Father
with his holy love. To entrust and submit one's
self to it unconditionally, that is *Religion*. Notwithstanding deep and humiliating acknowledgement of one's
own unworthiness and guilt and the weakness of others,
still to make God's law and right rule in the home, the
profession, the State, that is *Authority*. Not to be carried
away by impressions and impulses, but to trace God's
thoughts in the history of the Whole and of the Individual,

that is *Science*. Not to express imaginary pictures, but
divine reality—and in it the healthy as healthy and the
sick as sick, that is *Art*".[1]

It is this Calvinism which forms, as we already stated,
the bone and marrow of our Reformed Creed in its three
standards, the heart of the teachings, and the very spirit
of its Liturgy. It influences our conception of the other
distinctive principles and practices described in this Chapter. And we need not be ashamed of this Calvinism. Its
teachings, properly understood, are based upon the Word
of God. Its principles are the very warp of Holy Writ.
Every true Christian, even though professionally not accepting our Creed, is a Calvinist on his knees, in utter dependence on free grace. It still holds good and will as
long as the world endures, as Watson said in 1811 after
Bishop Tomlinson called Calvinism "dead": "such doctrines do not die; they only sleep", and as Froude expressed it: "Calvinism has appeared and re-appeared,
and in due time will re-appear again, unless God be an
illusion and man be as the beasts that perish".[2]

And Calvinism's *achievements* prove its value and
strength according to our Lord's declaration about a tree
being known by its fruit. "Calvinism has produced in all
countries in which it really dominated, a definite type of
character and conception of morals which was the
noblest that had yet appeared in the world."—*Carlyle*.

"Had it not been for the Puritans, political liberty
would propably have disappeared from the world. If ever
there were men who laid down their lives in the cause of
all mankind, it was those grim old Ironsides (of Crom-
well), whose watchwords were texts of Holy Writ; whose
battle-cries were hymns of praise. Those English Cal-

---

[1] Fabius, "Wezen van het Calvinisme", bladz. 31.
[2] "The Banner", March 22, 1917.

vinists didn't labor and die for themselves alone. They stood in the breach for all succeeding generations."—*John Fiske.*

"Out of this war (of Holland against Spain) of eighty years' duration, emerged a republic for two centuries the greatest in the world, a republic which was the instructor of the world in art and whose corner-stone was religious tolerance for all mankind."—*Campbell.*

"Calvinists have been the highest honor of their own age and the best models for imitation for every succeeding age."—*Encyclopedia Brittanica.*

§2. THE PSALTER IN DIVINE WORSHIP

Next to maintaing biblical Calvinism, the use of the *Psalter* in divine worship may well be called the second distinctive principle of the Christian Reformed Church. It is expressed in Article 69 of the *Church Order*: "In the churches only the 150 Psalms of David, the Ten Commandments, the Lord's Prayer, the Twelve Articles of Faith, the Songs of Mary, Zacharias, and Simeon, the Morning and Evening Hymns, and the Hymn of Prayer before the sermon shall be sung." The principle has been expressed in the motto: "In God's House nothing but God's Word, also in song." Calvin expressed this in still stricter way in the rule, published in 1542, that in the churches the Psalms of David alone should be used, because they were inspired by the Holy Spirit. "When we sing them we are certain of it that God puts these words into our mouth, as if He Himself sung in us to His own glory." The following replies may be given to the question: *"Why are you a Psalm-singing Church?"*

In the first place: there is *divine authority* for the use of the Psalter in divine worship. God's Word commands us: "Sing psalms to God and make a joyful noise." "Let us make a joyful noise to him with psalms." "Is any merry, let him sing psalms." Our second answer to the question, "Why sing Psalms?" is the *divine example* recorded in the Bible. They were used exclusively in the Old Testament Church, II Chron. 29: 30; Psalm 95: 2; Psalm 105: 2. Following the Old Testament examples we notice he example of our Lord Himself. At the close of the observance of the newly-instituted Lord's Supper: "they had sung an hymn." The "hymn" which was always sung in connection with the Passover was the Greal Hallel, consisting of Psalms 113 to 118, inclusive. It is generally agreed that Christ and His disciples used the Hebrew Psalter in their service of praise. There were no other sacred songs in existence. Christ Himself did not compose songs for religious worship nor direct others to do this work. He gave other important directions to the Church, but not one song did He give to be handed down to His followers. The example of Christ speaks volumes as to His will in the matter of praise.

The example of the *followers* of Christ is equally convincing. The apostles, when in prison, sang praises and the prisoners heard them. Is it a common sense idea to suppose that they composed the songs which they sang on that occasion? The only reasonable view is that they sang those inspired songs which they had been taught from their youth, and which were the long-established medium of praise for God's people. The early Christian converts, moreover, if they were Jews, would naturally use the Hebrew Psalter, and the gentile converts would, from the nature of the case, not be competent, all of a sudden, to compose a sacred hymnology. The "hymns" and "songs" mentioned in Eph. 5: 19 and Coll. 3: 16 evidently do not refer to human compositions, but to headings of various Psalms which in the Greek version, in use at the time, were named "hymns" and "songs". Thirty-four Psalms were called "songs" and five "hymns", while others had double titles, such as "psalm and song", "psalm and hymn", etc. No other compositions of this kind were extant in these early normative apostolic days. Moreover, the "Apostolical Constitutions", which show the customs of the Church from the times of the Apostles to the fourth century, inform us that "women, children, and the humblest laborers could repeat all the Psalms of David. They chanted them at home and abroad, and thus exercised their piety and refreshed their minds".[1]   Our third reason for singing Psalms is that they meet the great requirements of praise, exalting God in creation, providence, and redemption, while containing confessions of our unworthiness, expressions of our faith, our gratitude, our needs, etc. The Psalms are full of Christ in His Sonship, humanity, life, sufferings, atonement, offices, death, resurrection, ascension, heavenly glory, return to judge the world, etc. The Holy Spirit also is named in the Psalms repeatedly, as well as the heavenly Father. (Cf. Index of subjects in our U. P. Psalter, p. 368 ff.)

Dr. A. Kuyper gives the following additional reasons: In depth of spirituality the psalms excel the hymns; hymns have nearly everywhere crowded out the divinely-given collection, the Psalter; in the Psalms we hear the abiding, eternal, fundamental note of the pious heart resounding, whereas hymns are mostly of a temporary nature; hymns have nearly everywhere led to the introduction of choirs and to the silencing of the congregations, while in the struggle between hymns and Psalms, the indifferent all preferred the hymns and the pious the Psalms. They are the one set of songs to which all denominations should agree. They also bring out the oneness of the Church.

---

[1] Cf. A. M. Malcolm, Associate Presbyterian Magazine, August **1921.**

History shows us also that from the earliest times errorists have ever sought to make propaganda for their false teaching by means of hymns.

Finally, when the Psalms in public worship console and strengthen us, we can depend upon the promises which give us new courage: they are God's own words on which we can rely in life and in death.

It is on such grounds that the Reformed Churches have favored Psalmody—in divine worship in the churches, using the 150 Psalms of the Bible as their chief manual of praise. But they never occupied the exclusive standpoint of some of the Scotch churches in this regard. A few extra-psalmody selections have been found back of the Psalter ever since our fathers published their books of public praise, even as the Geneva Psalter of John Knox contained "spiritual songs".

The first complete Psalter used by our forebears during Reformation days was published in 1566 by Petrus Dathenus, already mentioned in Chapter I. This gifted though somewhat unsteady man based his metrical version on a French one published under Calvin's auspices. Its music is in part the work of BOURGEOIS, who lived and labored in Geneva in Calvin's days and of his Calvinistic colleague GOUDIMEL, once, at Rome, the teacher of the PALESTRINE. (Cf. *Stone Lectures*, p. 228.)

The version of Dathenus, though very rugged, endeared itself to our ancestors by precious associations and continued in use till 1773, when a new and much smoother versification appeared. It was this book which our pioneers carried with them to America, and the sweet, consoling, encouraging and New Testament spirit of this volume has not been equalled, much less surpassed by English versifications. Some of our German Churches use a Psalter version on the Dutch model, made by the Rev. M. Jorissen († 1823). Our American congregations employ the Psalter published in 1912 by the United Presbyterian Church, the work of a Joint Committee of nine American and Canadian Churches, on which our denomination was represented at first by the Rev. J. Groen, and later by the author of this book.[1] The music of the U. P. Psalter is varied and of excellent authorship as the superscriptions above each number indicate. (Cf. Indexes of tunes and composers, back of the Psalter, pp. 361—367.)

§3. PREACHING ON THE HEIDELBERG CATECHISM

The Christian Reformed Church in its Church Order, Article 68, insists on having the ministers of the congregations expound regularly the fifty-two Lord's Days of the Heidelberg Catechism, a division, by the way, dating from Reformation days. Regarding this rule some people have objected that it is man-made and unduly hampers the preacher in proclaiming such truths as the Spirit may lead him in or as the demand of the hour requires. Quite a common argument is that a man-made book like the Catechism is raised to the same level as the divinely-inspired Bible. Especially the Arminians of the days of the Synod of Dordrecht, 1618-1619, made much of the last mentioned objection.

Now in reply to these we might say that our fathers never meant the rule to be a strait-jacket. The general principle of our Book of Church Government about the *profit and edification* of the Church as a determining factor in the application of the rules, applies here also. Dr. Rutgers has brought that out beautifully in his *Geldigheid van de Oude Kerkenordening.* Moreover, preaching on

---

[1] A Psalter edition whose music had been arranged or composed by the Rev. H. Van der Werp (Chapter IV, §2) did not find denominational acceptance, although it is a meritorious production, more or less patterned after the Dutch Psalter. The U. P. Psalter was preferred as more simple, with classic tunes, greater variety and appropriateness, and more general usefulness.

the Catechism is not the only preaching to take place. As to the second objection—it rests on a misunderstanding. We do not preach on the Catechism in so far as it is a human document, but on the divine truths in it, "the sum of Christian Doctrine comprehended in the Heidelberg Catechism", as the Church Order expresses it, and that is taken from the Bible, in many instances transcribed literally. The objections, therefore, have no weight.

But on the other hand there are a number of weighty reasons in favor of obeying the rule of our fathers. If properly carried on, regular preaching on the Catechism, accompanied by constant and prayerful study, with application to the ever-changing conditions of Church and world, is a *boon* to the Church and ought faithfully to be continued. For which *reasons* ought this to be done? What *grounds* can be advanced for this distinctive practice?

(1) It keeps a living contact with the past of our people. Sermonic explanation of the "Heidelberger" is not an innovation, but a time-honored custom. In the same year in which Dathenus published the Catechism, a preacher in Amsterdam, Peter Gabriel, began to expound it every Sunday to his persecuted flock. The National Synod of The Hague, in 1586, prescribed that "the preachers must everywhere briefly explain the Heidelberg Catechism at the Sunday afternoon services." The Synod of Dordrecht in 1618-1619 also spoke in a similar way, insisting on it that this expounding should be so plain that the children of the Church could grasp the exposition, as well as the older ones—an exhortation not always borne in mind we fear. A time-honored custom this preaching certainly has become. And our reverence for the fathers, our obligations to Reformation days, our respect for the wisdom of our ancestors, should lead us to keep up this living contact with the past of our people.

(2)   Catechism-preaching constitutes a living bond of
union between the different congregations of a denomination, and the different divisions of Reformed Christendom.
The Roman Catholic Church demands that Mass everywhere be said in the Latin tongue, so that Roman Catholics
can go anywhere and everywhere to hear the same words,
and thus manifest the Catholicity or general character of
their Church. Among us as Reformed people, not a dead
language constitutes such a truly Catholic bond of union,
but the preaching of the living truths of the Bible of which
the Catechism is essentially a compendium. That means
a great deal in a world full of change. It means real, living uniformity of belief, amid the various nations and different churches, such as no Confession can bring about.
Confessions are but seldom read, whereas a Catechism explained regularly, gets into the very warp and woof of our
intellectual and spiritual life.

(3)   Catechism-preaching presents the truths of the
Bible as a *system*. The doctrines of God's Word form one
systematic whole. They form an unbroken chain. If one
link of truth is dropped, the whole system suffers. And
the Church is entitled to know, to feel, to hear, that what
it believes to be saving truth is not an aggregation of opinions, like a heap of sand is a pile of unconnected grains,
but an organic whole. Such will prevent shallow and indefinite thinking, with its sad lack of harmonizing of
doctrines.

(4)   Catechism-preaching safeguards the preacher
from one-sidedness in his treatment of Bible truth. It is a
well known fact that ministers have their doctrinal pref-
erences. Their characters differ also. One naturally is stern,
and feels like magnifying the Law as another John the
Baptist. A second one, with a nature of St. John the Divine, has much more love for the Gospel and its sweet
breathings of love. One is more philosophical, another

more practical. And so in still more variations there is marked difference between the servants of God.

But the preaching of the Catechism is a great help to deliver from one-sidedness and to develop an all-around appreciation and exposition of the many-sided truths of the Bible.

(5)   The usefulness of Catechism-preaching is shown in the fact that unpleasant as well as pleasant things can be presented without shocking the congregation. No one will deny that an exposition of the Seventh Command is necessary in our world of sin. So is the divine behest: "Thou shalt not steal", etc. Now, if a preacher should happen, all of a sudden, to announce that he is going to preach on the sin of adultery or theft, he is likely to set many tongues wagging and arouse many suspicions, whereas the exposition in the regular course of events, will drive the truth home without needless excitement. This has reference to all truths which men naturally dislike. For instance, also the one of total depravity, predestination, etc.

(6)   Catechism-preaching is useful because it magnifies religion as a living, soul-saving revelation, requiring personal embracing of God's truth and God's Savior. The direct, personal tone of the Catechism: "What is thine only comfort?", and the answer: "That I belong unto my faithful Savior", cuts off a great deal of verbose, empty, head-religion. And not only that, but the fact that the Catechism magnifies the living Christ as the great center of saving knowledge, as the indispensable, ever blessed Redeemer, renders it ever attractive, ever new and fresh. Because it satisfies the ever new longings of the human heart.

(7)   The systematic preaching of the Heidelberg book equips a church-member for holding his ground and de-

fending and spreading his principles. It calls his attention in a *systematic way* to the very deepest foundations
of our holy religion. It shows him what a firm foundation
the saints of the Lord have in the Word of God, in the
truth they embrace. It affords weapons to defend the
faith as well as means to carry on active warfare for God
and His Kingdom. It enables to quickly detect error in the
preaching of the unorthodox, and teaches to distinguish
between the precious and the vile. (Jer. 15: 19.)   Wise,
fresh, whole-souled, earnest preaching on the system of
truths of our Catechism has been an inestimable blessing
for countless numbers of people of the past. May it ever
continue such, generation after generation! (Cf. *The Banner,* January 2, 1913.)

§4.   CATECHETICAL INSTRUCTION

Not alone the congregation as a whole is to be faithfully and regularly instructed in the fundamentals of the
Christian religion—the youth of the Church in particular
is to be trained in these truths. That is another distinctive
principle and practice of the Christian Reformed denomination. From the beginning it laid emphasis on catechetical instruction, even as the Church of the fathers did.
This peculiar name for this religious education is, like the
word Catechism itself, derived from a Greek word of
which the word "echo" is a cognate form. The etymology,
however, suggests a descending rather than a reverber-
ating sound. Whether that "descending" had to do with
the raised platform of the teacher or the authority vested
in him, is a matter of dispute. Possibly both of these
ideas are correct. In the general sense of imparting oral
information, related words are used in Luke 1: 4; Acts
18: 25; 21: 21; Rom. 2: 18, etc. Inasmuch as oral instruction in the fundamentals of Christianity was the original
method to prepare people for baptism, the terms came into

use to designate the elementary religious instruction as imparted by the Church. Catechetical instruction is based on Holy Writ. God had known Abram, the Bible tells us, to the end that he might command his children to keep the way of Jehovah (Gen. 18: 19), and in the Old Testament the duty is stressed time and again. Jesus impressed on Peter the feeding of the lambs of the fold, John 21: 15. In harmony with this we find catechetical instruction in all churches of Christendom, and that not alone in the Old World but also in the New. Some have decried our instruction of this kind as "Dutch", and consequently un-American. But this is far from being the case. The Pilgrim Fathers and Puritans brought their catechisms along and faithfully instructed their young people in their truths. The *New England Primer* was a catechism, and "it contributed perhaps more than any other book, except the Bible, to the molding of those sturdy generations that gave to America its liberty and its institutions" (Betts, *History of Religious Education,* p. 37; 1923). Watts' catechisms have been in use a long time among the best American people, and the Westminster Catechism is being faithfully taught to the Presbyterians of the South, and to the Covenanters of the North—Americans of the oldest and sturdiest stock. In fact, in recent years, the confession is made repeatedly in American denominational journals, that churches which allowed catechetical instruction to be neglected, made a fatal mistake and in the "week-day religious instruction classes" there is revived, under a new name and with improved methods, what our fathers have maintained, thank God, to this day—*catechetical instruction.*

This may be defined as the educational work of the Church through its ministry, to bring the children of the Covenant of grace to spiritual and ecclesiastical maturity, to a walking in Covenant ways, to inherit the blessings of the Covenant, to build up the Church and to assist in carrying out its mission. The sacred, essential truths are to be imbedded and anchored in the mind; the emotions are to be aroused to take a living interest in them, the will is to be bent so that it may come to embrace God's truth, and accept the God of that truth as Sovereign and Father in Christ, and to devote the entire life, its talents and its possessions, to the service of God in the coming of His Kingdom. All of this is aimed at in the blessed work, "that the man of God may be perfect, thoroughly furnished unto all good works", II Tim. 3: 17. Prof. W. Heyns, whose definition of the subject we adapted, states in his *Catechetiek*, that the *basis* of the work lies in the Covenant of grace. The children of the Church belong to that Covenant, are partakers of its blessings, and consequently are under its ministry. The *character* of this religious education is religious, ecclesiastical, authoritative, and elementary. By religious is meant that its contents are not to be those of secular education, but distinctly of spiritual things, pertaining to the Covenant of grace. Ecclesiastical signifies that the Church as such, through its ministry, imparts the instruction, and because of this it is authoritative with Christ's commandment back of it (Matt. 28: 19; Mark 16: 16), and attendance upon it a matter of sacred duty, to which, moreover, in the Reformed Churches, the parents openly bind themselves as a part of the vows made at the baptism of their children. That the instruction is to be elementary is a matter of course. The aim of the work is not to train the ministry of the Church by means of this. The Theological School serves that purpose. (Chapter VI, §1—§4.)

Its aim is rather to bring the children of the Church to their maturity, their majority, as ordinary church-members in full communion, to know the fundamentals of religion, to walk in the ways of the Covenant, to inherit its blessings and then give themselves in personal, believing consecration, to the upbuilding of the Church formed by God's Covenant people, and to assist in the carrying out of its mission. This is a glorious objective, although a difficult one. But *very essential*. Especially in our country and age, with winds of all kinds of doctrines blowing, much superficiality abroad, and but little time somehow, for thorough study of fundamentals, the importance of this branch of Kingdom activity can not easily be overemphasized. The 1922 Synod was reminded of "the great importance of this instruction for our youth, the dangers that threaten this institution in our country, and the possibility that we ourselves enhance these dangers by neglecting to improve the instruction. Hence the expressed desire for obtaining greater unity in the matter, a graded system adapted to the gradually increasing intellectual, moral and spiritual needs of the children, as well as for improvement in the matter of promotion, methods of instruction and equipment. The Synod of 1912 decided that the higher Catechetical classes were to study the "Compendium" and the "Catechism", (Chapter VIII, §1). For classes conducted in English the Synod recommended the series of Catechetical books published by the Revs. H. Beets and M. J. Bosma: *Borstius' Primer of Bible Truths, Sacred History for Juniors, Sacred History for Seniors,* and *Compendium of the Christian Religion Enlarged.*

May catechetical instruction, the sheet-anchor of a truly Reformed Church, ever be our cherished asset. Even outsiders have come to "recognize that the Christian Reformed Church has a most excellent program of Christian education based on sound principles and operating most effectively". But our motto should be: "Excelsior'..

§5. CHRISTIAN EDUCATION

In Chapter VI, §6, we mentioned that the principle of education in Christian Schools is a part of the Church Order, Article 21. In regard to this matter also we may speak of a distinctive *principle* and practice of the Christian Reformed Church, for which good reasons can be advanced. That *principle,* a very fundamental one, is given by Mr. B. J. Bennink as follows:

"This principle circles around the simple but important question: The child, whose is it? Now its answer is readily given and agreed to by all: the child naturally belongs to the parents who gave him birth.

"In Socialistic circles the old Platonic idea that children belong to the State may still be held, and the Roman Catholic may sanction the idea that the Church owns the child, the man whose mind is unbiased will unhesitatingly declare, surely the child belongs to the parents, and—they are its responsible educators.

"Let us grasp and hold to this basic truth, it settles the right of existence for the Christian School fundamentally and radically.

"The State is greatly interested in the coming generation as its future citizens, but they are 'minors', and as such entirely in charge of the parents to whom their bringing-up is left, both as to body and mind, and only in case of extreme neglect may the State interfere in behalf of the delinquent.

"Of course, the State as well as the Church is entitled to supervision of the work of the parents in educating the child, but both Church and State should refrain from taking the children away from their parents and function as schoolmaster.

"Thus the school originates from the parents; they erect and maintain it, engage a teacher and pay him, and determine the quality and quantity of instruction to be given. State and Church watch with deep interest these doings of the parents, give advice, if necessary, so as to produce the wished-for results, but in no way should they molest the parents in the execution of their most important and undeniable right to educate their own children.

"From this sound principle springs forth the free and independent school of a free and independent people. But there is more.

"We do not only call our school *free,* but also *Christian.* These two qualifications are essential. The adjective 'Christian' in our days has a general and a specific meaning. Its general meaning is quite well synonymous with civilized, and as such it may be attributed to anything not pagan. But Reformed people have an altogether different conception of the word christian. They take it in the only real, Biblical sense, and then its meaning is directly and absolutely connected with the conception they have of the *Christ,* revealed as the Son of God, the Redeemer of His people, whom they acknowledge and honor as their Prophet, Priest, and King; Christ, the 'last Adam', in the Covenant of Grace, in whom their children are sanctified because they are born as the children of that Covenant."

In the *Young Calvinist,* September, 1923, the Rev. H. J. Kuiper mentions as an additional scriptural principle that *all* knowledge and science should be in harmony with the Bible.

"One of the principal functions of a school is to give *instruction* in various branches of study of which the child must have some knowledge to be equipped for its task in life. It must be able to read and write and figure. It must know something about its own body, the earth, its country and its history. The underlying and guiding principles in all these branches of study (relating, for example, to the origin of the earth, the origin and purpose of government) are matters of *faith.* Here the ways of the believer and the unbeliever must part. The true believer finds these principles in Scripture, which the unbelieving world does not receive because it is blind and hostile to

the truth. Our children cannot arrive at "a life and world
view" which is in harmony with the truth as revealed in
the Word of God unless the *instruction* which they receive
is permeated with the fundamental principles of this
Word.

"Scripture teaches that the fear of the Lord is the beginning of wisdom and of knowledge. Without the fear
of the Lord, as taught in Scripture, and (in the subjective
sense) as present in the heart, true knowledge, knowledge
of the origin and meaning and purpose of all things, is
simply impossible. This text plainly shows how inseparable the connection is between true *religion* and true
science. Without religion (the fear of the Lord) no real
knowledge or science. One may know many facts and
have much learning, but unless he is a Christian, he has
no *knowledge,* in the deepest sense of the word."

On the basis of these fundamental principles, we can
name several *reasons* to substantiate and affirm them.

(1)   The vow made by parents at the baptism of their
children to see the children instructed and brought up in
the aforesaid doctrines of our religion.

(2)   Our love of the Word of God demands a place for
it in the day school as well as in the home, and in the
Sunday school.

(3)   As lovers of christian song we want our children
to sing of their Redeemer as well as of their Creator,
something which state institutions do not allow.

(4)   We want prayer made in Christ's name in the
school, and for obvious reasons this, too, cannot be done in
public schools.

(5)   We desire religion to permeate not alone all of
our life, but likewise all of the education of the Covenant
children. We want to make "religious education an in-

tegral part of the child's education throughout the whole period of its plastic development, building religious concepts, attitudes, and habits into the expanding life from the first, so that they may become an inseparable part of its structure". (G. H. Betts, *New Program of Religious Education*.)

(6) Our conception of the aim of life differs radically from that of the world. We consider its chief aim to glorify God and to enjoy Him forever. Secular education under state control cannot very well aim higher than good citizenship and success.

(7) Our view of mankind as fallen and in absolute need of the regenerating power of the Holy Spirit, pledged to our children in Baptism, is radically different from that of the world, especially as it is under the spell of the evolutionary hypothesis.

(8) As christian patriots we demand religious training as a basis for morality. The "Father of his country" already warned us to "indulge with caution the supposition that morality can be maintained without religion", and history has proven time and again that Washington was right on the subject. Without religious authority morality is built on sand. (Compare the Ordinance of the Northwest, 1787.)

(9) The acknowledged purpose of education being training of character and training for leadership, we believe that religion should be an integral part of this training, that there may be a proper reckoning with God, His revelation and His judgment-day.

(10) The avowed purpose of our people's coming hither (Chapter I, §8) obligates us to give our children a christian education.

Since it is impossible, in fairness to our fellow-citizens who hold entirely different views concerning the above-named important matters, to have the public schools thoroughly christian, the only alternative left us is to erect and maintain free christian schools.   May all orthodox christians come to see this, also as a matter of consistency, since all denominations believe in having secondary and higher schools of a christian character at home and christian primary schools in foreign mission fields.   This is also in accordance with American tradition since the founders of our national life maintained christian schools, as history shows and such books as the *New England Primer,* named in §4, abundantly prove.

§6.   THE SEPARATED LIFE: SECRET ORDERS AND WORLDLY AMUSEMENTS

The Word of God calls God's children a "peculiar people", a people of God's own possession (Titus 2: 14; I Peter 2: 9) ; "unspotted from the world" (James 1: 17). While this cannot be carried out fully in this dispensation, "for then ye must needs go out of the world" (I Cor. 5: 10), in which we must be a salt and a leaven (Matt. 5: 13), it must be the aim of the christian to keep himself aloof as much as possible from sinful entanglements. "Be not unequally yoked with unbelievers" is the apostolic injunction (II Cor. 6: 14).   This applies to marriages and other relationships of life.   The Christian Reformed Church has been led to apply this principle of separation especially to two matters: Secret orders and worldly amusements.

Secret Orders have from the beginning been condemned as fellowships to be avoided as incompatible with membership in good standing, and as we related, this stand has been repeatedly affirmed.   Secret Orders or Socities have been *defined* as human, public organizations which conceal their principles and practices, more or less, from the public.   We distinguish, of course, between

privacy and secrecy. Privacy relates to the judicious con-
cealment from public view of that which concerns ourselves only, as individuals, families, or societies. Secrecy
as applied to secret societies, relates to the intentional con-
cealment by a public institution of that which in some
measure concerns all of us. But why oppose them and insist on the separated life of the membership of the Church
in this regard? We reply: *Secret societies are contrary
to the Word of God.*

(1) Principally, because their initiation oaths, binding to things not yet made known to the candidate for admission, are unscriptural. (Lev. 5: 4-6; Matt. 14: 6-10.)
The oath is the bond of society in promoting trustworthi-
ness among men. It accomplishes this in various ways:
In solemnizing covenants, Gen. 14: 22, 23; 26: 26-29; in
solemnizing testimony, Ex. 22: 10, 11; Num. 5: 19-24;
Heb. 6: 16; in confirming vows of loyalty to sovereigns and
leaders, Eccl. 8: 2; 2 Kings 11: 4; 2: 2; in promoting fidel-
ity to official trust, 1 Sam. 12: 5. The oath should therefore be considered very solemn, only to be uttered when
the God-ordained magistrates or God's honor and the
safety of our fellowmen require it. Now it is very evident that the heads of the different lodges are not "God-
ordained magistrates", and therefore have no authority to
administer oaths.

It is also plain that the honor of God or the safety of
our fellowmen does not necessitate such solemn oaths.

*These oaths are therefore unwarranted; and being so,
are sinful. And this puts the case but mildly.* Some of
the oaths administered in Masonic degrees are open to
even far more serious objection, so that the epithets of
"terrible" and "fearful" have not unjustly been applied
to them.

(2) The secrecy of these societies in general is unscriptural, John 3: 19-21; 18: 20. Good things should be

revealed; bad things should not be concealed. The Church of Christ is an open institution, Isaiah 55: 1; Rev. 22: 17.

(3)   Their selfishness is unscriptural, Luke 10: 30-37; Eph. 6: 10; 1 Peter 5: 17; Gal. 5: 2. The Church of Christ inculcates the spirit of unselfishness and love to all men, whereas the "charity" of lodges is nothing higher than that of the publicans of which the Savior spoke, Matt. 5: "If ye love them which love you, what reward have you?" We look upon the beneficiary efforts as simply "business" propositions. Only a certain class of people is admitted into the lodge, at a certain age, in good health, and those admitted only get out of it on an average what has been put in, minus the salaries of the officers, etc.

Now we do not condemn it that the beneficiary work is put on a solid basis—far from it. But that those features which are business propositions pure and simple are time and again heralded as "charity", that is what we object to.

(4)   Their binding together in a common brotherhood the godly and the ungodly is unscriptural, 2 Cor. 6: 14. The Church of Christ binds together in a common brotherhood all true believers who are made one in character and life through Christ, 1 Cor. 10: 17; John 6: 48.

(5)   There are grounds to fear that the lodge at times has tried to be "an empire within and empire" to the detriment of justice to all and special privileges to none, to say the least. History testifies to this in America. And from as far away as the Philippines, the dailies of November 20, 1923, carried the news that municipal officials of these islands were forbidden to join secret orders because as stated: "In such organizations members are inclined, in accordance with secret vows or rituals, to enforce the law less rigorously whenever fellow-members are affected unfavorably".

(6)   Our sixth objection is *the nomenclature of most lodges. We consider some of that immodest, if not lu-*

dicrous, and unrepublican, and some even blasphemous.
That different officers and members call themselves chan-
cellor commanders, knights, sir knights, nobles, princes
and potentates is to our mind most immodest and un-re-
publican, if not ridiculous and bombastic, savoring too
much of child's play and unworthy of serious men. The
same can be said of some paraphernalia. But our greatest
objection is against names which we consider blasphemous. These are found especially among the Masons.
To call a child of dust a "worshipful master", like the head
of a local Masonic lodge is called, we consider sinful.
The same is true of titles like the following: "Mystic Order of Veiled Prophets of the Enchanted Realm", "Thrice
Illustrious Knights of the Cross", "Princes of Jerusalem",
"Degree of Perfection or Grand-Elect Perfect and Sublime
Masons", etc. It seems to us any Christian who weighs
each of these names well will admit that they are not
alone contrary to all modesty but, as we said, of a blasphemous character. No sinner (as each of us is) ought to
dare to assume such names and titles, full of the most
solemn significance.

(7)   Another objection to the secret societies is: *many
of their ceremonies are either too frivolous for an earnest
christian to engage in, or too dangerous,* and therefore
contrary to the spirit of God's command, "Thou shalt not
kill". The frivolity of some ceremonies is too evident to
need any illustration, and the daily papers time and again
contain notices of accidents and deaths caused by different
initiation ceremonies.

(8)   Our eighth objection is *the use or rather abuse of
the Bible in the lodge ritual.* In the ritual of the Woodmen some texts are quoted which are far too exalted in
meaning to be used as such. For instance, when it speaks
of the apple-tree and the north wind, taken from the Song

of Solomon, and commonly explained to refer to no less
hallowed ones than our Savior and the Holy Spirit.

In the Odd Fellows' ritual an unwarranted use is made
of the parable of the Samaritan. Similar things could be
stated in regard to other lodges. And to this unwarranted
use of the Word of God we are strongly opposed. The
Bible is far too sacred a book to be used to lend dignity
and solemnity to meetings not exclusively christian and
certainly not intended to be meetings for divine worship.

(9)   Finally, our objection against the lodge is that,
*while Christ as the Savior is virtually excluded, deceased
members are nevertheless often declared saved when the
burial service is read.* The ritual of the Woodmen, e.g.,
contains the expression: "He shall live in the eternal
glories of his Maker." This is read alike over the remains
of unbelievers as well as of saints, and since Christ's is
the only name under heaven by which we are to be saved,
therefore we consider it unwarranted and soul-deluding
that any such statements are uttered, Tim. 3: 15, 16; John
8: 32; Matt. 28: 20.

Of course, we do not claim that secret societies are all
equally objectionable. They have many members who are
better than the systems themselves. But on the grounds
given, membership in them is incompatible with that of
membership in the denomination whose stand we
described.

Worldly Amusements, such as *card playing, theatre-
going* and *dancing* are also held to be contrary to the demands of a really separated life. Why?

I.   Each has its peculiar element of danger.

(1)   The fascination of *cards* is the so-called element
of chance. Chance is that which happens without any
known cause. The reason that card playing is more popu-

lar than other games of chance is "because this strange assembly of pasteboards, with their varying values, admits of infinite multiplying and balancing of chances." In every normal person four faculties of the soul are the basis of conduct—reason, conscience, affections, and will. The element of chance hinders and attacks the free operation of these faculties. The mind is thrown into confusion and feverish excitement, and hopes against hope. "Constant playing produces aggravated stimulations which amount to intoxication. This, again, produces enervation and effects for evil the whole intellectual and moral nature. Card-playing finally leads to gambling, by dem in.l-ing the added excitement of possible gain, and gambling to all kinds of dishonesty and deception". Moreover, as Dr. Kuyper puts it (*Stone Lectures,* p. 93), "Card-playing fosters in our heart the dangerous tendency to look away from God, and to put our trust in Fortune or Luck, placing Fortune above the disposition of God, and the hankering after Chance above the firm confidence in His Will. To fear God, and to bid for favors of Fortune, seems to the Calvinist as irreconcilable as fire and water."

(2) The fascination of the *theatre* is the element of entertainment. The theatre is a playhouse. Education, morality, public welfare—everything is subordinated to the one demand for entertainment. In providing this the theatre too frequently appeals to the unreal and sensational, and provides plays that exalt vice and debase virtue. The entertainers frequently are or become men and women of loose character, involving moral sacrifice which ruins souls and strikes at the foundation of society, while the constant and ever-changing presentation of the character of other persons hampers the molding of one's own personal character. (Cf. *Stone Lectures,* p. 94).

(3) The fascination of *dancing* is the element of sex. Dancing is the only amusement demanding for its popu-

larity the participation of both sexes. Sex invests it with
its chiefest charm. "Passion, however skillfully veiled,
lies at the basis of the modern dance". The impure suggestion is often more manifest in the afterthought than in
the act of dancing. To defend the modern dance from the
Scriptures (Eccl. 3: 4) is to manifest ignorance and to be
almost guilty of sacrilege.

II.   All three have objectionable elements in common.

(1)   They are alike perversions of good things, namely, the lot, fiction, and the social mingling of the sexes. It
is evident that they are perversions because they render
wholesome amusements tame and unsatisfying.

(2)   They are alike worldly and should not be classed
as "questionable". The fruit borne by them shows that
their origin is not good. Matt. 7: 17, 18.

(3)   They are alike hostile to true religion in its in-
ception and progress. It seems impossible to be devoted to
them and at the same time be whole-heartedly consecrated
to God and His service. Gal. 5: 16, 17; Matt. 6: 24.

(4)   They are alike in seeking the ruin of the young.
Eccl. 11: 9.

III.   All three are condemned as unfit for Christians.

(1)   By God's Word. 1 Cor. 10: 31; Heb. 12: 1; Matt.
6: 24; Rom. 12: 2; 8: 5-8; 1 John 2: 15-17; Col. 3: 1, 2; Gal.
5: 19-25; 6: 7, 8.

(2)   By the Church of Christ. 1 Peter 2: 9.

(3)   By the enlightened Christian conscience. Rom.
14: 23.

(4)   By the exacting judgment of the unconverted.
2 Sam. 12: 14; Rom. 2: 24.[1]

---

[1] We are considerably indebted regarding the material given in
§6 to the "Manual of Doctrine", (Reformed Presbyterian Church),
edited by Rev. C. McLeod Smith, published in 1911.

TEST QUESTIONS

1. What do you understand by Calvinism?
2. What does Dr. Warfield say about the nature of Calvinism and the things it emphasizes?
3. Why do we use the Psalter as our chief manual of public praise?
4. What can you say about the Psalter version in use among us?
5. Why does the Church insist on Catechism preaching?
6. What is the nature and purpose of Catechetical instruction? Which benefits have you derived from it?
7. What are the fundamental principles underlying the Christian education movement?
8. Which of the ten reasons based on these principles appear the strongest to you?
9. Which are our chief reasons for our stand against secret orders?
10. Why does the separated life involve a shunning of worldly amusements?

REFERENCES

Dr. A. Kuyper, "Calvinism, Six Stone Lectures."

Dr. S. L. Morris, "Presbyterianism, Its Principles and Practice."

N. S. McFetridge, "Calvinism in History."

"Calvin and the Reformation", by Doumergue, Lang, Bavinck and Warfield.

Prof. L. Berkhof, "Subjects and Outlines."

Prof. W. Heyns, "Handboek voor de Catechetiek."

Dr. M. Reu, "Catechetics."

Dr. J. McNaugher, et. al., "The Psalms in Worship."

Dr. D. T. Bonner, "The Psalmody Question."

Books by Dr. Charles A. Blanchard and others on Secret Orders, published by the National Christian Association, 850 West Madison Street, Chicago, Illinois.

CHAPTER X

THE CHRISTIAN REFORMED CHURCH GOVERNMENT AND CHURCH ORDER

INTRODUCTORY: THE WHY OF CHURCH GOVERNMENT AND CHURCH ORDER

THERE HAVE been and are people who, on principle, are opposed to any such rules and regulations as involved in this Chapter. The Quakers and Plymouth Brethren hold that the Church is an exclusively spiritual body, destitute of all organization, bound together only by their mutual relation to their common Lord. The Church, according to this theory, so far as outward bonds are concerned, is only an aggregation of isolated units, saints, brethren, disciples. This view confounds the visible with the invisible Church. The people speaking of "optional Church government", hold a related theory. The form of Church polity is simply a matter of expediency. Each body of believers may adopt such methods of organization as it considers most convenient and efficient—thus opening the door to all kinds of arbitrariness.

Over against this the great majority of Christians have always held to the necessity of some form of outward organization and rules and regulations governing it. As a flock needs a shepherd, a body and a family a head, so with the flock of Christ, the body of believers, the household of God. The necessity of this is seen at once if we consider that believers have many common interests, a common task, and sometimes are confronted by a common foe. Lack of all outward organization would render it impossible to fulfill its calling properly. Therefore we find our Lord instituting the apostolate even before the Church in its New Testament form was constituted. Moreover, the Bible speaks of *ruling* elders, of "governments", (1 Cor. 12: 28), and Paul admonishes that "all things be done decently and in order". 1 Cor. 14: 40. (Cf. Article XXX, Confession of Faith.)

In a notable address given at a meeting of the Federation of Reformed Churches of Germany, Sept., 1923, in the historical city of Emden, §4 below, Dr. H. Bouwman, of Kampen, deduced the necessity of church federation (kerkverband) from the fact of the unity of the Church in Christ, John 15; Eph. 4: 6; Coll. 2: 19; the need the one church has of the others, Rom. 15: 26; II Cor. 8: 1; I Cor. 12: 27; and the maintaining of the liberty of local churches in the face of the possibility of having its office-bearers lord it over it. A church arbitrarily keeping itself apart from the rest, is apt to degenerate into a sect. Moreover, different things should not be disposed of by one local church, viz. those pertaining to their relation to others, (gemeenschapsleven) and the fixing of general principles of doctrine, liturgy, and discipline.

§1.   OTHER SYSTEMS OF CHURCH GOVERNMENT

While the Church of all ages has been a unit, or practically so, in deeming church government a necessity, there is great diversity as to the *kind* of organization called for. And just like in civil government we have several types, so as to that of the Church. Governments in a political sense are of three general forms: the monarchial, the aristocratic, and the democratic. A *monarchy* signifies a country "ruled by one", having one person at the head, either ruling with absolute power, or limited by a constitution. Of this type is the Roman Catholic Church government, headed by the Pope. The term "hierarchy" or priest-rule has at times been applied to describe this and kindred types of government. An *aristocracy*, also called *oligarchy*, that is. rule by the "best" or by the "few", places the government into the hands of a small number of chief persons. The Episcopalian denominations belong to this type. *Democracy* indicates rule by the people. All denominations following the *Independent* order of church government aim at a democracy in the full sense. The "people, that is, the membership of the various congregations, rule the churches. The leadership and authority of the office-bearers as representing Christ as the head of the church, are practically set aside. Popular sovereignty is embodied in this form of Church polity. Each local congregation is absolutely autonomous, that is, independent of its sister or other organizaitons. Church assemblies of wider scope have no more than advisory power. Hence the name "Council" or "Conference", bodies without legislative authority whatever. Confessional statements are merely "Declarations", of what at the time happen to be the doctrinal views of the majority of the brethren in conference. Historical continuity is thus practically broken. Individualism predominates. The opposite of this Independent extreme is *Collegialism,* in which central government ("Besturen") infringes unduly upon the autonomy or self-rule of the local churches. (Cf. Chapter I, §6.)

§2. THE PRESBYTERIAN SYSTEM AND ITS PRINCIPLES

A combination of the three types just named forms what is called the Reformed or Presbyterian System or Order of Church government. It is also named: Presbyterial-Synodal. "Presbyterian" is derived from the Greek word "presbyter", indicating an elderly person. The name in the connection here discussed signifies: rule by elders, i.e. teaching and ruling elders of the congregations. Historically the name came into prominence as opposed to rule by bishops as church prelates, although originally the words elder and bishop were synonymous. (Compare Acts 20:17 and Acts 20:28; Titus 1:4, 7.) This Presbyterian system, held by practically all Reformed Churches (hence the name *Reformed* system), is *monarchial* because it considers Christ the sole and sovereign Head of the Church. (Compare Chapter I, §4.) It is *aristocratic* in so far as it holds that Christ's authority is delegated to his representatives and instruments: the teaching and ruling eldership. And it is *democratic* because it accords to all communicant members in good standing the right to share in the government of the church by voting for its officers and in other ways coöperating in the activities of the congregation. There is no difference between ordinary church-members as "laymen", and others who compose the "clergy", even as the "parity" of the ministers is a fundamental principle of the system. (See Article 84 of the Church Order and compare Chapter I, §4.) The following may be called the chief *principles* underlying the Presbyterian order of church government.

(1) The Sovereignty of God. (Compare Chapter IX, §1). Christ has sovereignly been "set" as *King* over Zion, (Psalm 2:6), and God's Word is the Constitution of the Church. "For the *Lord* is our Judge, the *Lord* is our Lawgiver, the *Lord* is our King". (Isaiah 33:22.)

(2) Christ exercises His authority by means of His *office-bearers*. They are His "ministers" or servants, His instruments. Their power is not original. They have no authority for legislating laws not found in or based on the Word of their Lord. Their power is only declarative, regulative, executive, subject to the Word, under guidance of the Holy Spirit.

(3)   These office-bearers are called, in the sense of being designated, by the various churches as instruments, not deriving their authority from the congregations however—(such would be a form of popular sovereignty)—but from Christ whom they represent.

(4)   The various churches are considered complete local manifestations of the body of Christ.   There is a parity of churches as well as of office-bearers, (Article 84, Church Order) and each congregation possesses *autonomy* (self-rule), except in so far as it has transferred some of its rights to other church judicatories in the interests of Federation in *classical* or *synodical* organizations.   The Reformed system in this regard stands midway between the extremes of a closely-knit monarchy, exemplified by the *Collegialistic* and other systems, and that of the *Independents* whose Confederacy has no more than advisory power   (*The Banner,* February 5, 1920.)

In a negative way we may deduce from these principles that no decisions may be taken by the authorities which infringe on the sovereignty of the Church's head, or conflict with the parity of the office-bearers or churches. Arbitrary rule of one brother over another or one church or judicatory over another, is forbidden also. No church-rule may arbitrarily burden the members, infringing on their christian liberty.   Each regulation made must be promotive of the order and profit or welfare of the church. (1 Cor. 14: 40; Eph. 4: 12.)   Regulations are to be made with "common consent", that is by majority vote of the properly delegated members of the respective judicatories.

§3.   CHURCH JUDICATORIES ACCORDING TO THE PRESBYTERIAN ORDER

The Bible does not alone furnish authority for the fundamental ideas of the Presbyterian system outlined above, but also for the various church courts or *judicatories* belonging to it. In the 15th chapter of Acts we read of the church at Antioch disturbed by a question of rites and ceremonies, a question which could not be settled locally. Hence it was referred to a broader assembly at Jerusalem, composed of apostles and elders. After much deliberation a decision was made and that decision was not simply to affect Antioch, where the question arose, but the entire Church. "And as they went through the cities, they delivered them the decrees to keep which had been ordained of the apostles and elders that were at Jerusalem." Acts 16: 4. In the Christian Reformed Church the following judicatories exist. The first is the *consistory*, composed of the elders, both teaching and ruling, in small churches augmented by the deacons. These consistory members are chosen by the communicant members in good standing. (Compare Acts 1: 13-26.) In our Church Order rules governing the consistories are found in Articles 37—40.

Delegates from consistories comprising certain *groups* of churches, meet from time to time in a *Classis* or Presbytery, the second judicatory. (1 Tim. 4: 14.) Its duties, etc., are outlined in Articles 41—45 of the Church Order. Only teaching and ruling elders are eligible to represent their consistories, though in exceptional circumstances deacons may be accorded a seat. Specified numbers of both teaching and ruling elders in equal numbers, are delegated by the classical judicatories to meet as a third judicatory called a *Synod*. In the case of the Christian Reformed Church the Synod comprises the representatives of all the Classes of the entire denomination. See Article 50 of the Church Order. Larger denominations have Particular Synods as distinguished from General Synods or General Assemblies, the broadest kind of church judicatories. (For Particular Synods see Articles 47—49 of the Church Order.)

§4. HISTORY, CHARACTER AND AUTHORITY OF THE CHURCH ORDER

The foundations of the Church Order of the Reformed Churches of Dutch origin were laid during the terrible days of the bloody Spanish and Romish persecution when martyr fires were burning in the Netherlands, but when men like Dathenus, de Bray, Marnix, and others held their synodical meetings in Antwerp and elsewhere, already in 1563. A "Convent" of exiled pastors and elders meeting at Wesel, 1568, was particularly active in laying down certain regulative principles, and still more the Synod of 1571, held in the East Friesian city of Emden, the haven of refuge of many of our exiled forebears. Other Synods followed, to revise, condense and augment these articles as the case might be, until at the great Synod of Dordrecht, 1618-'19, the Church Order was once more gone over thoroughly by this National Synod of the Church of our fathers, see Chapter I, §6. But not all the Netherland churches were allowed by the civil government to conduct their affairs according to its regulations, even though some of them accorded more authority to the "magistracy" than the principle of the separation between Church and State (see Chapter V, §6) allowed. The reorganization of the Netherland Church under King William I, (Chapter I, §6), practically shelved the Church Order of Dordrecht. But the fathers of the Dutch Secession restored it to authority, barring things pertaining to the civil government's interference and other obsolete matters. It was this Church Order, with the reservations or changed referred to above, that was adopted when the Christian Reformed Church effected its separate organization in 1857, as related in Chapter II, §7.

The *character* or essence (wezen) has been said to be that of a collection "of *general rules* for the good order of church life",to be distinguished from ecclesiastical resolutions (decrees), and customs. A church resolution or decree furnishes the application of a general principle in a given case. A custom is a usage which by means of long observance has obtained a certain stability or fixedness.

The *authority* of the Church Order is built on the command regarding subjection to office-bearers. Like children are owing obedience to their parents, Eph. 6: 1-3; Col. 3: 20; and subjects to magistrates, Rom. 13: 1-7, so the Lord demands obedience to church authorities, as evident from Matt. 16: 19; 18: 18; John 20: 21, 23; Acts 15: 27-29; and especially Heb. 13: 7 and 17: "Obey them that have the rule over you, and submit to them; for they watch in behalf of your souls, as they that shall give account."

The Church Order's authority, however, while it has an ecclesiastical character, is not conscience-binding in an absolute sense. The Lord alone can bind the conscience, James 4: 12: "One only, is the Law-giver and Judge, even He who is able to save and to destroy."

Church rules are of a regulating character and bind the conscience only in so far as they are taken from the Scriptures. But since it is assumed that they are founded on the Word of God, until or unless the contrary is proved, they are of a binding character on ecclesiastical domain and obligate the members and office-bearers of the churches to observance. (J. Jansen, *Kerkenordening,* 1923, p. 2). Compare for the above Articles 1, 41, and 86 of the Church Order and Articles 27—32 of the Confession.

To once more quote from Dr. Bouwman's address (Introductory paragraph above) : A Church Order is to regulate the functioning of the offices of the Church, by Calvin called the eye, ear, and hand through which the Church manifests itself; it should contain the principles of Church government; should reveal the confessing nature of the Church; and it should maintain its holy character by means of the chief rules governing the administration of the Word, the Sacraments, and Discipline.

§5. OUTLINE OF THE CHURCH ORDER OF 1914

After repeated attempts to bring the Church Order of Dordrecht closer to American church life, a revision was adopted by the Synod of 1914. It adheres closely to the original, more so than the elaborate proposal laid before the Synod of 1912, which, with its outline as reported to the 1910 Synod will, we presume, some day be appreciated more than at the time it was laid before our people. Particularly regarding the handling of cases of discipline, those proposals contained valuable directions. Of the 1914 edition of the Church Order, the main divisions are *four* in number: of the offices, Articles 2—28; church assemblies, Articles 29—52; of Doctrines, Sacraments and other Ceremonies, Articles 53—70; of Censure and Ecclesiastical Admonition, Articles 71 to the end. We may outline this as follows:

(1) Under *"offices"* are subsumed articles touching the teaching elders or ministers (Articles 3—17), and the professors or "doctors" of the Church (Article 18), students for the ministry, (Articles 19 and 20), Christian Schools, Article 21). Matters pertaining to the ruling elders are contained in Articles 22, 23, and 27; to the deacons, Articles 24—26, and 27, while the relation to civil authorities is defined in Article 28.

(2) Under *"Assemblies"* are found general regulations (Articles 29—36), consistorial regulations (Articles 37—40), rules pertaining to the Classis (Articles 41—46), to the Particular Synods (Articles 47—49), to the Synod (Article 50), missionary work (Article 51), and linguistic rules (Article 52).

(3) Under *"Doctrines, Sacraments* and *Ceremonies"* we find regulations pertaining to doctrine (Articles 53—55), Baptism (Articles 56—60), Communion (Articles 61—63), and other matters pertaining to divine services and matrimony (Articles 65—70).

(4) The part about *Censure and Admonition* covers rules concerning the discipline over members (Articles 71—78), office-bearers (Articles 79—81), letters of dismissal (Article 82), the poor (Article 83), the parity of churches and office-bearers (Article 84), and about churches differing from us in usage (Article 85). The closing Article 86, covers the authority and possible revision of the Church Order, even as the opening Article spoke of its purpose and outlined its contents.

(For the text of the Church Order and annotations we beg to refer to the book on the subject published in 1921, whose authors are the Revs. W. Stuart and G. Hoeksema. Publishers, The Van Noord Book & Publishing Co., Grand Rapids, Mich.)

§6. CHURCH VISITATION RULES

This institution is based on Article 44 of the Church Order which reads as follows:

"The Classis shall authorize at least two of her oldest, most experienced and competent Ministers to visit all the Churches once a year and to take heed whether the Minister and the Consistory faithfully perform the duties of their office, adhere to sound doctrine, observe in all things the adopted order, and properly promote as much as lies in them, through word and deed, the upbuilding of the congregation, in particular of the youth, to the end that they may in time fraternally admonish those who have in anything been negligent, and may by their advice and assistance help direct all things unto the peace, upbuilding, and greatest profit of the churches. And each Classis may continue these visitors in service as long as it sees fit, except where the visitors themselves request to be released for reasons of which the Classis shall judge."

Church visitation is an old ordinance of the Christian Church. It was regulated as early as 347 by the Council of Sardica to promote the good order in the congregations. From the very beginning of regular church life among the Reformed people of the Netherlands, it has been continued to the present day.

The Synod of 1922 approved of the following RULES FOR CHURCH VISITATION.

"The Visitation which, according to Article 44 of the Church Order, must take place in the Churches, in order to proceed properly, calls for the observance of the following particulars:

(1) Every Classis appoints from its midst at least two ministers as visitors, and an equal number of alternates.

(2) At least one week prior to their coming the visitors notify the Consistory of the day and the hour of their visit.

(3) On the intervening Sunday the approaching visitation is publicly announced to the congregation.

(4) All members of the Consistory give diligence to be present at the meeting arranged for the visitation. Every member who remains absent is to acquaint the meeting with the reasons for his absence. If one-half of the members are absent, the visitation cannot take place.

(5) The Consistory sees to it that all the books of the Church are brought to the meeting for inspection by the visitors.

(6) At the meeting one of the visitors functions as president, and the other as clerk. The visitors record their findings and doings in a book for refer-

ence at future visitations, to be retained in the archives of Classis.

(7) If abnormal conditions in a church make it desirable, the visitors shall repeat their call as soon and as often as necessary.

(8) After all the churches have been visited, the visitors shall, with all necessary discretion, prepare a report of their findings and doings, and present the same to the next Classis.

GUIDE FOR THE EXAMINATION

Questions to the Full Consistory

(1) Do you have preaching services at least twice on each Lord's Day, once from a text the choice of which is left free, and once after the order of the Heidelberg Catechism, so that no Lord's Day is omitted?

(2) Does the Consistory determine what shall be read at reading services?

(3) Is the Lord's Supper celebrated at least four times a year, and is it preceded by a preparatory sermon and followed by an applicatory sermon?

(4) Does the Consistory see to the regular holding of catechetical classes, and to their faithful attendance?

(5) Are the members of the Consistory elected in accordance with Articles 22 and 24 of our Church Order?

(6) Are the Forms of Unity signed by all the members of the Consistory, minister, elders, and deacons?

(7) Does the Consistory meet at stated times according to the needs of the church?

(8) Are all matters calling for the attention of the Consistory dealt with according to our Church

Order, and are the acts of the Consistory properly recorded and kept?

(9) Do the members of the Consistory, before each celebration of the Lord's Supper, exercise Christian censure among themselves?

(10) Is Church Discipline administered faithfully in accordance with the Word of God and the Church Order?

(11) Is the Consistory aware of the presence in the congregation of members of secret societies, and if there are such, are they dealt with according to Church Discipline?

(12) Do the members of the Consistory, as their office demands, regularly visit the families, the sick, and the poor?

(13) What is the spiritual condition of the Church? Do unity, peace, and love prevail?

(14) Do the youth of the Church, coming to years of discretion, seek admission to the Lord's Table?

(15) Is the Church to the extent of its ability diligent towards the extension of God's Kingdom?

(16) Are the collections, prescribed by Classis and Synod, taken according to the respective regulations?

(17) Are all the funds and legal papers, both of the Church and of the poor, kept in a safe place, in such a way that there can arise no occasion for distrust, and that a change in office, through death or otherwise, can occasion no difficulties; and is the Church properly incorporated? Are the archives in good order?

(18) Do the parents as far as possible send their children to Christian Schools?

QUESTIONS TO THE ELDERS AND DEACONS IN THE ABSENCE OF THE MINISTER OR MINISTERS

(1) Does the Minister faithfully exercise his office in preaching and administering the Sacraments, in

adherence to God's Word, the Forms of Unity, and the Church Order?

(2) Does he in the discharge of his ministry use the Forms of the Church, and does he conduct public worship in an edifying manner?

(3) Does he catechize regularly, is he faithful in visiting the sick, and does he take part in the visitation of the families?

(4) How does he manifest himself in his domestic and public life?

(5) Does his work as a teacher and preacher give evidence of diligent study, particularly his preaching of the Catechism?

(6) Does he devote himself as exclusively as possible to the discharge of his official duties?

(7) Does he receive a sufficient income proportionate to the needs of a well-ordered family?

QUESTIONS TO THE MINISTER OR MINISTERS IN THE ABSENCE OF THE ELDERS

(1) Are the Elders regular in their attendance at the meetings of the Church and of the Consistory?

(2) Do they from time to time visit the catechetical classes for the purpose of observing how they are conducted and attended, and do they upon request assist the Minister in catechizing?

(3) Are they doing their part in administering Christian discipline and in maintaining decency and order in all matters?

(4) Do they, according to their ability, visit, comfort, and instruct the members of the Church, and do they try to prevent or remove all offense?

(5) Do they, both at home and in public, lead a life exemplary for the congregation?

QUESTIONS TO THE MINISTER OR MINISTERS AND ELDERS IN THE ABSENCE OF THE DEACONS

(1) Are the Deacons regular in their attendance at the meetings of the Church and of the Consistory, and also, if such are held, of the Deacons?

(2) Are they diligent in collecting alms, and do they faithfully discharge their duties in caring for the poor and the distressed, and in comforting them?

(3) Are the collections counted in the presence of the Minister or of one or more of the Elders?

(4) Do they wisely administer the funds in consultation with the Minister and Elders; do they keep a double record of receipts and disbursements, and do they at stated times render an account thereof?

(5) Do they in their life at home and in public manifest themselves as exemplary Christians?

TEST QUESTIONS

1. Why is Church government and a Church Order a necessity?
2. Which are the three main system of church government outside of the Presbyterian or Reformed?
3. Give the leading principles of the Presbyterian System?
4. Which are the Church Judicatories according to the Presbyterian Order.
5. What can you say about the History of our Church Order?
6. What do we hold about the character and authority of the Rules and Regulations of the Church Order?
7. What is embraced under Part I of the Church Order?
8. What matters are covered under Parts II, III, and IV?
9. What is meant by Church Visitation?
10. Which do you think are the five most important questions of the Rules for Church Visitation?

REFERENCES

Rev. M. J. Bosma, "Exposition of Reformed Doctrine", Chap. VI.
Dr. H. Beets, "Compendium Explained", Chapter XVI.
Dr. S. L. Morris, "Presbyterianism", Chapter IV.
Revs. W. Stuart and G. Hoeksema, "Church Order".

APPENDIX I

Grandrapids 29 April 1857

Aan de Eerwaarde Synodale vergadering der Christelijke afgeschei-denen in Nederland!

Eerwaarde en geliefde Broeders! in ons verheerlijkt hoofd en Eeuwige Koning Jezus Christus! hij die is, was, en zijn zal, de ge-trouwe Imanuël en heerschappij voerende over Zijne Kerk zij met Zijne godheid, Majesteit, genade en Geest, in het midden der verga-dering en geve in liefde maar ook in opregtheid en getrouwheid te handelen in alle voorkomende zaken, en legge veel van zijne hoogheid op aller harten opdat men niet vermag af te wijken ter regter of linkerzijde van wege dezelve.

Onze innige verkleefd en gebondheid aan Christus Kerk op aarde waar dezelve zig ook mogt openbaren, gevoelende, zoo gevoelen wij met een het pijnlijke van het rekken van dien band, waarmede wij gebonden zijn aan UEW. die als vertegenwoordigers dier Kerk ver-gadert zijt. De uitgeleide gemeente, afgescheiden van **alle** protes-tantsche genootschappen, hebben wij bij Godlijk ligt leren kennen, als de Bruid en het wijf des Lams, en het was door genade dat wij op eene dag van 's Heeren Heirkragt, onze halse bij vernieuwing mogten buigen onder dat zagte en zalige juk van Jezus Christus, om onder verdrukking en vervolging (waarvan ook wij ons deel in Nederland genoten) het Lam te volgen door bezaaide en onbezaaide landen: Ge-liefde Broeders! dat standpunt, afgescheiden van **alle** protestant-sche genootschappen is, hoewel verre van Nederland verwijdert, nog hetzelfde bij ons: het is waar dat wij voor een tijd dit standpunt hier in America hadden verlaten dog dit was slegts door misleiding: Wij, onbekend met alles, werden onderrigt, dat de zich noemende Dutch Reformed Churs, in leer en regeering volkomen was overeenstem-mende met de Gereformeerde Kerk zooals dezelve vroeger in Nederl. bestond, dus ook met de afgescheidene: ter goeder trouw hebben wij ons daarop aan dat genootschap aangesloten. Dog nu het ons open-baard werd, dat dit genootschap in sommige zaken, nog Liberaalder was dan de Hervormde Kerk in Nederl. en dat vele, ja overstromende fondamenteele dwalingen waren heerschende en de weg van protes-teren voor ons werd gesloten, hebben wij na rij beraad, onze verbin-tenis aan dat kerkgenootschap moeten opzeggen, en vinden ons voor den Heere verpligt, tot ons vorig standpunt terug te keren, en zoo wenschen wij weder een deel te zijn van de door den Heere uitgeleide gereformeerde Kerk.

Die ons vroeger gekend hebben weten hoe wars wij waren van af-scheiding van de Kerk, en hoe wij niet anders dan Gods ongenoegen voorspelden op het vermenigvuldigen van gemeententjes naast de Kerk. Hier in zijn wij nog dezelfden; die vrijzinnige begrippen wor-den door ons verfoeid, den Bijbel en onze daarop gegronde formulie-ren van Eenheid leren ons anders. Wij zeggen met Vader Brakel, men moet zig bij de **Kerk** voegen, en bij dezelve blijven. Dog wan-

neer er overstromen fondamentele dwalingen komen, dan houd die
vergadering op de Kerk te zijn, alle gelovigen zijn verpligt zij afte-
scheiden, en God trekt de zijnen als dan ook zelve daaruit: Nu is
de groote vraag. Zijn er overstromende fondamentele dwalingen uit
de Boeken der zig noemende Dutch Ref. Churs voortkomende? De
agt nagttekenen voortkomende in de Wagterstem, zullen daaromtrent
wel eenig antwoord geven. Ook eene Samenspraak gezonden aan den
Weleerwaarde Ds. Joffers, ja al was het niet anders dan de doordrij-
ving eener algemeene verzoening, waren er dan al niet fondamentele
dwalingen? Want welk fondamenteel leerstuk kan men staande hou-
den, de algemeene verzoening lerende? en wij zijn in staat te bewijzen dat studenten op de Semenarium dit leerstuk zonder tegenspraak
der onderwijzers verdedigen, en de Synode verspreiding van boeken
met dit leerstuk, bevorderen. Meer zullen hier nu niet van schrijven,
zijnde reeds vroeger door ons gedaan, welke brief door Curatoren der
Theologische School te Kampen is gelezen, welke van een en ander
wel mededeeling zullen willen doen.—

Broeders! geene scheuring, maar vereeniging is dat geen wat onze
wensch en Bede uitmaakt. Daarom is het dat wij ons met deeze tot
UEw. wenden, met vriendelijk verzoek ons te erkennen, als een deel
der afgescheidenene Gereformeerde Kerk in Nederland en ons in
voorkomende gevallen zoovel mogelijk met raad en hulp bijstaan: de
afscheiding neemt hier toe. De Heere opent meer en meer de ogen
zijns volks, het merendeel der gemeente hier te Grandrapids [is]
met Ds. H. G. Klijn afgescheiden. Ds. K. van den Bosch met bijna
zijne geheele gemeente, te uitgezondert zes of zeven huisgezinnen.
Alle te Polkton alle te Vriesland, Zeeland enz. neemt dezelve meer en
meer toe: het is eene zaak welke alom weerklank vind in het hart van
Gods volk. Dringend is dan ook aller verzoek, vereeniging met de
kinderen van een zelfde Moeder.

Wij kunnen niet verwagten van UEw. eene koele afzetting met
het ben ik mijns broeders hoeder? integendeel hopen en geloven wij
dat daar een en dezelfde band ons bind, gij ons met opene armen
ontvangt, en het begeerde ons zult bewijzen.—

Eene andere begeerte mogen en kunnen wij ons niet verzwij-
gen, en die is, (het is de bede van den Groten Hoogepriester, dat zij
allen één zouden zijn, gelijk hij met den Vader één was. en daar er
nog veele van Godskinderen tegen ons overstaan, om welke redenen
dan ook) dat UEw. pogingen mogte aanwenden, om scheuring, welke
door de Scheiding tusschen ons Hollandsche volk is ontstaan, onder
's Heeren genadigen zegen te helpen heelen, hoe onmooglijk dit aan
ons oog mooge schijnen, de Heere welke door middelen wil werken
konde het met zijnen zegen besproeien, ons te samen eenen weg doen-
de bewandelen.—

het moet gewis verwondering baren bij UEw. dat wij opname en
vereeniging verzoeken bij UEw. die zijn afgescheiden van een kerkgenootschap hetwelk mooglijk ook tot UEw. komt, hunne vereeniging
te kennen gevende, en ook nog wel ondersteuning schenkende: Dog
die verwondering zal spoedig ophouden, indien slegts op de **beginse-**

len gezien word. Wij gaan uit van het Gereformeerd beginsel dat een Kerk kenbaar word uit zijne kenmerken, en dat die Kerk meer één is, en de Heere aldaar en ook aldaar alleen, den zegen belooft, en het leven tot in Eeuwigheid, en die kenmerken bij de afgescheidene in Nederland vindende, zoo mogen wij niet terug blijven, maar komen, met verwerping van alle andere genootschappen.—

Daar de andere uit dat Liberale beginsel werken: overal is de Kerk, en slegts Nederlandsch afgescheidene zoeken, gelijk zij zoeken de vereeniging met Baptist, Methodist, Episcopal, en andere dwalende sexte: onder de schone naam van Evangelische Eenheid. Dog is niets anders dan Evangelie verdringende verbroedering.

Aangenaam zal het ons zijn een gunstig antwoord van UEw. te ontvangen, waarmede wij zijn, naa toebidding van 's Heeren dierbaarste zegen.

UEw. Liefhebbende Broeders in Christus
H. G. Klyn presis.
K. van de Bosch Sriba.

APPENDIX II

De **"Acht Nachtteekenen"** bovengenoemd, in "De Wachterstem", 15 Jan., 1857, noemen het invoeren van 800 gezangen, waardoor de Psalmen worden verdrongen, het ophouden van catechismus prediking, catechisatie en huisbezoek, het prediken eener algemeene verzoening, het uitnoodigen tot het Avondmaal van alle gezindheden, de Roomschen alleen uitgesloten, het uitgeven van allerlei boeken met andere kerkengroepen, het openen van den predikstoel voor predikanten van allerlei gezindheden, het tegenspreken der Afscheiding, het afraden om de kinderen verschilpunten met andere genootschappen in te prenten en het verwerpen van de leer der Verkiezing als te calvinistisch.

Waar negen "Nachtteekenen" worden genoemd, berust het noemen van "Agt" zeker op onnauwkeurige memorie.

H. B.

INDEX